THE VALUES
CAMPAIGN?

The Catholic Church and the Nation-State: Comparative Perspectives, Paul Christopher Manuel, Lawrence C. Reardon, and Clyde Wilcox, Editors

The Christian Right in American Politics: Marching to the Millennium, John C. Green, Mark J. Rozell, and Clyde Wilcox, Editors

Faith, Hope, and Jobs: Welfare-to-Work in Los Angeles, Stephen V. Monsma and J. Christopher Soper

Of Little Faith: The Politics of George W. Bush's Faith-Based Initiatives, Amy E. Black, Douglas L. Koopman, and David K. Ryden

School Board Battles: The Christian Right in Local Politics, Melissa M. Deckman

Uncompromising Positions: God, Sex, and the U.S. House of Representatives, Elizabeth Anne Oldmixon

The Values Campaign? The Christian Right and the 2004 Elections, John C. Green, Mark J. Rozell, and Clyde Wilcox, Editors

THE VALUES CAMPAIGN?

The Christian Right and the 2004 Elections

Editors
JOHN C. GREEN
MARK J. ROZELL
CLYDE WILCOX

Georgetown University Press
Washington, D.C.

As of January 1, 2007, 13-digit ISBN numbers will replace the current 10-digit system.
Paperback: 978-1-58901-108-3
Cloth: 978-1-58901-109-0

Georgetown University Press, Washington, D.C.

Library of Congress Cataloging-in-Publication Data

The values campaign? : the Christian right and the 2004 elections / John C. Green, Mark J. Rozell, and Clyde Wilcox, editors.
    p. cm. — (Religion and politics series)
    Includes bibliographical references and index.
    ISBN 1-58901-109-0 (hardcover : alk. paper) — ISBN 1-58901-108-2 (pbk. : alk. paper)
    1. Presidents—United States—Election—2004. 2. Elections—United States. 3. Religious right—United States. 4. Christian conservatism—United States. 5. United States—Politics and government—2001– I. Green, John Clifford, 1953– II. Rozell, Mark J. III. Wilcox, Clyde, 1953– IV. Religion and politics series (Georgetown University)
JK5262004 .V35 2006
324.973'0931—dc22

2006003009

This book is printed on acid-free paper meeting the requirements of the American National Standard for Permanence in Paper for Printed Library Materials.

13 12 11 10 09 08 07 06   9 8 7 6 5 4 3 2
First printing

Printed in the United States of America

Contents

Tables

PART ONE

The Christian Right Movement in 2004

The March Goes On

The Christian Right and the 2004 Values Campaign

JOHN C. GREEN, MARK J. ROZELL,
AND CLYDE WILCOX

THE CHRISTIAN RIGHT NEVER CEASES TO SURPRISE PROFESSIONAL observers of American politics. Since its inception in the late 1970s, this social movement among conservative Christians has been the subject of numerous obituaries and revivals. The "values campaign" is a good example: After the 2000 election the Christian Right was widely perceived to be moribund—only to be declared a major factor in the 2004 election results. Behind these volatile assessments lies a deeper reality. The Christian Right has been engaged in a long and torturous march from outsider status into the mainstream of regular politics. The "values campaign" reveals that the march goes on.

This volume is the fifth in a series of research reports on the state-level activities of the Christian Right, beginning with *God at the Grassroots* (Rozell and Wilcox 1995) and followed by *God at the Grassroots, 1996* (Rozell and Wilcox 1997); *Prayers in the Precincts* (Green, Rozell, and Wilcox 2000); and *The Christian Right in American Politics: Marching to the Millennium* (Green, Rozell, and Wilcox 2003). We have served as conveners of a community of scholars who have followed Christian Right activities at the state level; this volume includes contributions by several scholars who have been involved since 1994, as well as insights from several new colleagues.

These state-level studies have focused on the electoral and organizational activities of the Christian Right, adding an important dimension to the extensive literature on the movement. This broader literature includes descriptions of the religious communities that form the movement's core and peripheral constituencies in the mass public (Wilcox 1992; Leege and Kellstedt 1993; Kohut et al. 2000; Layman 2001); the attitudes and activities of the leaders of these constituencies, especially pastors (Jelen 1991; Guth et al. 1997); and the characteristics of the movement's corps of activists (Wilcox 1992; Rozell and Wilcox 1996; Green et al. 1996; Green, Rozell, and Wilcox 1998; Oldfield 1996).

What accounts for the prominence of the Christian Right in the 2004 "values campaign" and its continued political march? The case studies in this volume suggest that three factors were especially important: alterations of the movement's motives, means, and opportunities (see Green, Guth, and Hill 1993; Green, Guth, and Wilcox 1998; and Green, Rozell, and Wilcox 2003 for fuller discussions of these themes).

From its inception the Christian Right has been motivated by a desire to restore traditional morality to public policy. In this regard, many of the movement's activities have been reactions to policy changes. For example, Christian Right activists have sought to reinstate legal restrictions on abortion, protect religious expression in public institutions, and limit the expansion of gay rights (Wilcox 1992, 2000). Although some of the movement's goals have been proactive, such as support for school vouchers and faith-based social service providers, the level and intensity of Christian Right activity are explained in large measure by policy shifts away from traditional morality. Such a shift occurred in 2004: legalization of same-sex marriage in Massachusetts and the fear that other states would follow suit. This change provided a powerful motivation for movement activity.

This change in motives was followed by expanded means for Christian Right operations—including, as in the past, organizational innovations (Rozell and Wilcox 1996). On one hand, many existing Christian Right groups gained new vitality; on the other hand, new groups were founded at the state and national levels. Some of these groups were specific to the 2004 campaign, but others were more general-purpose organizations that may persist in the future. Indeed, a lasting effect of the "values campaign" may be expansion of the movement's organizational infrastructure. Thus, in addition to a newly prominent issue in 2004, the movement's activities also enjoyed new prominence.

These new motives and means came together with new political opportunities in 2004 (Green, Rozell, and Wilcox 2003, 10–13). The same-sex marriage issue spawned a serious of state ballot initiatives that gave focus to the movement's activities. Although these state-level efforts were important in their own right, they also had implications for the rest of the ballot—especially President George W. Bush's reelection bid. Moreover, the presidential campaign itself presented an important opportunity: The contest was very close, so movement efforts could make a significant differ- ence, and movement members strongly preferred Bush over the Democratic nominee, Senator John Kerry. Because Bush had been renominated without opposition, old animosities between the Christian Right and other Repub- lican factions were largely absent in 2004. Other opportunities included several U.S. Senate seats, especially in the South. By and large, movement- backed candidates prevailed in the primaries and the general election, with some significant exceptions. Thus, the special mix of political opportunities in 2004 contributed to the movement's prominence as well.

The chapters that follow illustrate these changes in motives, means, and opportunities. Because of the nature of the 2004 campaign, this vol- ume departs from its predecessors in that it begins, in part I, with several general chapters on the Christian Right. In chapter 1, Mark J. Rozell and Debasree Das Gupta review the role of moral issues in the 2004 "values" campaign. Indeed, hardly had the balloting ended before the nation's pun- ditry engaged in an acrimonious debate about the meaning of the election, occasioned by an exit poll finding that the largest groups of voters had voted on the basis of "moral values." Rozell and Das Gupta sort through the claims and counterclaims, and they conclude that although the close election was about many things, moral issues were crucial to a significant minority of voters who were key to the Republican victories up and down the ticket. This analysis reveals the importance of such issues to conserva- tive Christians—a key element of the GOP base.

In chapter 2, John Green, Kimberly Conger, and James Guth look at the Christian Right activist corps in 2004—the people who supplied much of the means by which the movement operated. Although these activists closely resemble movement activists of the past, this group was somewhat more pragmatic and diverse—continuing a trend of the preceding decade. Indeed, Green, Conger, and Guth find five clusters of movement activists that differ on issue positions and political style. These "agents of value" were uniformly opposed to same-sex marriage and hostile to the judiciary. Although these activists were highly involved in the 2004 campaign, their level of activity did not appear to be dramatically greater than in the recent past. Green, Conger, and Guth speculate that the perceived increase in movement activity may have arisen from activity by new groups, clergy, and the Bush campaign's aggressive efforts to mobilize conservative Christians.

Part I concludes with a review by Clyde Wilcox, Linda M. Merolla, and David Beer of the state-level marriage amendments. Wilcox, Merolla, and Beer argue that same-sex marriage transformed the Christian Right in 2004; it was the first new issue to engage the movement since the early 1990s. Moreover, in contrast to much of the Christian Right's agenda, a majority of Americans support "protection" of traditional marriage, open-ing an avenue for cooperation with religious communities that had not embraced the movement in the past. The issue also reinvigorated existing movement organizations and spawned a new set of state-level groups, and it generated new resources, especially from clergy and congregations. All of these changes were healthy for the Christian Right, although it is far too soon to tell if this transformation will endure. Although state marriage initiatives appear to have had little effect on the presidential race in most of the states with initiatives on the ballot, they may have mattered in a few battleground states.

Part II of the book turns to state case studies, which are presented roughly in order of competitiveness in 2004 but alternating between states with Republican and Democratic success. Not surprisingly, the most com-petitive states are located in the Midwest, followed by southern and west-ern states. The case studies begin with Ohio; in chapter 4, John Green discusses the role of the Christian Right in the state that settled the presi-dential election. The movement was unusually prominent in 2004, largely because of ballot Issue 1, the strictest of the state marriage amendments. Prodigious activity put Issue 1 on the ballot and helped secure its passage by a large margin. Much of this activism overlapped with a strong effort to reelect the president, including an aggressive mobilization of conservative Christians by the Bush campaign. This chapter concludes that on balance Issue 1 provided a modest benefit to Bush's very small victory margin. The new vitality of the "Bible and Buckeye State" may continue into future elections.

In chapter 5 James Penning and Corwin Smidt consider the Chris-tian Right in Michigan, a highly competitive state that narrowly stayed in the Democratic column in 2004. Unlike Ohio, Michigan has had a set of prominent state-level movement organizations for some time, and they were quite active in 2004. These organizations campaigned vigorously for Bush and a state marriage amendment and against a gambling proposition. This "war on the home front" fell short of its goals, however. Although conservative Christians were a significant voting bloc, the victory was lim-ited to the marriage amendment, which passed by a large margin. Penning and Smidt conclude that the Michigan Christian Right is "powerful but not dominant" and has become a major constituency of the state's Repub-lican Party.

In chapter 6 Kimberly Conger and Don Racheter analyze Iowa—one of the few states that shifted from "blue" to "red." Conger and Racheter report that the Christian Right was a factor in Bush's narrow victory in this very competitive state. Indeed, the Hawkeye State has one of the strongest state chapters of the Christian Coalition. The successful effort on behalf of the president was not mirrored in down-ballot races, however—especially in state legislative races, where Iowa Republicans lost seats. These difficulties point to the uneasy relationship between Christian conservatives and other elements of the Republican coalition. Because of Iowa's high level of electoral competitiveness, Republicans will have to present a united front to keep the state in the "red" column in the future.

In chapter 7 Christopher Gilbert takes up the case of Minnesota, which narrowly remained in the Democratic column despite recent Republican gains. Indeed, the GOP recently obtained parity with the Democrat-Farmer-Labor Party, and the Christian Right made a significant contribution to this shift. Over the past decade the movement has been integrated into the state Republican Party, giving it access to party leaders, platforms, and policymaking. Although "battleground" politics sets stern limits on Republican success, it also makes GOP control of state government a possibility. Gilbert notes that such a result was "hardly foreseeable twenty years ago in the early days of Christian Right activism."

The key state in the 2000 election, Florida, is the subject of chapter 8, written by Kenneth Wald, Richard Scher, Matthew DeSantis, and Susan Orr. Republicans enjoyed great success in Florida in 2004: winning a narrow but clear victory for Bush, picking up a U.S. Senate seat, and continuing their dominance of state government. The Christian Right was an important part of this success, having become a "durable faction" in the state GOP. Wald et al. note, however, that the movement is "so near and yet so far" in its quest to change public policy in the Sunshine State. An apt illustration of this limitation is the case of Terri Schiavo and the legal attempts to prevent removal of the brain-damaged woman's feeding tube. Although in many ways this case was tailor-made for Christian Right success, the movement did not prevail, in part because "the American political system has a genius for resisting radical change."

Another disappointment for the movement is reported in chapter 9, in which Carin Larson takes up the case of Colorado. The Centennial State has become a focus of attention for the Christian Right because one of the most prominent movement organizations, Focus on the Family, is headquartered in Colorado Springs. Yet Colorado is a diverse and growing state where Christian conservatives are just one part of the Republican coalition. In 2004 the movement was very active and helped secure a narrow victory for President Bush. At the same time, however, the GOP lost a U.S. Senate seat and control of the state legislature. The Senate primary race represented a classic contest between Christian conservatives and moderate Republicans; the eventual nominee, Peter Coors (of beer company fame), came from the latter camp. The movement's lack of enthusiasm for Coors may have been a factor in his narrow general election loss to Democrat Ken Salazar—underscoring the need for party unity in highly competitive races.

Notably, the major Christian Right failure in 2004 occurred in Illinois. In 1998 the movement scored a major victory in the U.S. Senate race when Republican Peter Fitzgerald defeated the incumbent Democrat, Carol Moseley Braun, who was mired in an ethics scandal (Jelen 2000). Yet Fitzgerald proved to be so unpopular in the Land of Lincoln—in part because of his social issue conservatism—that he chose not to seek reelection in 2004. After his Republican replacement was forced to leave the race because of a sexual scandal, state GOP candidates recruited former United Nations Ambassador Alan Keyes, a prominent movement leader and former senatorial and presidential candidate. Although Keyes' prospects were slim from the beginning, his outspoken views on social issues—many of which were widely shared by movement activists—quickly devastated his campaign, allowing moderate Democrat Barack Obama to win the election in a landslide. The Keyes campaign was a classic example of a Christian Right "purist" approach, and it starkly reveals the limits of explicit movement candidates.

In chapter 10 Shad Satterthwaite reports on the 2004 election in Oklahoma. Here the Christian Right was involved in a high-profile U.S. Senate race between two members of Congress: conservative Republican Tom Coburn and moderate Democrat Brad Carson. Coburn, a movement ally, described the contest as a "race between good and evil"—an assertion in line with his very conservative positions on social issues. With help from the Christian Right, Coburn held the seat for the GOP. Movement efforts also helped secure passage (by a large margin) of a state marriage amendment, as well as a measure increasing the tax on tobacco (by a small margin). As Satterthwaite notes, however, "good" did not triumph uniformly over "evil" in the Sooner State: Despite fierce opposition from Christian conservatives, ballot measures on a lottery and gambling passed by large margins.

Christopher Soper and Joel Fetzer cover California in chapter 11, analyzing the 2004 campaign as well as the 2003 recall election that made Arnold Schwarzenegger governor. Although the Christian Right has long been active in California, its success has been sharply curtailed by the social liberalism of the state. The recent campaigns were no exception. Despite considerable movement activity, Bush lost the Golden State to Kerry by a large margin, and Proposition 71—an initiative to provide public funding for embryonic stem-cell research—passed by a comfortable margin. Indeed, Proposition 71 was a direct challenge to one of President Bush's signal actions in support of the Christian Right's agenda: a limit on federal dollars for stem-cell research. Moreover, the proposition was endorsed by none other than Governor Schwarzenegger. Christian conservatives had reluctantly backed

Schwarzenegger in the 2003 recall election, reversing a pattern of intraparty division. Schwarzenegger proved that social issue moderation was important for statewide victories in California and thereby revealed the limits of movement influence on policy. The Christian Right did benefit from its support of Schwarzenegger, however, in fall 2005 when he vetoed legislation that would have legalized same-sex marriage in California.

In chapter 12 James Guth discusses the Christian Right in South Carolina, one of the states where the movement has enjoyed the most success. Although there was hardly a presidential campaign in the Palmetto State (Bush won in a landslide), there was an important U.S. Senate race, in which Republican Jim DeMint defeated the state's most attractive Democratic candidate, state Superintendent of Education Inez Tenenbaum. DeMint won the Democratic nomination in a crowded primary in which all the candidates sought the support of social conservatives. Guth notes that the Christian Right has "deposited a distinct but fairly well-integrated residue in the state GOP," and "although the party is not in Christian Right hands, it is clearly in conservative Christian hearts." Nonetheless, the movement still confronts challenges with regard to implementing its policy goals, leaving some doubt about its future impact.

In some respects, the California and South Carolina cases set the outside limits of the influence of the Christian Right. In the former, a political environment that is hostile to the movement's goals means that even extensive activity will produce only modest results, but supporting moderate Republicans is key to even minimal success—as revealed by Governor Schwarzenegger's veto of same-sex marriage legislation. In the latter, a favorable political environment allows the movement to exert considerable influence—but not enough to dictate all policy outcomes.

These limits suggest that the "value campaign" in 2004 was not an aberration but a consistent part of national politics, albeit strengthened by the same-sex marriage issue and the close presidential campaign. Thus, moral traditionalism is likely to continue to be one factor—though hardly the only factor—in elections. Although the exact impact of the 2004 campaign on the Christian Right is uncertain, there is every reason to believe that the movement's long march into regular politics will continue in the near future.

References

Green, John C., James L. Guth, and Kevin Hill. 1993. "Faith and Election: The Christian Right in Congressional Campaigns 1978–1988." *Journal of Politics* 55:80–91.

Green, John C., James L. Guth, and Clyde Wilcox. 1998. "Less than Conquerors: The Christian Right in State Republican Parties." In *Social Movements and American Political Institutions*, ed. Anne N. Costain and Andrew S. McFarland. Lanham, Md.: Rowman and Littlefield, 117–35.

Green, John C., James L. Guth, Corwin E. Smidt, and Lyman A. Kellstedt. 1996. *Religion and the Culture Wars: Dispatches from the Front*. Lanham, Md.: Rowman & Littlefield.

Green, John C., Mark J. Rozell, and Clyde Wilcox. 1998. "Religious Constituencies and Support for the Christian Right in the 1990s." *Social Science Quarterly*. 79:815–27.

———. 2000. *Prayers in the Precincts: The Christian Right in the 1998 Elections*. Washington, D.C.: Georgetown University Press.

———, eds. 2003. *The Christian Right in American Politics: Marching to the Millennium*. Washington, D.C.: Georgetown University Press.

Guth, James L., John C. Green, Corwin E. Smidt, and Lyman A. Kellstedt. 1997. *The Bully Pulpit: The Politics of Protestant Clergy*. Lawrence: University Press of Kansas.

Jelen, Ted G. 1991. *The Political Mobilization of Religious Beliefs*. Westport, Conn.: Praeger Press.

———. 2000. "Illinois: Moral Politics in a Materialist Political Culture." In *Prayers in the Precincts: The Christian Right in the 1998 Elections*, ed. John C. Green, Mark J. Rozell, and Clyde Wilcox. Washington, D.C.: Georgetown University Press, 243–56.

Kohut, Andrew, John C. Green, Scott Keeter, and Robert Toth. 2000. *The Diminishing Divide: Religion's Changing Role in American Politics*. Washington, D.C.: Brookings Institution.

Layman, Geoffrey. 2001. *The Great Divide: Religious and Cultural Conflict in American Politics*. New York: Columbia University Press.

Leege, David C., and Lyman A. Kellstedt, eds. 1993. *Rediscovering the Impact of Religion on Political Behavior*. Armonk, N.Y.: M. E. Sharpe.

Liebman, Robert C. 1983. "Mobilizing the Moral Majority." In *The New Christian Right*, ed. Robert C. Liebman and Robert Wuthnow. New York: Aldine Press, 49–73.

Oldfield, Duane. 1996. *The Right and the Righteous: The Christian Right Confronts the Republican Party*. Lanham, Md.: Rowman & Littlefield.

Rozell, Mark J., and Clyde Wilcox, eds. 1995. *God at the Grassroots: The Christian Right in the 1994 Elections*. Lanham, Md.: Rowman & Littlefield.

———. 1996. *Second Coming: The New Christian Right in Virginia Politics*. Baltimore: Johns Hopkins University Press.

———, eds. 1997. *God at the Grassroots, 1996: The Christian Right in American Elections*. Lanham, Md.: Rowman & Littlefield.

Wilcox, Clyde. 1992. *God's Warriors: The Christian Right in 20th Century America*. Baltimore: Johns Hopkins University Press.

———. 2000. *Onward Christian Soldiers: The Christian Right in American Politics*, 2nd ed. Boulder, Colo.: Westview Press.

CHAPTER ONE

"The Values Vote"?

Moral Issues and the 2004 Elections

MARK J. ROZELL AND DEBASREE DAS GUPTA

IN THE INSTANT ANALYSES THAT INEVITABLY FOLLOW U.S. ELEC-tions, many observers of the 2004 contest said that successful mobilization of the religious right was the key to understanding the scope of the GOP triumph. A national exit poll asked voters to identify the most important issues in making up their minds on election day. Among a list of leading issues, the most frequently cited answer was "moral values." Exit poll data also showed a significant increase in voting among conservative evangelicals in 2004. Furthermore, these voters were even more solidly Republican than they had been in 2000. The presidential nominees had clashed over moral issues such as abortion and stem cell research, and media coverage gave substantial emphasis to these controversies during the campaign. Eleven states held anti–gay marriage referenda, and all of these measures passed easily.

It is no surprise, therefore, that leading political analysts referred to the 2004 elections outcome as "the values vote." Is the GOP triumph so easily explained, however? The evidence suggests the following: First, the 2004 election does not represent a sea change in U.S. politics that demonstrates the triumph of moral issues. The election outcomes do validate the existence and continuation of certain voting trends, including the increased Republicanism of evangelical and Catholic voters, as well as heightened electoral polarization. Second, moral values were a key component of the campaign, but one-dimensional interpretations of the GOP triumphs do not adequately explain the election outcome. President Bush's victory and those of many Republican candidates throughout the country were the result of other key factors as well, including security issues, incumbency, home state advantage, and lack of voter enthusiasm for Democratic presidential nominee John F. Kerry. In this chapter, we describe and explain the role of moral issues in the 2004 campaign, with particular emphasis on the impact of the religious right. We also review the evidence about whether the 2004 election outcome was a "values vote."

The 2004 Election: A "Moral Values" Campaign?

Some observers, such as *New York Times* columnist David Brooks, said that 2004 would be a "values" election, and data from the Zogby poll seemed to confirm that assessment. Brooks said that "Americans want to be able to see their leaders' faith." When voters were asked to name their most important voting criterion, 54 percent said having a president who shares their values, 29 percent said having a president who can best provide for their safety, and only 13 percent said having a president who will improve their personal finances. In the summer of 2004, Brooks wrote that John Kerry's deep flaw was that only 7 percent of Americans (in a *Time* magazine poll) had identified the Democratic nominee as "a man of strong religious faith." Brooks regarded faith as so key to voting decisions that Kerry was doomed to lose if he could not change this perception of him as a secular candidate (Brooks 2004). Indeed, polling data showed that the regular churchgoing population was heavily Republican, and the less religiously observant population was strongly Democratic.

Furthermore, during the 2004 campaign many observers suggested that the country had become unusually divided and that supporters of Bush and Kerry shared little in common. There is some evidence to support the divided electorate thesis. A Zogby International poll found that whereas two-thirds of Kerry supporters had watched the controversial film *Fahrenheit 911*, only 3 percent of Bush supporters had done so. Half of Bush's supporters said they had seen the film *The Passion of the Christ*, whereas only 15 percent of Kerry supporters had done so. With regard to the statement, "We were better off in the old days when everyone just knew how they were expected to behave," 61 percent of Bush supporters agreed, but only 18 percent of Kerry supporters agreed; 75 percent of Bush supporters said that a president should emphasize his religious values, and 96 percent of Kerry supports said that religion is a private matter that does not belong in public discourse (Zogby International).

Political divisions also were evident as a result of the growing identification of evangelical Protestants with the Republican Party—a trend that began with the Reagan administration but became even more pronounced during President George W. Bush's first term. A 2004 Pew survey found that whereas 38 percent of the public identified as Republican, the number went up to 56 percent for evangelicals. In the same poll, 68 percent of respondents said that it is important for a president to be a person with strong religious beliefs; 87 percent of evangelicals held this position. In 2003, when merely 47 percent of all respondents supported Bush's reelection, 69 percent of evangelicals backed the president (www.pewcenter.org).

Despite such support for Bush, Republican strategists remained worried throughout 2004 because of the tepid turnout among conservative evangelicals in 2000. Surprisingly, in 2000 the turnout among this group was significantly lower than it had been in 1996. The moderate GOP candidate Bob Dole, whom President Clinton defeated easily, had done a better job at mobilizing the core constituency of the religious right in 1996 than the victorious and more conservative Bush in 2000. To Republicans, this fact made the evangelical turnout in 2004 the true wild card of the election (Rozell 2004).

Indeed, the Bush campaign caused a stir when reports revealed that it had asked thousands of churches to turn over membership directories for the purpose of political contacting. The evidence suggests, however, that this effort was not needed, as evangelical clergy across the country discussed the election from the pulpit and prominent evangelical leaders also expressed their preferences and urged supporters to vote moral values in the election. For example, Focus on the Family chairman James Dobson personally endorsed Bush, even though he had never made a public endorsement of a presidential candidate before (Cooperman and Edsall 2004). Many conservative evangelical leaders similarly engaged in personal signaling of their vote preferences to help Bush.

Simultaneously, a grassroots mobilization of social conservative voters seemed to take off largely on its own, rather than being directed by any interest group organization such as the Christian Coalition. Indeed, whereas many previous studies of the Christian Right have emphasized the top-down nature of the mobilization of religious conservative voters, the 2004 election may be the best evidence yet that locally directed, grassroots efforts around the country added up to a large-scale political mobilization without any national group or campaign coordinating the strategy. Reports in the campaign made clear that the same-sex marriage issue was a major factor in mobilizing grassroots activists. A 2003 Massachusetts state supreme court decision sanctioning same-sex marriage and the defiant act by San Francisco's mayor of illegally marrying thousands of same-sex couples planted the seeds of a major mobilization by evangelical Protestants and conservative Catholics. Although President Bush had initially wavered about whether to support a constitutional ban on gay marriage, a few weeks after the action of the San Francisco mayor the president stated his support. "A few judges and local authorities are presuming to change the most fundamental institution of civilization. Their actions have created confusion on an issue that requires clarity," he declared (Cooperman and Edsall 2004). After the election, conservative Christian leaders beamed that the cultural issues had delivered victory to Bush. According to Roberta Combs of the Christian Coalition, "There is no doubt that because four radical left-wing Massachusetts judges ruled that homosexual marriages are constitutional last year, there was a conservative backlash which played a major role in the election outcome" (AFP 2004).

Ultimately, the November 2004 election delivered President Bush victory by a clear margin and made him the first candidate to win a majority of the popular vote since his father in 1988. A majority of the initial analyses attributed Bush's success to the values/morality issue, emphasizing a religious and cultural divide in which the religious right and the gay marriage issue played prominent roles in energizing Bush's vote base. Many subsequent analyses, however, shifted the focus away from the values theme to issues such as incumbency, terrorism, and security. In the following section we consider the major arguments against the belief that 2004 was a values-based election outcome.

Offsetting the Values

Exit polling data first suggested the importance of values to the 2004 election outcome. The leading factor voters cited was "moral values" (cited by 22 percent of the electorate). The inclusion of moral values as one of six options in "the one issue that mattered most" came under extensive criticism, however—so much so that ABC's director of polling, Gary Langer (2004), among others, has argued that a "poorly devised exit poll question and a dose of spin are threatening to undermine our understanding of the 2004 election."

Observers have challenged the salience of moral values in influencing the election outcome primarily on two grounds. First, the phrase "moral values" itself has been deprecated as open to interpretation and at best fuzzy compared to other issue options such as taxes or the economy. Opponents of the values thesis argued that the phrase is amorphous in its meaning and therefore easier to choose than any other specific issue choice. For social conservatives, "moral values" are about sexual behavior, abortion, and stem cell research. For many moderate and progressive voters, "moral values" are about peace, social justice, and economic fairness.

Second, some commentators have dismissed the case for moral values as the foremost factor as a function, rather than a finding, of the closed-choice or forced-choice format of the exit poll question. As a rebuttal, analysts have cited preelection polls in which, in an open-ended format, only 10 percent of respondents chose moral values. Furthermore, some commentators have pointed out that if the exit poll question had been framed to combine some of the issue options, the results would have been different and the significance of moral values would have been trumped by, for example, terrorism (20 percent) and Iraq (19 percent) or economy/jobs (20 percent) and taxes (5 percent).

The triumph of the anti–gay marriage initiatives further supported the conclusion that morality/values was the significant factor affecting vote choice and turnout. Gay marriage referenda were on the ballot in eleven states, and in each of these states the ban passed by overwhelming margins (between 57 percent and 86 percent). Hillygus and Shields (2005) examine the relative importance of moral values against factors such as party identification, the economy, and the Iraq war and find, however, that positions on gay marriage and abortion were not the significant predictor of vote choice for independents in either gay-marriage states or battleground states.

Yet even if moral values do not predict vote choice, issues such as gay marriage and abortion may have affected voter turnout. Indeed, voter turnout was significantly higher in 2004 than in 2000 across the country, except in a few noncompetitive states. Ansolabehere and Stewart (2005) provide evidence that polarization on gay marriage and higher voter turnout in 2004 did not work in Bush's favor; instead, these factors aided his opponent, even though overall Bush came out particularly strong in counties that were clearly pro-Bush in 2000 and in which there also was an anti–gay marriage initiative. They find that in states without a gay marriage initiative, Bush's vote share in 2004 over 2000 increased uniformly across counties in these states. In states with gay marriage referenda on the ballot, however, whereas Bush augmented his vote share in counties that voted Republican in 2000, in clearly Democratic and more evenly divided counties of 2000 the reverse was true. Because the outcome from this voting pattern was a net shift of 2.6 percentage points away from Bush, Ansolabehere and Stewart (2005) conclude that the gay marriage initiative mobilized voters on both sides, and negatively affected Bush.

In direct contradiction to Ansolabehere and Stewart's (2005) finding is Burden's (2004) analysis. Although Burden shares the view that Bush did significantly worse in battleground states, he posits that Bush did benefit from higher voter turnout. According to Burden's analysis, Bush gained by a whole percentage point for every 4 percentage points that turnout increased in 2004 over 2000. Burden maintains, however, that although higher turnout helped Bush, there is no aggregate effect from anti–gay marriage initiatives on turnout; according to Burden, the initiatives mobilized voters on both sides of the issue. Hillygus and Shields (2005) draw a subtle but very important distinction in this respect—that "voters may have cast a ballot based upon foreign policy once they entered the voting booth, as our analysis indicates, but the salience of gay marriage and/or abortion sparked interest in individuals who were otherwise unlikely to vote on Election Day."

Burden (2004) explains Bush's victory and the outcome of the election in light of the decreased gender gap—which, at 3 percent, was less than half of what it had been in 2000. He provides an alternative hypothesis according to which Bush's share of the vote went up because of increased support from married, white women, presumably because of their concern for national security.

There is evidence, however, that moral issues did play a role in driving up Bush's support among women. A preelection survey by Mason Dixon Polling & Research offered moral and family values as one of the options in its issue question and found that voters who selected this alternative were overwhelmingly female—indicating that Bush's strength among these voters increased in 2004.

Finally, one must be cautious in making sweeping claims about increased Christian Right turnout because exit polls do not permit direct comparison between evangelical turnout in 2000 and 2004. In 2000 voters were asked, "Do you consider yourself part of the conservative Christian political movement, also known as the religious right?" In 2004, however, this question was changed to, "Would you describe yourself as a born-again or evangelical Christian?" The latter wording probably taps a larger pool of voters and seems likely to produce larger estimates of Christian Right turnout.

Values Mattered

Howard Schuman (2005) points out that "[T]o the extent that 'moral values' is meaningful to a substantial number of Americans in deciding how to vote, it is a legitimate alternative." Therefore, according to Schuman, irrespective of whether the phrase "moral values" is as tangible or defined as other issues, it does convey to voters a meaningful choice. In addition, he notes that open questions suffer from salience effects in which people coming up with their own options usually opt for the most heard or discussed issue. Iraq and terrorism had dominated the election debate and remained in the news much more than the phrase "moral values." Schuman supports the closed-choice question used in the exit poll because it provides respondents with an even platform from which to choose (Schuman 2005).

So, was "moral values" significant in how Americans voted, and was it a factor that contributed to the increase of Bush's popular vote total over 2000? Exit poll data suggest that it was. Voters who chose moral values as the most important issue (22 percent of the electorate) overwhelmingly backed Bush—80 percent to 18 percent. For the next most important issue, "economy/jobs," the vote was reversed: 80 percent to 18 percent against Bush. This split in the voting pattern does validate moral values as crucial for Bush voters electing him in 2004. A *Los Angeles Times* exit poll similarly found that independents voting for Bush were twice as likely as Kerry supporters to choose "moral/ethical values" from among twelve issue choices.

A good indicator of voter preferences in 2004 was church attendance. Among voters who attend services more than once per week (16 percent of the electorate), two-thirds supported Bush. Among those who attend weekly (26 percent), 58 percent voted for Bush and 41 percent for Kerry. Bush broke about even with Kerry, however, among voters who attend services a few times per month (14 percent of the electorate). Kerry prevailed strongly among nonchurchgoers and those who merely attend a few times per year (43 percent of voters). Among the 42 percent of the electorate that said abortion should be illegal in most or all cases, voters favored Bush over Kerry by a 3–1 margin.

In 2000, when only 14 percent of voters self-identified as members of the "religious right," 72 percent voted for Bush and 27 percent for Al Gore. In 2004, white evangelicals and born-again Protestants accounted for 23 percent of the electorate; they favored Bush over Kerry by 78–21 percent and accounted for 35 percent of total votes received by Bush. Although the exit poll questions in 2000 and 2004 were not the same, the evidence suggests that there was a much stronger turnout in 2004 among white evangelical conservatives and that these voters were more solidly Republican than in 2000. According to a survey conducted at the University of Akron, evangelical turnout in 2004 increased by 9 percent from 2000. This increase translated into a 4 percent increase in Bush's evangelical vote share.

Bush won all fifteen states with the largest evangelical populations, garnering a total of 121 electors toward the 270 needed for victory. More important, in some of the crucial swing states the evangelical margin for Bush was far more than his margin of victory. In Iowa, for example, one-third of the voters were white evangelicals. In Colorado, one-fourth of all voters were evangelicals, and 86 percent voted for Bush (Waldman and Green 2004). In all of the swing states combined, moral values voters supported Bush over Kerry by 84–15 percent—even larger than the national average. A study of the elections data by Lewis (2005) concludes "that attitudes toward same-sex marriage had a statistically significant and meaningful impact on both individual voters and state vote totals." Lewis notes that widespread disapproval of same-sex marriage also "may have contributed to party switches by New Hampshire and New Mexico."

Voter turnout in 2004 was much higher than in most recent elections. At 60.34 percent, turnout was marginally lower than the 1992 level of 60.6 percent. For the eleven states with gay marriage referenda—Arkansas, Georgia, Kentucky, Michigan, Mississippi, Montana, North Dakota, Ohio, Oklahoma, Oregon, and Utah—the aggregate turnout rate was 61.9 percent; in the remaining 39 states and the District of Columbia, this rate was 60.2 percent—a difference of limited impact, no doubt. Compared to 2000, however, aggregate turnout rose by 7.5 percentage points in the states holding marriage referenda, compared to 5.1 points in the rest of the country. Thus, the anti–gay marriage referenda seem to have improved voter turnout by 2.4 percentage points (Althaus 2005; McDonald 2005).

All eleven states that had these bans on the ballot passed them by significant margins. Among voters who say that there should be no legal recognition of same-sex relationships (37 percent of voters), this group voted 70–29 percent for Bush over Kerry. The result was reversed among those who favor legal recognition of gay marriage (25 percent), with Kerry prevailing 77–22 percent. In Ohio—the state that decided the presidential election outcome—62 percent favored the referendum banning gay marriage, and this number rose to 86 percent among evangelicals (2004 exit polls at www.beliefnet.com). Some postelection analyses suggested that these referenda were responsible for higher Christian Right turnouts, although the evidence is not conclusive. Thus, it is important to avoid overstating the impact of anti–gay marriage referenda across the country, as some postelection analyses did.

A Broader Coalition

Bush's defeat of John Kerry was not merely a Christian Right triumph. Many voting groups contributed to his victory. Bush also had devoted considerable effort to courting regular church-attending Catholics in his first term, and there is evidence that this effort paid off. Bush increased his vote share among all Catholics from about 47 percent in 2000 to 52 percent in 2004. Much of this improvement, unsurprisingly, was among white church-going Catholics, who supported Bush with 58 percent of the vote. Bush's improvement in the Catholic vote in Ohio from 2000 to 2004 was about 172,000— larger than his approximately 130,000 vote margin in that decisive state.

Thus, one can plausibly argue that the Catholic vote delivered victory to the president just as much as the religious right vote. Bush also improved his showing among Jews (17 percent in 2000, 25 percent in 2004). Ultimately, Bush won a broad-based victory, improving his showing among all religious groups in 2004, except for "other faiths"—which went more heavily for Kerry in 2004 than for Gore in 2000, largely as a result of the switching allegiances of Muslims who were included in this category in the exit polls. Kerry won two-thirds of voters who identified their religious affiliation as "none"—an improvement over Gore's 61 percent with this group in 2000.

Thus, the key to Bush's success was his ability to mobilize conservative evangelicals while also appeal to churchgoing Catholics and many moderate voters. Indeed, although Bush won a commanding margin among conservative voters, he also received 45 percent of the moderate vote. Bush demonstrated an ability to speak to different audiences at the same time. Rather than discuss abortion directly, he used phrases such as "the culture of life" to appeal to social conservatives without appearing threatening to moderates at the same time. This strategy has fit a pattern of his presidential rhetoric; he frequently has used language that connects deeply with co-religionists while flying under the radar of nonreligious Americans (e.g., his use of phrases such as "wonder working power," his references to "evil" and "evildoers").

Perhaps the biggest surprise in 2004 was the disappearance of the "gender gap." Bush heavily won the support of married women and significantly improved his vote share from 2000 among single women. Exit polling data suggest that security issues and values were the key factors in explaining Bush's support among women voters. Women disproportionately made up the percentage of voters who said in exit polls that they based their vote decision on social issues in 2004.

Bush also gained significantly from 2000 among Hispanics and blacks, and values issues probably were important factors for both of these groups. Indeed, 22 percent of black Protestants who attend church more than weekly voted for Bush in 2004, and his overall share among blacks increased from 9 percent in 2000 to 16 percent in 2004. Many black Protestant ministers throughout the country actively supported bans on same-sex marriage, and this issue did appear to resonate with many black voters who normally would vote Democratic in much higher numbers than they did in 2004.

Conclusion

One can credibly suggest that strong support from religious conservatives was critical for President Bush's reelection in 2004. Not surprisingly, the core of this winning constituency was evangelicals who cast their ballots emphatically in favor of Bush. Yet Bush significantly increased his vote share among other religious groups as well. What is noteworthy is that a broader religious base developed around the evangelical core, comprising mainly white Catholics and a substantial increase in support among black Protestants. The major theme resonating within this winning coalition was the values agenda. Given this outcome, what can the country expect in the coming years: Will the culture war on the electoral side be carried over to the policy side as well?

Given the successful organizing by the Christian Right, the movement can lay claim to being a major player in President Bush's win. Thus, many movement activists have been quick to assert that they also could lay legitimate claim to a significant portion of Bush's second-term agenda, although at this writing in 2006, Bush has not made any major push on the social issues agenda.

Indeed, the victory of the Christian Right in 2004 may have been more defensive than anything. That is, the election result ensured that the push for civil unions or gay marriage is temporarily stopped, that prochoice judges are less likely to be appointed to the federal courts, that the ban on federal funding of family planning services overseas is maintained, that late-term or "partial-birth" abortions continue to be prohibited, and that the federal government may be less likely for some time to fund broader stem cell research than is currently allowed. These victories are significant in themselves, as the GOP retains strong control of the federal government and the Democratic Party remains in splinters and struggles with its strategies for dealing with moral issues in future campaigns.

References

Agence France Presse (AFP). 2004. "U.S. Christian Right Exultant after Bush Re-Election." November 5. Available at www.religionnewsblog.com/9261-.html (accessed February 5, 2006).

Althaus, Scott L. 2005. "How Exceptional Was Turnout in 2004?" *Political Communication Report* (Winter). Available at www.ou.edu/policom/1501_winter/commentary.htm (accessed April 19, 2006).

Ansolabehere, Stephen, and Charles Stewart III. 2005. "Truth in Numbers." Available at www.bostonreview.net/BR30.1/ansolastewart.html (accessed July 1, 2005).

Brooks, David. 2004. "A Matter of Faith." *New York Times*, 22 June, A19.

Burden, Barry C. 2004. "An Alternative Account of the 2004 Election." *The Forum* 2, no. 4:1–10.

Cooperman, Alan, and Thomas B. Edsall. 2004. "Evangelicals Say They Led Charge for the GOP." *Washington Post*, 8 November, A1.

Hillygus, D. Sunshine, and Todd G. Shields. 2005. "Moral Issues and Voter Decision Making in the 2004 Presidential Election." *PS: Political Science and Politics* 38, no. 2 (April): 201–10.

Langer, Gary. 2004. "A Question of Values." Available at www.nytimes .com/2004/11/06/opinion/06langer.html (accessed April 19, 2006).

Lewis, Gregory B. 2005. "Same-Sex Marriage and the 2004 Presidential Election." *PS: Political Science and Politics* 38, no. 2 (April): 195–99.

McDonald, Michael. 2005. "2004 Voting-Age and Voting-Eligible Population Estimates and Voter Turnout." *United States Election Project.* Available at http:// elections.gmu.edu/Voter_Turnout_2004.htm (accessed April 19, 2006).

Rozell, Mark J. 2004. "Bush's Wild Card: The Religious Vote." *USA Today*, 22 September, A21.

Schuman, Howard. 2005. "The Morals Choice." *Public Opinion Pros.* Available at www.publicopinionpros.com/op_ed/2004/nov/schuman.htm (accessed February 5, 2006).

Waldman, Steven, and John C. Green. 2004. "It Wasn't Just (Or Even Mostly) the 'Religious Right.'" Available at www.beliefnet.com/story/155/story_15598_1.html (accessed February 5, 2006).

Zogby International. 2004. "Zogby/Williams Identity Poll." Conducted 11–16 August. Obtained by author.

CHAPTER TWO

Agents of Value

Christian Right Activists in 2004

JOHN C. GREEN, KIMBERLY H. CONGER,

AND JAMES L. GUTH

WITHIN THE INTENSE DEBATE OVER THE MEANING OF THE 2004 election there was a clear point of consensus: The Christian Right was a key player in the campaign. Indeed, the ballots had hardly been counted when a series of liberal pundits blamed Christian conservatives for the outcome (see Marshall 2004)—an accusation that conservative Christian leaders eagerly accepted, gladly taking credit for the Republican victory (Cooperman and Edsall 2004). Although a full explanation of the role of religion in this close election is far more nuanced (Muirhead et al. 2005), the Christian Right was as prominent in 2004 as in any national campaign since 1980.

Christian Right activists helped put initiatives banning same-sex marriage on the ballot in eleven states and then waged strong grassroots campaigns on their behalf (Hook 2004). In addition, there was an unusually close link between the Bush reelection campaign and conservative Christians. The former built its own network of church liaisons to achieve Karl Rove's goal of increasing turnout among evangelical Protestants and other religious traditionalists (Cooperman 2004). The latter deployed new voter mobilization efforts, such as the "I Vote Values" campaign, alongside older tactics, such as voter guide distribution in congregations. In fact, these broader mobilization efforts of the "religious right" revitalized the embryonic "religious left," anxious to arouse the faithful on behalf of Democrats (Myers 2005).

Who were these movement activists in the 2004 campaign? How did they differ from movement activists in the recent past? This chapter offers a tentative answer to the first question and an educated guess on the second.

Christian Right activists in the 2004 campaign can be fairly described as "agents of value," both because they were motivated by traditional moral values and because they were valuable assets in the contest. Although the 2004 activists resembled their predecessors in many ways, they appear to be somewhat more diverse and pragmatic than in the past. That degree of internal diversity gave the Christian Right many faces in national politics. Although they were heavily engaged in 2004, they apparently were only modestly more active than in the past. Thus, the Christian Right's prominence in 2004 may reflect the perception that key "values" were at stake in the contest, the movement's close relationship to the Republican Party and the Bush campaign, and a broad effort to mobilize conservative Christian voters.[1]

The Christian Right Activist Corps

The foregoing conclusions are cautious for a reason: The Christian Right activist corps is difficult to study. Because political activists make up only a small portion of the mass public—and Christian Rightists are only a small portion of the activist corps—surveys of the citizenry do not generate samples large enough for analysis. Thus, special studies of activists are required. Unfortunately, there is no "national registry" of movement activists, and the formal lists that do exist rarely are available to scholars. An alternative strategy is to study activists appearing in public documents, such as campaign finance disclosure forms, or among public officials, such as national convention delegates. However, the very processes that make such individuals public can introduce biases into the study. In short, constructing an adequate sample of movement activists is a challenge—which numerous scholars have taken on.[2] Although we must take care in appropriating this previous work for our purposes, it reveals some key expectations about the characteristics of the Christian Right activist corps.

Expectations from Past Studies

Not surprisingly, religion is the defining characteristic of the Christian Right: Studies have found that activists are mostly highly traditional evangelical Protestants. Nevertheless, scholars have found considerable diversity among them, such as differences among self-identified fundamentalists, Pentecostals, charismatics, and "plain vanilla" evangelicals.

Indeed, individual movement organizations often have been based in a particular evangelical subtradition (Wilcox 1988; Smidt et al. 1994).

In demographic terms, Christian Right activists have looked much like other political activists: white, older, well-educated, affluent, and with high-status occupations (Guth et al. 1994); some studies have found a special role for clergy (Guth 1996). Although Christian Rightists typically have a slightly lower social status than regular party activists, they differ more in other respects; for example, they include more women and members of traditional nuclear families and are more likely to live in the South and in rural areas (Green and Guth 1988).

In political terms, movement activists have been conservative and Republican, with a very strong emphasis on moral issues—especially abortion and school prayer (Wilcox 1992). Some studies also have found Christian Rightists to be part of the "hard right"—strong supporters of free market economics and anticommunist foreign policy. Others found a bit more variation on nonmoral issues, especially social welfare (Guth and Green 1989). Movement activists often have opposed the "rights agenda" of liberal groups, including feminists, gays and lesbians, and environmentalists. Some scholars, however, have reported that the movement has adopted "rights" language, with an emphasis on protecting conservative social groups—including traditionally religious people (Moen 1992).

Like many social movements, the Christian Right initially was known for a strident political style. Activists often were "purist" in orientation, uncooperative in politics, and even intolerant of cultural differences (Bruce 1988). Subsequent studies, however, have found evidence of an evolving, pragmatic style, with a more cooperative spirit and increased tolerance (Rozell and Wilcox 1996). Similarly, many movement activists initially were reluctant to engage in politics, preferring to seek social change by spiritual means; they became mobilized by perceived threats to their values (Wilcox, Linzey, and Jelen 1991). There is some evidence that these activists have become more enthusiastic about political engagement recently, although the political environment has become no less threatening to their values (Green 1999).

Whatever their initial reluctance, Christian Rightists have been very involved in politics (Green, Guth, and Fraser 1991). Their activities have included favorite movement tactics, such as distributing voter guides, signing petitions, and participating in boycotts, but they also have participated in more conventional politics, from contacting public officers to serving as party officers. Many Christian Rightists also have helped sustain movement organizations, although the transience of such groups has demonstrated the difficulties in building permanent political entities (Green, Rozell, and Wilcox 2003).

The Study

The foregoing findings provide some perspective for the present study, which is based on a survey of Christian Right activists in 2004. Most of the present sample was randomly drawn from lists of donors to federal political action committees associated with the movement and from members of movement organizations.[3] Random samples were taken from each list, based on the relative size of the original sources. This sample was then surveyed by mail, using a modified version of the "Dillman technique" (Dillman 1978). Four mailings between the 2004 election and early spring 2005 produced 612 usable returns—a response rate of 48 percent (excluding undeliverable mail). The margin of error on the survey is plus or minus 4 percentage points. Although there was no evidence of response bias when respondents were compared to the original sample, the results must be viewed with caution because the sample may not be fully representative of Christian Right activists. Nevertheless, the data represent a reasonable approximation of the most visible activists in 2004.

The Christian Right Activist Corps in 2004

A useful way to describe these Christian Right activists is by their sentiments toward several organizations associated with the movement or its main religious constituents. The first column of table 2.1 lists the percentage of respondents who felt "very favorable" toward each of a wide range of organizations, as well as the percentage claiming to be "members."

The two most popular groups were Focus on the Family, headed by James Dobson, and the Family Research Council, an advocacy group founded by Gary Bauer and now headed by Tony Perkins. Although formally separate, Focus on the Family and the FRC work closely together and are linked to state-level counterparts. Roughly 70 percent of respondents held highly favorable views of these organizations, and about one-fifth claimed to be members.

The next three organizations were viewed positively by three-fifths of the respondents, with about one-sixth claiming membership: the American Center for Law and Justice (a litigating organization focusing on constitutional law, founded by Pat Robertson and headed by Jay Sekulow); the National Right to Life Committee (the flagship organization of the prolife movement, allied with the Christian Right); and Concerned Women for America (an antifeminist evangelical women's organization founded by Beverly LaHaye, wife of longtime movement activist and best-selling author Tim LaHaye).

Table 2.1 Christian Right Activists in 2004: Organizational Favorability and Membership

% Very Favorable	All	Core	Hard Right	Pan-Evangelical	Pro-Family	Peripheral
Percentage of Sample	**100.0**	**31.3**	**10.8**	**12.7**	**14.7**	**30.5**
Focus on the Family	**70.7**	99.0	35.4	79.5	97.8	32.5
% Focus Member	*21.2*	*35.9*	*13.6*	*20.5*	*35.6*	*2.1*
Family Research Council	**69.8**	98.4	30.5	82.9	96.6	25.2
% FRC Member	*19.3*	*32.8*	*9.1*	*11.5*	*35.6*	*4.8*
American Center for Law and Justice	**61.8**	79.5	55.4	70.0	66.3	36.0
% ACLJ Member	*17.3*	*24.6*	*22.7*	*21.8*	*18.0*	*5.9*
National Right to Life	**59.0**	80.4	78.5	69.6	31.2	32.7
% NRLife Members	*14.0*	*23.7*	*20.3*	*12.8*	*6.7*	*5.9*
Concerned Women for America	**58.1**	80.9	72.7	62.0	50.0	26.3
% CWA member	*15.2*	*19.9*	*30.3*	*15.4*	*15.6*	*4.8*
Christian Coalition	**53.7**	73.8	70.3	70.8	21.6	28.9
% CC Member	*15.4*	*22.5*	*22.7*	*14.1*	*8.9*	*9.1*
American Family Association	**51.0**	73.2	46.0	72.5	53.2	10.5
% AFA Member	*15.7*	*23.0*	*19.7*	*15.4*	*19.1*	*5.4*
Alliance Defense Fund	**48.2**	65.7	20.4	50.0	76.7	17.0
% ADF Member	*14.1*	*21.6*	*6.1*	*14.3*	*23.3*	*4.8*
Traditional Values Coalition	**34.9**	56.9	40.3	55.1	4.3	7.6
% TVC Member	*7.8*	*13.6*	*15.2*	*9.0*	*1.1*	*2.1*
Operation Rescue	**26.9**	32.9	48.4	47.5	1.4	13.4
% OR Member	*3.6*	*4.3*	*7.6*	*5.2*	*1.1*	*2.1*
National Association of Evangelicals	**17.1**	20.5	5.4	47.5	13.0	5.5
% NAE Member	*1.3*	*1.6*	*0.0*	*1.3*	*3.3*	*0.5*
Catholic Alliance	**10.2**	11.6	5.6	24.1	2.9	8.1
% CA Member	*1.0*	*0.5*	*1.5*	*1.3*	*0.0*	*1.6*
Evangelicals for Social Action	**8.1**	0.0	0.0	54.3	0.0	0.0
% ESA Member	*1.0*	*1.6*	*0.0*	*3.9*	*0.0*	*0.0*
Bread for the World	**8.0**	0.0	0.0	51.4	0.0	0.0
% BFW Member	*1.3*	*0.0*	*0.0*	*10.4*	*0.0*	*0.0*

Source: Survey by authors.

The next three organizations were viewed favorably by about half of the respondents, with membership claimed by roughly one-sixth. The first is the Christian Coalition, surely the best-known movement organization. Founded by Pat Robertson[5] and initially run by Ralph Reed, it is now directed by Roberta Combs. The relatively weak support for the Coalition may reflect its difficulties after the departures of Reed and Robertson, including a decline in the number of state affiliates, but our sample may also underrepresent the Coalition's following.[4] The other organizations in this grouping are the American Family Association (which opposes obscenity in the media and public life and is headed by Rev. Donald Wildmon) and the Alliance Defense Fund (another litigating organization founded by James Dobson and other movement leaders, now headed by Alan Sears).

Some other movement organizations were not regarded as favorably (although few activists reported highly unfavorable assessments, opting instead for neutrality), with less than one-tenth claiming to be members. The Traditional Values Coalition (specializing in opposition to gay rights and headed by Rev. Lou Sheldon) was viewed positively by about one-third of the sample, and Operation Rescue (best known for civil disobedience against abortion clinics; founded by Rev. Randall Terry and now headed by Rev. Philip Benham) was viewed favorably by roughly one-quarter. In addition, only about one-tenth held favorable views of the Catholic Alliance, originally founded by the Christian Coalition and continued independently under the direction of Ray Flynn, a former mayor of Boston and U.S. Ambassador to the Vatican.

Lower favorability extended to the National Association of Evangelicals—the umbrella group for evangelical churches but not part of the Christian Right. Even less popular were two liberal groups associated with parts of the evangelical community: Evangelicals for Social Action, a "progressive" group founded by seminary professor Ron Sider, and Bread for the World, an antihunger lobby founded by Missouri Synod Lutheran pastor Arthur Simon. Only a handful of respondents claimed to belong to any of these groups.

Activist Categories

These connections were used to create five categories of movement activists (first row in table 2.1).[5] "Core Activists" constituted a little less than one-third of the sample and were characterized by highly favorable views of all of the movement organizations except Operation Rescue; between one-fifth and one-third also reported being members of these groups. In contrast, "Peripheral Activists" were characterized by low levels of both favorability and membership in all the organizations; they made up another one-third of the sample. As we will see, these activists were "peripheral" to the Christian Right but not necessarily peripheral to politics.

The remaining one-third of the sample was made up of three small but distinctive categories, falling between the Core and Peripheral Activists. "Pan-Evangelical Activists" (about one-eighth of the sample) were characterized by high favorability toward *all* the groups listed and substantial membership in many. Indeed, they gave the highest positive evaluations of groups clearly outside the Christian Right, including the National Association of Evangelicals, the Catholic Alliance, Evangelicals for Social Action, and Bread for the World. Thus, these activists were the warmest toward all forms of evangelical political expression, although they were not always moderate on issues.

"Hard Right Activists" (about one-tenth of the sample) reported high favorability and membership in the National Right to Life Committee, Concerned Women for America, and the Christian Coalition but low favorability for Focus on the Family and FRC. This group was the most conservative, emphasizing a traditional moral order. In some respects, their opposite were the "Pro-Family Activists" (about one-sixth of the sample), who exhibited very high favorability and membership in Focus on the Family, the FRC, and the Alliance Defense Fund but were cool toward the Christian Coalition, the National Right to Life Committee, and especially Operation Rescue.

The Christian Right clearly has many faces in national politics. This diversity of organizations, goals, and strategies also underscores the movement's commitment to democratic politics.

Religious Characteristics

Religious characteristics are a good place to begin describing these activists (table 2.2). In 2004 the Christian Right activist corps apparently was still concentrated among evangelical Protestants, though with a somewhat more diverse religious following than in the past. Core Activists included the largest proportion of evangelicals, and Peripheral Activists incorporated the largest contingent from other traditions.

Overall, more than two-thirds of respondents belonged to evangelical Protestant churches. Evangelicals were most numerous among Core Activists (more than three-quarters) and least common among Peripheral Activists (slightly more than half). The strongest evangelical affiliation was with nondenominational or independent churches, which accounted for more than one-third of the sample overall and in each of the five cat-

Table 2.2   Christian Right Activists in 2004: Religious Characteristics

Denomination	All	Core	Hard Right	Pan-Evangelical	Pro-Family	Peripheral
			%			
Evangelical Protestant	**68.6**	78.0	69.7	69.2	74.4	55.2
Nondenominational	***35.9***	*37.7*	*36.4*	*32.1*	*43.3*	*31.7*
Baptist	***19.8***	*24.6*	*25.8*	*17.9*	*15.6*	*15.3*
Pentecostal, Holiness	***5.3***	*7.3*	*3.0*	*14.1*	*0.0*	*2.7*
Other evangelicals	***7.6***	*8.4*	*4.5*	*6.4*	*15.6*	*5.5*
Mainline Protestant	**19.4**	16.8	9.1	21.8	21.1	24.0
Roman Catholic	**11.0**	5.2	21.2	7.7	3.3	18.6
Other traditions	**1.0**	0.0	0.0	1.4	1.1	21.1
Total	**100.0**	100.0	100.0	100.0	100.0	100.0
Movement						
Evangelical only	**27.1**	35.4	13.6	28.2	37.8	17.6
Evangelical and Fundamentalist	**15.0**	15.1	12.1	20.5	17.8	12.3
Spirit filled	**11.3**	14.6	18.2	10.3	8.9	7.0
Fundamentalist only	**6.9**	7.8	12.1	3.8	1.1	8.0
Mainline sectarians	**11.6**	11.5	4.5	12.8	17.8	10.7
Bible literal word of God	**70.8**	78.4	73.8	74.7	77.0	56.8
Greater than weekly worship	**45.8**	53.7	43.9	55.8	43.3	34.8
Gifts of the spirit	**20.1**	22.4	23.1	30.6	18.8	12.9

Source: Survey by authors.

egories; Pro-Family Activists included the largest contingent (more than two-fifths). Baptists of all sorts contributed about one-fifth of the sample in general and were most concentrated among Core and Hard Right Activists. Pentecostal and Holiness churches accounted for just 5 percent of the activists overall; their members were most numerous among Pan-evangelical Activists. All other evangelical churches together accounted for roughly one-twelfth of the respondents and were found most frequently among Pro-Family Activists.[6]

About one-third of the sample was affiliated with nonevangelical churches, with one-fifth in mainline Protestant denominations, most commonly among Peripherals (but also with Pro-Family and Pan-Evangelical

Activists). Catholics constituted a little more than one-tenth of the respondents but were twice as numerous among Hard Right and Peripheral Activists (about one-fifth of each). Other religious traditions (such as Latter Day Saints and Eastern Orthodox) provided few members and were concentrated among the Peripherals.

What about identification with religious movements long associated with the Christian Right? More than one-quarter of activists were members of evangelical churches who also self-identified as "evangelical" (most common among Pro-Family Activists); another one-sixth identified as both "evangelical" and "fundamentalist" (a combination that was most common among Pan-Evangelical Activists). "Spirit filled" identifications (Pentecostal and charismatic) made up 11 percent and "pure" fundamentalist 7 percent of the sample; both were concentrated among Hard Right Activists (18 percent and 12 percent, respectively). Finally, about one-eighth of the respondents were mainline Protestants with sectarian identifications (typically "evangelical"); this group was found most often among Pro-Family Activists.

As in past studies, these movement activists held orthodox religious beliefs and engaged frequently in traditional religious practices. For example, 70 percent claimed to be biblical literalists, and more than two-fifths reported attending worship once a week or more. In both cases, Peripheral Activists were exceptions; they were slightly less likely to be literalists and frequent attendees. Finally, one-fifth of all respondents reported practicing the "gifts of the spirit," such as speaking in tongues or faith healing. These practices were most common among Pan-Evangelical Activists and least common among Peripherals.

Demography

As in previous studies, this survey found that 2004 movement activists had relatively high social status, although with the special social traits long associated with the Christian Right. There were some modest demographic differences across the five categories, however.

SOCIAL TRAITS

As table 2.3 shows, activists were overwhelmingly white and tended to be male and middle-aged or older, despite some variation across the categories. Core and Hard Right Activists were roughly evenly divided between men and women; Pro-Family Activists and Peripherals counted more men (three-fifths and two-thirds, respectively). Hard Right Activists had the most senior citizens, with almost half older than 65 years, and Pro-Family

Table 2.3 Christian Right Activists in 2004: Social Traits

	All	*Core*	Hard *Right*	Pan- *Evangelical*	Pro- *Family*	*Peripheral*
				%		
Race						
White	**95.5**	95.1	98.3	95.9	95.5	94.7
Age						
Under 35 years	**3.5**	2.1	7.7	3.8	3.4	3.3
35–50 years	**24.8**	28.6	13.8	19.2	31.5	23.8
51–65 years	**35.0**	38.0	32.3	34.6	40.4	30.4
Over 65 years	**36.7**	31.3	46.2	42.3	24.7	42.5
Gender						
Male	**58.3**	52.4	49.2	55.8	60.7	67.8
Marital status						
Married	**76.6**	80.1	68.2	71.8	82.2	75.3
Remarried	**6.3**	6.8	7.6	5.1	3.3	7.1
Widowed	**6.9**	6.3	12.1	10.3	3.3	6.0
Single	**10.2**	6.8	12.1	12.8	11.2	11.6
Children at home	**28.8**	29.1	13.8	19.5	45.5	29.6
Children attend						
Public school	*43.5*	*30.9*	*20.0*	*53.8*	*35.0*	*62.7*
Christian school	*23.2*	*30.9*	*30.0*	*15.4*	*25.0*	*15.3*
Parochial school	*6.8*	*7.3*	*20.0*	*7.7*	*2.5*	*6.8*
Home school	*26.5*	*30.9*	*30.0*	*23.1*	*37.5*	*15.3*

Source: Survey by authors.

Activists, understandably, were the youngest on average, with three-fifths between ages 35 and 65.

Not surprisingly, most respondents belonged to traditional nuclear families: Three-quarters were married and never divorced, and more than one-quarter reported having children at home. Pro-Family Activists scored highest on both of these measures. Overall, about two-fifths reported that their children attended public schools; one-third said their children attended Christian or parochial schools, and one-quarter reported that their children were home schooled. A majority of both Pan-Evangelical and Peripheral Activists patronized the public schools, a plurality of Core and Hard Right Activists favored religious education, and a plurality of Pro-Family Activists home schooled their children.

GEOGRAPHY AND SOCIOECONOMIC STATUS

Table 2.4 reports the geographic location and socioeconomic status of respondents. As one might expect, Christian Right activists reside most often in the South (more than one-third) and least often in the Northeast (less than one-sixth), with many in the Midwest and West (roughly one-quarter each). Again, there is some variation across categories: Hard Right Activists were the most southern, and Pan-Evangelical Activists were most midwestern. This pattern may represent a more varied regional distribution than in the past.

Christian Right activists were overrepresented in nonmetropolitan areas. More than one-quarter lived in rural areas; if small cities were included, almost half lived outside of metropolitan areas. Overall, just one-fifth lived within major cities and about one-third in suburbs around such cities. There were modest differences across categories. Core Activists were least urban and most suburban; Pan-Evangelical Activists had the most rural residents—but also the largest proportion living in major cities.

Overall, Christian Right activists have high socioeconomic status. More than two-thirds reported family incomes of more than $50,000, and about one-fifth had incomes of more than $150,000. Pro-Family Activists were the most affluent and Pan-Evangelical Activists the least affluent. In addition, these activists were well educated, with nearly three-quarters college graduates and two-fifths having postgraduate degrees. There was very little educational variation within the sample, although Pro-Family Activists had the highest educational attainment (four-fifths college degrees or better) and Pan-Evangelical Activists the lowest (three-fifths).

Given respondents' high levels of education, it is not surprising that many of these activists were in high-status occupations. More than one-fifth were "knowledge professionals" (e.g., lawyers, teachers, journalists). Another one-fifth were "technical professionals" (e.g., engineers, computer programmers, accountants), and about as many were business managers or small business owners. About one-tenth held blue-collar or clerical jobs or were homemakers. Surprisingly, only a few were religious professionals, such as clergy—just 3.7 percent of the sample. The remaining one-quarter were retired. There also was some modest variation by category: Pro-Family Activists had the most business managers; Pan-Evangelical Activists accounted for the most small business owners and blue-collar workers; Hard Right Activists comprised the most homemakers; Core Activists had the highest proportion of technical professionals; and Peripherals had the most retirees.

Table 2.4   Christian Right Activists in 2004: Geography and Socioeconomic Status

Variables	All	Core	Hard Right	Pan-Evangelical	Pro-Family	Peripheral
				%		
Region						
Northeast	**13.2**	12.0	15.2	11.5	14.4	13.9
Midwest	**26.9**	26.0	27.3	32.1	23.3	27.3
West	**22.8**	24.0	15.2	20.5	25.6	24.1
South	**37.0**	38.0	42.4	35.9	36.7	34.8
Place						
Rural, small town	**28.7**	29.4	28.8	33.8	31.8	24.2
Small, medium city	**29.2**	27.8	30.3	27.3	26.1	32.6
Suburbs	**31.7**	35.3	28.8	23.4	32.9	32.0
Major city	**10.4**	7.5	12.1	15.6	9.1	11.2
Education						
High school or less	**9.5**	6.8	12.3	15.6	6.7	9.9
Some college	**19.4**	16.9	23.1	24.7	13.5	21.3
College graduate	**32.2**	36.5	29.2	19.5	43.8	28.4
Postgraduate	**39.0**	39.7	35.4	40.3	36.0	40.4
Occupation						
Knowledge professional	**19.2**	19.7	19.0	18.9	19.1	19.0
Religious professional	**3.7**	2.1	6.3	6.8	5.6	2.3
Technical professional	**18.0**	22.3	9.5	12.2	18.0	19.0
Business manager	**9.7**	7.4	6.3	4.1	16.9	12.1
Small business	**6.5**	4.8	6.3	9.5	5.6	7.5
Blue collar, clerical	**8.7**	10.1	9.5	12.2	4.5	7.5
Homemaker	**10.9**	15.4	15.9	9.5	15.7	2.3
Retired	**23.3**	18.1	27.0	27.0	14.6	30.5
Income						
Under $50,000	**29.1**	29.6	36.3	37.3	26.7	23.6
$50,000–$99,999	**33.8**	35.2	29.1	29.8	28.0	38.2
$100,000–$149,999	**15.9**	17.3	14.5	17.9	13.3	15.3
$150,000–$250,000	**10.1**	8.6	16.4	3.0	14.7	10.2
Over $250,000	**11.2**	9.3	3.6	11.9	17.3	12.7

Source: Survey by authors.

Political Views

Like their counterparts in past studies, the 2004 Christian Right activists were strongly conservative and Republican, highly critical of government institutions, and focused on traditional morality. Core Activists were most likely to reflect these tendencies and Peripherals the least likely to do so. Yet these activists were hardly monolithic: There was considerable variation in views across categories, even on moral issues.

POLITICAL IDENTIFICATIONS

Table 2.5 reports the basic political views of the Christian Right activists in this survey. Overall, about one-third labeled themselves "extremely conservative" and more than one-half as "conservative"; very few self-identified as moderates or liberals. Hard Right Activists, naturally, were the most right-wing (almost one-half extremely conservative), followed closely by Pan-Evangelical Activists. In contrast, Pro-Family Activists had the fewest extremely conservative members (one-fifth) and Peripherals the most moderates and liberals (one-twentieth).

Overall, almost half of the activists identified as "strongly Republican" and another one-third as "Republican"; there were few independents and Democrats. Pan-Evangelical Activists were the most strongly Republican (three-fifths), followed closely by Hard Right Activists. Pro-Family and Peripheral Activists had the weakest Republican identification (two-fifths), and Peripherals counted the most independents and Democrats (one-sixth).

These activists gave President Bush positive ratings at the beginning of his second term: About one-fifth rated his performance as "excellent," two-fifths as "good," and another one-fifth as "fair." Coming from one of Bush's strongest constituencies, however, these numbers are not extremely high: More than 90 percent of the activists voted for Bush, and even the Constitution Party[7] vote surpassed John Kerry's 2 percent (data not shown). Pan-Evangelical Activists were warmest toward Bush (one-third rated his performance as "excellent"), followed closely by Hard Right Activists. Pro-Family Activists and Peripheral Activists were least positive about the president.

Whatever the strength of their approval of Bush, Christian Rightists had very negative views of the two other branches of the federal government—both also controlled by Republicans. Overall, almost three-quarters had mixed or poor evaluations of Congress. Pro-Family Activists were most negative (four-fifths) and Core Activists least negative (roughly two-thirds). Their views of the Supreme Court were even more negative: More than 90 percent gave the Court mixed or poor evaluations. Here Core

Table 2.5   Christian Right Activists in 2004: Ideology, Partisanship, and Job Approvals

Ideology	All	Core	Hard Right	Pan-Evangelical	Pro-Family	Peripheral
				%		
Extremely conservative	**34.3**	38.0	46.2	44.2	21.3	28.0
Conservative	**52.5**	52.6	44.6	42.9	62.9	54.3
Slightly conservative	**10.2**	7.3	7.7	11.7	13.5	12.0
Moderate, liberal	**2.5**	2.1	1.5	1.3	2.2	5.8
Partisanship						
Strong Republican	**48.1**	49.7	59.7	61.0	40.4	40.5
Republican	**32.8**	33.5	29.0	20.8	42.7	33.5
Lean Republican	**10.3**	12.6	4.8	11.7	7.9	10.4
Independent, Democrat	**8.8**	4.2	6.5	6.5	8.9	15.7
JOB APPROVAL						
Bush						
Excellent	**22.3**	23.6	29.2	33.3	14.6	17.5
Good	**42.4**	50.3	30.8	34.6	51.7	49.7
Fair	**18.2**	17.8	21.5	19.2	20.2	15.8
Mixed, poor	**12.1**	8.3	18.5	12.9	13.4	17.0
Congress						
Excellent	**0.8**	0.0	1.5	0.0	0.0	2.2
Good	**7.8**	9.9	9.2	5.2	4.5	7.7
Fair	**17.7**	20.8	10.8	22.1	12.4	17.6
Mixed, poor	**73.7**	69.2	78.4	72.8	83.1	72.5
Supreme Court						
Excellent	**0.0**	0.0	0.0	0.0	0.0	0.0
Good	**2.3**	1.6	3.1	0.0	1.1	4.4
Fair	**6.1**	2.1	3.1	5.2	6.7	11.5
Mixed, poor	**91.5**	96.4	93.8	94.9	92.1	84.0

Source: Survey by authors.

Activists were almost completely negative and Peripherals again were least so, though still quite critical.

Table 2.6 explores these activists' views of government from another perspective: the extent to which they regarded governmental units as "a threat to Christian values." The U.S. Supreme Court topped the list; more than two-thirds of the activists regarded it as "very threatening." Pan-Evangelical Activists were most hostile to the high court (more than three-quarters), Peripherals least negative (about three-fifths).

Public schools came in second in this category; two-thirds of the respondents regarded them as most threatening. Hard Right Activists were most concerned about the schools (about three-quarters); interestingly, Pro-Family Activists were least negative (three-fifths), followed closely by Peripherals. State courts came in third; half of the respondents regarded them as threatening, with Pro-Family Activists most worried and Peripherals least concerned.

Fewer than half of the activists regarded the remaining institutions as threatening: federal agencies (two-fifths), Congress and state legislatures (roughly one-quarter each), state governors (about one-fifth), and local government (at less than one-fifth overall). Generally speaking, Pan-Evangelical Activists tended to be most negative toward these institutions, and Pro-Family Activists and Peripheral Activists were least negative.

ISSUE PRIORITIES AND POSITIONS

Table 2.7 summarizes the respondents' issue priorities. As one might expect, three-fifths named "moral issues," such as abortion and same-sex marriage,

Table 2.6   Christian Right Activists in 2004: Institutional Threats to Christian Values (% "very threatening")

Governmental Units	All	Core	Hard Right	Pan-Evangelical	Pro-Family	Peripheral
U.S. Supreme Court	69.3	72.6	64.1	77.3	72.4	62.5
Public schools	66.8	72.0	76.9	64.4	59.8	61.9
State courts	50.0	52.2	50.0	50.0	53.4	45.9
Federal agencies	41.4	39.7	45.9	39.1	35.3	45.6
U.S. Congress	28.3	24.7	29.7	36.6	27.3	28.6
State legislatures	24.7	28.6	23.0	27.5	21.8	21.4
State governors	19.2	19.1	22.2	25.0	12.0	19.3
Local government	18.5	17.5	21.3	25.7	14.8	17.3

Source: Survey by authors.

Table 2.7   Christian Right Activists in 2004: Issue Priorities and Positions

Positions	*All*	*Core*	*Hard Right*	*Pan-Evangelical*	*Pro-Family*	*Peripheral*
Issue Priorities						
Moral issues	**59.0**	68.0	61.0	68.0	60.0	41.0
Foreign policy	**28.0**	22.0	30.0	20.0	24.0	40.0
Economic	**7.0**	3.0	6.0	7.0	9.0	12.0
Political process	**6.0**	7.0	3.0	5.0	7.0	7.0
	100.0	100.0	100.0	100.0	100.0	100.0
Structural Agenda[a]						
Judges should only interpret the law	**98.0**	97.0	95.0	100.0	98.0	98.0
Pro–school vouchers	**85.0**	94.0	85.0	87.0	92.0	72.0
Pro–marriage amendment	**81.0**	93.0	88.0	90.0	87.0	61.0
Support Israel	**78.0**	88.0	66.0	88.0	82.0	64.0
Pro–Patriot Act	**37.0**	54.0	34.0	32.0	43.0	19.0
Spread democracy abroad	**30.0**	45.0	34.0	38.0	31.0	9.0
General Conservatism[a]						
Anti–environmental protection	**70.0**	75.0	88.0	64.0	65.0	62.0
More to welfare spending	**54.0**	63.0	54.0	35.0	56.0	52.0
Oppose United Nations	**44.0**	52.0	66.0	30.0	31.0	41.0
Raise taxes to balance budget	**42.0**	48.0	52.0	30.0	47.0	33.0
Moral Agenda[a]						
Restrict abortion	**94.0**	97.0	100.0	91.0	92.0	90.0
Regulate pornography	**29.0**	43.0	26.0	39.0	36.0	7.0
Pro–prayer amendment	**29.0**	40.0	32.0	42.0	9.0	21.0

[a]Percent "strongly agree."
Source: Survey by authors.

as the "most important problem" facing the country. Foreign policy concerns came in a distant second (more than one-quarter), and economic and political process priorities were rare. There were some significant internal variations, however: Core and Pan-Evangelical Activists were most concerned with moral issues and Peripherals least concerned; the latter split their top priorities nearly evenly between moral and foreign policy concerns.

The rest of table 2.7 reports the percentage of strongly conservative responses to an extensive battery of issue questions. In this table and subsequent ones, the "strongly agree" figures are presented to capture nuances among respondents. On balance, these activists tended to hold conservative views on nearly all these issues. Where relevant, we discuss the full range of opinion in the text.

Factor analysis revealed three underlying dimensions to these data.[8] The first might be called a "structural agenda" because the items reflected the movement's new concern with the structure of public policy, whether domestic (judges, marriage) or foreign (support for Israel and spreading democracy abroad). The second dimension captured "general conservatism," including issues such as environmental protection and balancing the federal budget. The final dimension was a "moral agenda," comprising issues motivating the movement from its inception: abortion, pornography, and school prayer.

As one might expect, activists were nearly unanimous that judges should "only interpret the law" rather than make it. Overall, about four-fifths supported school vouchers, a constitutional amendment to prohibit same-sex marriage, and the state of Israel. On these issues, Core Activists were most conservative and Peripheral Activists least so. Only about two-fifths of the respondents strongly supported the Patriot Act, however, and less than one-third strongly agreed that America should "spread democracy abroad." On these matters, Core Activists were most conservative—that is, most likely to support the Patriot Act and efforts to spread democracy abroad—and the other categories less so, with Peripherals taking moderate or even liberal positions.

Christian Right activists were less consistent in their support for general conservatism. Overall, 70 percent strongly opposed more environmental regulation. About half strongly opposed new initiatives to fight poverty, and two-fifths opposed cooperation with the United Nations and raising taxes to balance the budget. Hard Right Activists took the most conservative stances on these items, and Pan-Evangelical Activists were least conservative. (Notably, Peripheral Activists also were among the most conservative on these issues.)

Turning to the moral agenda, these activists were strongly in favor of restricting abortion, across all categories. Only about one-quarter, however, strongly favored restrictions on pornography or passing a constitutional amendment to allow prayer in public schools. On these matters, the biggest backers (Core and Pan-Evangelical Activists) failed to muster a strong conservative majority, and the other categories held more moderate positions (such as members of the Hard Right and Peripheral Activists on pornography and Pro-Family and Peripheral Activists on school prayer).

Hence, even within the moral agenda there were some differences among Christian Rightists.

PROTECTING RIGHTS

A final set of political attitudes concerned protecting rights. Respondents were asked whether particular groups needed "more protection," "less protection," or if existing protection was "about right." Table 2.8 reports a "net protection score," with positive figures indicating a desire for increased protection and negative figures *decreased* protection of the group's rights. (On most items, "about right" was the modal category.)

Factor analysis of these items also revealed three dimensions of opinion.[9] The most important dimension might be called "families and order" because it included increased protection for traditional families, combined with decreased protection for groups perceived as the cause of disorder. The second dimension concerns the rights of women in the workplace and the rights of African Americans. The third dimension was about the rights of conservative social groups.

More than fourth-fifths of the sample supported more protection for traditional families. In contrast, more than three-fifths wanted fewer pro-

Table 2.8 Christian Right Activists in 2004: Views on Protecting Rights (net support for increased protection, %)

Categories	*All*	*Core*	*Hard Right*	*Pan- Evangelical*	*Pro- Family*	*Peripheral*
Families and Order[a]						
Traditional families	85	89	89	83	83	81
Gays and lesbians	–64	–69	–71	–68	–63	–54
Atheists	–53	–55	–62	–42	–45	–56
Criminal defendants	–50	–53	–54	–36	–54	–48
Muslims	–27	–29	–45	–38	–17	–20
Women and Blacks						
Women in workplace	–2	–17	–3	–4	–3	3
African Americans	–14	–11	–25	–14	–7	19
Conservative Rights						
Religious people	75	89	71	76	79	58
Home schoolers	74	83	86	74	71	63
Victims of crime	73	73	72	65	81	74
Gun owners	43	45	50	40	33	42

[a]Positive = more protection needed; negative = less protection needed.
Source: Survey by authors.

tections for gays and lesbians, and more than half desired less protection for atheists and criminal defendants. Only about one-quarter, however, supported less protection for Muslims, who did better than other unpopular groups. Hard Right Activists were most opposed to protecting rights; Pan-Evangelical Activists were least opposed. Christian Rightists were largely neutral on the rights of women in the workplace and the rights of African Americans—subjects of intense liberal political action in the recent past. Overall, there was only a slight preference for less protection. Two categories stand out, however: one-quarter of Hard Right Activists opposed increased protection for African Americans, whereas Peripherals favored *more* protection for blacks and women.

These movement activists did favor increased protection for conservative social groups, however. For example, three-quarters favored more protection for "religious people," home schoolers, and victims of crime. Core Activists tended to score highest and Peripherals lowest, with only modest variation between them. Only two-fifths of the activists, however, favored increased protection for gun owners—often regarded as allies of the Christian Right (Rozell and Wilcox 1996). Hard Right Activists were most in favor of Second Amendment rights (half) and Pro-Family Activists least (one-third).

Political Style

Movement activists appeared to be somewhat more pragmatic in 2004 than they had been in the past. One reason may be a thoroughgoing commitment to political engagement and a strong sense that political action can help restore traditional moral values. Nevertheless, on these matters there was considerable variation among these activists.

PURISTS AND PRAGMATISTS

Table 2.9 reports several self-assessments of political style. For example, three-quarters of the activists claimed that political engagement by religious people was "not divisive," and just one-tenth said it was "very divisive." When respondents were asked a parallel question about the attitudes of others toward "religious people," half reported that the two groups can get along "with ease." When they were asked directly whether religious people were "purists" or "pragmatists" in politics, more than one-quarter said "purists," a little less than one-fifth said "pragmatists," and the remaining half claimed "some of both."

This mix of attitudes holds for a direct measure of electoral pragmatism found in Table 2.9: Slightly more than one-quarter of the sample said

Table 2.9   Christian Right Activists in 2004: Political Style

Political Style	All	Core	Hard Right	Pan-Evangelical	Pro-Family	Peripheral
				%		
Religious people in politics						
Very divisive	**10.5**	10.2	9.4	15.3	5.8	11.6
Somewhat divisive	**14.6**	14.0	18.8	13.9	10.5	16.2
Not divisive	**74.9**	75.8	71.9	70.8	83.7	72.3
Others get along with religious people?						
Very difficult	**20.5**	16.0	19.0	25.0	27.9	20.2
Some difficulty	**27.3**	30.5	25.4	27.8	32.6	21.4
With ease	**52.3**	53.5	55.6	47.2	39.5	58.3
Religious people in politics						
Very pragmatic	**17.0**	17.3	15.9	20.0	11.9	18.3
Very purist	**27.4**	27.2	33.3	14.7	26.2	31.4
Some of both	**55.6**	55.5	50.8	65.3	61.9	50.3
I support my party's nominee						
Under all circumstances	**29.1**	26.6	28.3	38.9	14.5	35.2
Only when I believe in the candidate	**54.9**	52.7	66.7	47.2	67.5	50.0
Only when holds right issue positions	**16.0**	20.6	5.0	13.9	18.1	14.9
Religious people should						
Stay focused on politics	**82.6**	87.0	75.4	85.7	78.9	80.9
Withdraw for nonpolitical activities	**2.0**	2.1	3.1	1.3	1.1	2.2
Some of both	**15.4**	10.9	21.5	13.0	20.0	16.9
Best way to solve social problems						
Religion should be engaged in politics	**60.2**	68.6	64.1	59.7	56.2	52.0
Religion should help nonmembers	**26.2**	22.2	21.9	23.6	30.3	31.0
Religion should help members	**13.4**	8.6	14.1	16.7	13.5	17.0
Main goal of religious politics						
Transform society overall	**44.2**	49.7	39.7	35.5	45.8	43.0

Table 2.9   (continued)

Political Style	All	Core	Hard Right	Pan-Evangelical	Pro-Family	Peripheral
				%		
Correct specific problems	**33.5**	29.6	38.1	38.2	36.1	32.6
Proclaim distinctive values	**22.3**	20.7	22.2	26.3	18.1	24.4
Politics and traditional morality						
Politics can help restore morality	**76.5**	82.8	81.5	85.7	60.7	71.6
Politics unlikely to restore morality	**22.0**	16.7	15.4	11.7	37.1	27.3
Politics can't restore traditional morality	**1.5**	0.5	3.1	2.6	2.2	1.1

Source: Survey by authors.

that they support their party's nominee "under all circumstances," and only one-sixth claimed that their support was contingent on the candidate taking the right issue positions. The remaining half chose the intermediate stance of backing the party "only when it offers candidates I believe in." All told, these movement activists appear somewhat more pragmatic in their support for candidates than in the past.

There were important differences across the categories, however. Hard Right Activists were most likely to report the presence of purists, and Pan-Evangelical Activists were most likely to report pragmatists. The most interesting pattern, however, was for the Pro-Family Activists: They were least likely to regard religious people as a source of political division—but also least likely to expect easy cooperation between religious people and others, to identify religious people as pragmatists, and to back their party under all circumstances. Peripherals, interestingly, reported the most party loyalty.

VIEWS OF THE POLITICAL PROCESS

These Christian Rightists were quite positive toward the political process—probably more so than in the past. Overall, more than four-fifths agreed that "religious people should stay focused on politics" rather than give equal or greater priority to nonpolitical activities. Three-fifths regarded political action, as opposed to nonpolitical efforts, as the best way to solve social problems. More than two-fifths believed that the goal of politics should be to "transform society" as opposed to "correcting a specific problem" or "proclaim distinctive values" (each about one-third). Finally, three-quarters thought that politics can "help restore traditional values"—an astounding figure given the antipolitical views of evangelicals for much of the twentieth century.

Core Activists were most optimistic about politics; there was more variation across the other categories. Hard Right and Pro-Family Activists were least likely to give priority to politics over nonpolitical pursuits; Peripheral Activists were least likely to regard political engagement by religious people as the best way to solve social problems. Meanwhile, Hard Right and Pan-Evangelical Activists were least inclined to regard societal transformation as the goal of politics, opting for more incremental goals. Pro-Family Activists were most skeptical that politics could help restore traditional morality.

VALUES AND PROPOSITIONS

Table 2.10 reports strong agreement with values and propositions associated with political style. Again, factor analysis reveals three dimensions of opinion.[10] The first dimension might be called the "civic gospel": beliefs that justify political involvement by conservative Christians to protect moral values (see Guth et al. 1997). This "civic gospel" differs from the "social gospel" of liberal Christians, which also justifies political engagement but also differs from the "individual gospel" of evangelism and conversion; the latter long discouraged political engagement by conservative Christians. The second dimension might be called "Christian militancy" because it supports a strident role for conservative Christians in politics (Green et al. 1994). Finally, the third dimension might be labeled "cooperative values"—items that reveal a commitment to the political process over substantive policy goals.

More than three-quarters of the respondents strongly agreed with the civic gospel's key elements: that being a good citizen is part of being a "good Christian" and that Christians should engage in politics to "protect their values." Nearly as many agreed on a key motivation: that the main cause of social problems is "moral decay." Core Activists were most in agreement and Peripherals least so.

The activists also see other roles for religious people in the political process: More than half strongly disagreed that "clergy should stay out of politics," but most strongly agreed that the "United States prospers when it follows God." Nearly half strongly believed that "God works through elections." On the other hand, only slightly more than one-quarter strongly agreed that "free enterprise is the only system compatible with Christianity." Differences between Core and Peripheral Activists also appeared on

Table 2.10   Christian Right Activists in 2004: Values and Propositions (% strongly agree/strongly disagree)

Values	All	Core	Hard Right	Pan-Evangelical	Pro-Family	Peripheral
"Civic Gospel"						
Being a good citizen is part of Christianity	**78.0**	91.1	75.8	85.9	73.0	63.6
Christians should do politics to protect values	**76.0**	88.5	75.8	82.1	68.5	63.4
Cause of social problems is moral decay	**69.7**	82.1	75.8	69.7	60.7	58.2
Disagree: Clergy should stay out of politics	**56.2**	63.2	50.0	66.2	60.0	44.6
U.S. prospers when it obeys God	**52.3**	64.4	59.1	63.6	39.8	37.6
Gods works through elections	**46.2**	53.6	40.9	57.1	48.9	33.5
Free enterprise only system compatible with Christianity	**28.3**	28.1	44.6	32.5	23.9	22.5
One correct Christian view	**21.0**	25.4	29.7	25.3	15.9	13.5
Christian militancy						
U.S. should be proclaimed a Christian nation	**7.1**	6.3	7.9	16.9	3.4	5.3
U.S. needs a Christian Party	**10.5**	8.4	18.8	16.0	8.0	8.8
Bring people to Christ and social ills will be solved	**32.1**	38.1	33.3	39.7	23.3	26.2
Disagree: Cause of problems poverty and discrimination	**44.9**	45.8	43.9	45.5	41.1	45.9
Cooperative values						
Disagree: Encourage social diversity	**14.7**	11.5	27.7	18.4	8.3	14.8
Cooperate in politics even if disagree on religion	**24.4**	25.4	12.3	32.9	24.1	24.4
Disagree: Tolerate diverse views of morality	**36.6**	43.2	56.9	38.2	23.6	27.5

Source: Survey by authors.

these items, with one major exception: Hard Right Activists were markedly less supportive of the first and third of these items, and most strongly in agreement with the fourth. The last item in this dimension is a measure of dogmatism—namely, that there is "one correct Christian view on most issues." By this measure, the activists were not particularly dogmatic: only one-fifth strongly agreed with this statement, with Hard Right Activists most dogmatic (still less than one-third) and Peripherals least dogmatic (about one-eighth).

In keeping with this relative lack of dogmatism, very few activists strongly subscribe to Christian militancy: Only 10 percent strongly agreed that the United States needs a "Christian political party," and just 16 percent agreed. Even fewer strongly agreed that the United States should be proclaimed a "Christian nation." Hard Right and Pan-Evangelical Activists had the highest numbers, though only about one-sixth of each group strongly supported these statements. These figures contradict a common view that most Christian Rightists have theocratic rather than policy aims (Marshall 2004).

In fact, this dimension of political style was most fully defined by its opposites. On one hand, two-fifths of the activists strongly disagreed with the idea that the main cause of social problems was "poverty and discrimination"—a key tenet of the social gospel. This "anti–social gospel" message was held uniformly across the activist categories. On the other hand, about one-third strongly agreed that "if enough people were brought to Christ, social problems would take care of themselves"—a central tenet of the individual gospel once common among evangelical Protestants (and still held by many). Pan-Evangelicals and Core Activists scored highest and Pro-Family and Peripheral Activists lowest on this measure.

Finally, these Christian Rightists could be described as "not uncooperative" on the third dimension. For instance, just one-third strongly disagreed that "diverse views on morality should be tolerated"—a less strident response than one might expect given the movement's concern with morality. Similarly, just one-quarter strongly disagreed that "religious people should cooperate in politics even if they disagree on religion." Only about one-sixth strongly rejected encouraging ethnic, racial, and religious diversity. Hard Right Activists were by far least cooperative.

Political Activity

By the standards of the mass public, the study respondents were quite active in politics, consistent with past studies. Interestingly, Core Activists were less engaged than Peripheral Activists, and Hard Right Activists were among the least engaged—a pattern that held for participation in movement organizations as well. Beyond these regularities, however, there was considerable variation.

POLITICAL ACTS

Table 2.11 lists respondents' self-report of sixteen activities in 2004. Given that the sample was drawn in part from donor lists, we should hardly be surprised that more than four-fifths reported making a campaign contribution. Contacting public officials (three-quarters) and signing a petition (two-thirds) also were very common activities. These activities are relatively easy for affluent and well-educated people to perform.

Not surprisingly, more arduous activities were less common. Roughly two-fifths of the respondents reported attending a public meeting or campaign rally, distributing voter guides in churches, or participating in a boycott in 2004. About one-third claimed to have joined a political group, raised funds, or written a letter to the editor; about one-quarter reported registering voters. More onerous tasks were even less common: About one-fifth campaigned door-to-door, and even fewer served as party officials. Finally, one-tenth canvassed churches or participated in a protest or demonstration, and less than one-tenth ran for public office. All told, this sample reported an average of six such political activities in 2004.

There were some interesting variations in political activity across the activist categories. Core Activists were most involved in the distinctive tactics of the Christian Right, such as signing petitions, distributing voter guides, and participating in boycotts. They also were most likely to contact a public official and make a campaign contribution. Core Activists (mean of 6.1 types of activity) were not the most active group overall, however; Peripherals and Pan-Evangelical Activists tied for this honor, with a mean of 6.5 types of activity.

Peripheral Activists were most involved in conventional political activities: attending public meetings and campaign rallies; joining political groups and raising funds; door-to-door campaigning; serving as a party official; and interestingly, participating in protests and demonstrations. Pan-Evangelical Activists were most engaged in registering voters, canvassing churches, and running for public office. By comparison, Hard Right and Pro-Family Activists were less involved: The former excelled only in writing letters to the editor, and the latter were least active overall, with a mean of 5.1 types of activity.

Evidence from within the survey suggests that Christian Rightists were only modestly more active in 2004 than in the past. This conclusion tends to fit with past studies in which comparable data are available. The respondents reported being more engaged on eight of the sixteen activities (making donations, contacting public officials, signing petitions, attend-

Table 2.11   Christian Right Activists in 2004: Political Activity

Activity	All	Core	Hard Right	Pan-Evangelical	Pro-Family	Peripheral
				%		
Made campaign contribution	**84.0**	87.5	78.8	80.8	82.2	84.5
Contacted public official	**75.9**	84.4	72.7	69.2	76.7	70.6
Signed petition	**67.5**	77.1	63.6	71.8	61.1	60.4
Attended public meeting	**42.1**	44.8	34.8	42.3	32.2	46.5
Attended campaign rally	**37.8**	33.3	33.3	35.9	34.4	46.5
Distributed voter guides	**37.7**	46.9	31.8	35.9	31.1	34.2
Participated in boycott	**37.6**	46.1	37.9	43.6	37.8	26.2
Joined political group	**34.9**	37.0	25.8	32.1	24.4	42.2
Engaged in fundraising	**33.3**	29.7	24.2	37.2	23.3	43.3
Wrote letter to editor	**30.7**	33.9	37.9	32.1	23.3	27.8
Registered voters	**27.4**	29.2	21.2	32.1	23.3	27.8
Campaigned door-to-door	**20.4**	17.2	22.7	20.5	10.0	27.8
Served as party official	**17.9**	12.5	19.7	15.4	11.1	27.3
Canvassed churches	**11.4**	13.0	13.6	15.4	7.8	9.1
Participated in protest	**11.4**	11.5	7.6	7.7	10.0	15.0
Ran for office	**6.7**	3.1	6.1	11.5	6.7	8.6
Mean types of acts	**6.0**	**6.1**	**5.5**	**6.5**	**5.1**	**6.5**
Year first active in politics						
Before 1960	**11.4**	7.8	20.7	16.7	6.7	11.9
1960s	**16.8**	16.2	15.5	18.2	16.0	17.9
1970s	**19.3**	21.6	19.0	19.7	17.3	17.9
1980s	**27.5**	28.1	25.9	18.2	30.7	29.8
1990s	**19.1**	20.4	17.2	16.7	21.3	18.5
2000s	**5.8**	6.0	1.7	10.6	8.0	4.0

Source: Survey by authors.

ing rallies, distributing voter guides, participating in boycotts, joining political groups, and registering voters). The level of involvement in two activities (fundraising and canvassing churches) was unchanged, and the remaining six items were less common in 2004. Only one, door-to-door campaigning, declined dramatically—perhaps a bit surprising given the intensity of the 2004 campaign.[11] Change in activity levels was fairly uniform across activist categories (data not shown).

Overall, few of the activists were recent recruits to politics; only about one-twentieth entered the process in 2000 or later. The largest number, a little more than one-quarter, were first activated in the 1980s, when the Christian Right appeared. About one-fifth became active in both the 1970s and 1990s, and the remaining one-quarter were involved before the 1970s. There were modest variations across activist categories. Pan-Evangelical Activists included the most recent recruits but also the most even distribution by decade. In contrast, Hard Right Activists counted the fewest new recruits and the most veterans from the 1950s. Pro-Family Activists and Core Activists had the fewest participating before 1970.

ORGANIZATIONAL ACTIVITIES

One of the most important types of activity by Christian Rightists is engagement in movement organizations. Table 2.12 reports on two aspects of organizational engagement for a particular group to which respondents belonged: their own activity within the organization and their report of the organization's collective activity.[12]

Overall, engagement level differed by type of activity. For instance, more than 90 percent of the respondents received a newsletter from their organization, and nearly as many paid dues or made financial contributions. Just two-fifths participated in organizational activities, however, and less than one-third worked with allied organizations or attended group meetings. As one might expect, even fewer held a group leadership position (about one-quarter). There were a few important differences across activist categories. Interestingly, Peripheral Activists reported the highest participation in organizational activities, attending meetings, working with allied groups, and serving in leadership positions. Pro-Family Activists resembled the Peripherals in this regard, usually outperforming the other categories. Pan-Evangelical Activists and Hard Right Activists were among the least involved in their organizations.

There also was wide variation in the collective activities of these organizations. Overall, 90 percent claimed their group was active in educating the public on issues, and about four-fifths reported mobilization of members to contact public officials, as well as contacting officials directly (presumably by means of a lobbyist). Two-thirds claimed that their organization was involved in issue campaigns, such as ballot initiatives. Almost half reported voter registration drives, and two-fifths named activity in electoral campaigns. Finally, a little more than one-quarter said that their organization was active in drafting legislation.

A final bit of information must be viewed with some caution: reports on sources of funding for the activist's organization. The activists in this survey overwhelmingly claimed that individual donations were a major

Table 2.12   Christian Right Activists in 2004: Engagement in Movement Organizations (% reporting activity)

Activities within a group	All	Core	Hard Right	Pan-Evangelical	Pro-Family	Peripheral
Receive a newsletter	**92.0**	95.3	90.4	94.6	88.7	88.8
Pay dues or donate	**88.4**	90.6	88.5	87.5	88.7	85.6
Participate in group activities	**40.8**	41.4	44.2	35.7	38.0	42.4
Work with allied groups	**30.7**	29.0	21.2	30.4	36.6	33.6
Attend group meetings	**30.7**	26.0	23.1	28.6	32.4	40.0
Hold leadership position	**26.4**	21.9	17.3	23.2	33.8	33.6
Group's political activities						
Educate citizens on issues	**91.1**	91.8	86.5	89.3	90.1	93.6
Urge members to contact officials	**83.7**	85.2	80.8	85.7	85.9	80.8
Contact public officials	**80.4**	83.5	76.9	82.1	77.5	78.4
Conduct awareness campaigns	**68.1**	71.0	55.8	76.8	67.6	65.6
Conduct voter registration drives	**47.5**	54.7	46.2	44.6	40.8	43.2
Participate in candidate campaigns	**42.4**	40.6	42.3	55.4	29.6	46.4
Draft legislation	**28.8**	30.2	30.8	25.0	28.2	28.0
Group funding sources						
Individual donations	**93.9**	92.4	96.2	85.7	95.8	97.6
Churches, ministries	**31.5**	33.1	26.9	39.3	33.8	26.4
Foundations, charities	**19.2**	21.3	7.7	19.6	23.9	18.4
Businesses	**18.6**	20.1	11.5	8.9	16.9	24.8
Allied groups	**15.6**	13.6	15.4	17.9	12.7	19.2
Political parties	**4.9**	1.2	7.7	1.8	1.4	12.0

Source: Survey by authors.

source of money (more than 90 percent overall). Churches and religious ministries came in a distant second (a little under one-third)—a pattern that may surprise some observers but is consistent with tax laws. Mentioned less frequently were foundations and businesses (less than one-fifth each), allied groups (one-sixth), and political parties (one-twentieth). If these perceptions are accurate, movement organizations are classic membership organizations, with only modest connections to outside patrons.

Here, too, there was some variation. Peripheral Activists were most likely to mention individual donations as a source of funds, but they also had the most mentions of foundations, businesses, allied groups, and political parties. This pattern may reflect the greater integration of these activists—and their organizations—into regular politics, but it also may reflect a wider variety of groups. Pro-Family Activists mentioned foundations most often, and Pan-Evangelical Activists reported churches and religious organizations most frequently. Hard Right Activists were notable for the relative lack of mention of funding from foundations, whereas Core Activists mentioned party funding the least often.

Agents of Value

What have we learned about these movement activists in 2004, and how did they differ from their counterparts in the past? We can offer a tentative answer to the first question and make an educated guess on the second.

These Christian Rightists were agents of value in the 2004 campaign. They were both proponents of traditional moral values and valuable assets in the contest. Like their predecessors, contemporary Christian Rightists in 2004 were drawn overwhelmingly from the ranks of highly traditional evangelical Protestants, although they do appear somewhat more diverse than in the past. They were middle-class and middle-aged, included more women, belonged to traditional nuclear families, and lived outside of major metropolitan areas—but may be more widely dispersed across the country.

In political terms, Christian Right activists were solidly conservative, strongly Republican, critical of government, and focused on traditional morality—as movement activists always have been. There may be somewhat greater diversity of opinion, however, on issues beyond the key moral concerns that have defined the movement. Perhaps the largest difference from their predecessors was in political style. These Christian Rightists appear to be somewhat more pragmatic than their counterparts in the past. Many adhere to a new civic gospel that justifies political action in defense of traditional morality. They certainly see politics as positive and efficacious—probably more so than in the past. This shift in political style may be the product of slow and steady integration of these activists into conventional politics.

Although these activists were heavily engaged in politics in 2004, they appear to have been only modestly more active than in the past; there is little evidence of a surge in their numbers in recent years. Thus, the Christian Right's prominence in media reports may not reflect a surge in the level and number of regular movement activists. Their greater cooperation with the Republican Party and the Bush campaign—both of which aggressively sought the support of conservative Christians—may have made the movement more prominent, however. Another factor may be the importance of same-sex marriage in the 2004 campaign, especially the state-level marriage initiatives. This issue may have generated additional activism outside the movement activist corps, including activity by new "promarriage groups" and expanded efforts by clergy and congregations (Cooperman and Edsall 2004). Interestingly, many of the activists in our study were not especially engaged in the movement organizations—a pattern that is consistent with the institutional instability that has long plagued Christian conservatives.

Our most interesting finding may be the diversity within the Christian Right activist corps. Core Activists embodied the most salient attributes of the movement, including a more pragmatic political style. Peripheral Activists were as numerous, less given to the movement's characteristic attitudes, and more active in politics. Meanwhile, the three remaining categories represented variations on movement themes: Hard Right Activists maintained a strong emphasis on traditional moral order; Pan-Evangelical Activists showed a special religious perspective on public affairs; and Pro-Family Activists reflected the salience of family issues. Thus, the Christian Right has many faces in national politics.

This internal diversity means that the Christian Right will not always speak with one voice. Although the movement was united behind George W. Bush in 2004 and is uniform in its backing for key social policy priorities, there is considerable disagreement on other matters. Given that many Christian Rightists are now enthusiastically committed to the political process, such differences may become more important in the future. A good test of their commitment may come in the 2006 mid-term elections and the 2008 presidential campaign, when Republicans will again need their support—perhaps for candidates less palatable to many movement activists.

Notes

1. The key targets of Christian Right activism, evangelical Protestants, turned out and voted for Republicans at record rates. See Green et al. (2005) for details.

2. Past studies of Christian Right activists can be characterized by their samples. Some scholars have surveyed members or leaders of movement organizations (e.g., Wilcox 1988; Wilcox, Linzey, and Jelen 1991; Smidt et al. 1994; Berkowitz and Green 1997; Rozell and Wilcox 1996; Green 2003; Racheter et al. 2003; Conger and Green 2002). Other studies rely on campaign contributors to Christian Right

groups or candidates (e.g., Guth and Green 1987; Green and Guth 1988; Green, Guth, and Fraser 1991; Wilcox 1992, 1996; Brown, Powell, and Wilcox 1995). Still other studies have looked at Christian Rightists among the clergy (e.g., Langenbach and Green 1992; Guth et al. 1997) or party activists (e.g., Layman 2001; Rozell, Wilcox, and Green 1998; Green, Jackson, and Clayton 1999). For good overviews of the role of activists in the movement, see Liebman and Wuthnow (1983), Bruce (1988), Hertzke (1993), Oldfield (1996), Green et al. (1996), Martin (1996), and Watson (1997).

3. The political action committees (PACs) included the Campaign for Working Families, the Eagle Forum, Concerned Women for America, the Madison Project, Government is Not God, and the Susan B. Anthony PAC. We obtained internal lists of group contributors from movement activists, on the condition of confidentiality. These lists were associated with Focus on the Family, the family research councils, and the Christian Coalition. Careful comparison of both kinds of lists found them to be similar in basic characteristics.

4. Our sample may miss state-level Christian Coalition activists, who were especially active in 2004. It is worth noting, however, that the American Center for Law and Justice was more popular than the Christian Coalition in this sample; the former is one of the few organizations with majority support in four of the five categories in table 2.1.

5. These categories were created by means of two-stage cluster analysis, using all the organizational affect and membership data in table 2.1.

6. These groups included Missouri Synod Lutherans, the Presbyterian Church in America, and other smaller evangelical churches.

7. The Constitution Party was a minor party with a strongly conservative agenda, including a heavy dose of conservative Christian doctrine. In 2004 it ran Michael Peroutka for president.

8. This analysis used principal components factoring with a varimax rotation; all factors had eigenvalues greater than 1.0 (2.8, 1.8, and 1.2, respectively), accounting for 45 percent of the variance.

9. This analysis used principal components factoring with a varimax rotation; all factors had eigenvalues greater than 1.0 (3.1, 1.6, and 1.1, respectively), accounting for 53 percent of the variance.

10. This analysis used principal components factoring with a varimax rotation; all factors had eigenvalues greater than 1.0 (3.2, 1.5, and 1.2, respectively), accounting for 40 percent of the variance.

11. The decline in self-reported door-to-door campaigning may reflect the reduced importance of geography in campaigning. Indeed, churches and religious organizations may be the "precincts" of contemporary elections.

12. These data on organizational engagement came from a special question in which respondents first were asked if they belong to "pro-family, pro-life, or Christian conservative organization" and then, if so, to name the organization. All of the organizations listed in table 2.1 were listed frequently, but there were a large number of other groups, many of them local. By this measure, 81 percent of respondents belonged to such a named group.

References

Berkowitz, Laura, and John C. Green. 1997. "Charting the Coalition: The Local Chapters of the Ohio Christian Coalition." In *Sojourners in the Wilderness: The Christian Right in Comparative Perspective*, ed. Corwin E. Smidt and James M. Penning. Lanham, Md.: Rowman & Littlefield, 57–74.

Brown, Clifford, Lynda Powell, and Clyde Wilcox. 1995. *Serious Money: Fundraising and Contributing in Presidential Nomination Campaigns*. Cambridge: Cambridge University Press.

Bruce, Steve. 1988. *The Rise and Fall of the New Christian Right*. Oxford: Clarendon Press.

Conger, Kimberly H., and John C. Green. 2002. "The Christian Right in the States: 2000." *Campaigns and Elections* 23 (1): 58–60, 64–65.

Cooperman, Alan. 2004. "Churchgoers Get Direction from Bush Campaign." *Washington Post*, 1 July, A6.

Cooperman, Alan, and Thomas B. Edsall. 2004. "Onward, Christian Soldiers." *Washington Post National Weekly Edition*, 15–21 November, 12

Dillman, Don A. 1978. *Mail and Telephone Surveys: The Total Design Method*. New York: Wiley.

Green, John C. 1999. "The Spirit Willing: Collective Identity and the Development of the Christian Right." In *Waves of Protest: Social Movements since the Sixties*, ed. Jo Freeman and Victoria Johnson. Lanham, Md.: Rowman & Littlefield, 153–68.

———. 2003. "Evangelical Protestants and Civic Engagement: An Overview." In *A Public Faith: Evangelicals and Civic Engagement*, ed. Michael Cromartie. Lanham, Md.: Rowman & Littlefield, 11–30.

Green, John C., and James L. Guth. 1988. "The Christian Right in the Republican Party: The Case of Pat Robertson's Supporters." *Journal of Politics* 50:150–65.

Green, John C., James L. Guth, and Cleveland Fraser. 1991. "Apostles and Apostates? Religion and Politics among Political Activists." In *The Bible and the Ballot Box*, ed. James L. Guth and John C. Green. Boulder, Colo.: Westview Press, 113–39.

Green, John C., James L. Guth, Lyman A. Kellstedt, and Corwin E. Smidt. 1994. "Uncivil Challenges? Support for Civil Liberties among Religious Activists." *Journal of Political Science* 22:25–50.

Green, John C., James L. Guth, Corwin E. Smidt, and Lyman A. Kellstedt. 1996. *Religion and the Culture Wars: Dispatches from the Front*. New York: Rowman & Littlefield.

Green, John C., John S. Jackson, and Nancy L. Clayton. 1999. "Issue Networks and Party Elites in 1996." In *The State of the Parties*, 3rd ed., ed. John C. Green and Daniel M. Shea. Lanham, Md.: Rowman & Littlefield, 105–19.

Green, John C., Mark J. Rozell, and Clyde Wilcox. 2003. "The Christian Right's Long Political March." In *The Christian Right in America*, ed. John C. Green, Mark J. Rozell, and Clyde Wilcox. Washington, D.C.: Georgetown University Press, 1–20.

Green, John C., Corwin E. Smidt, James L. Guth, and Lyman A. Kellstedt. 2005.
    "The American Religious Landscape and the 2004 Presidential Vote." Avail-
    able at www.uakron.edu/bliss/docs/TheAmericanReligiousLand.pdf.
Guth, James L. 1996. "The Politics of the Christian Right." In *Religion and the Cul-
    ture Wars: Dispatches from the Front*, ed. John C. Green, James L. Guth, Corwin
    E. Smidt, and Lyman A. Kellstedt. New York: Rowman & Littlefield, 7–29.
Guth, James L., and John C. Green. 1987. "The Moralizing Minority: Christian
    Right Support among Political Contributors." *Social Science Quarterly* 68:
    598–610.
———. 1989. "God and the GOP: Varieties of Religiosity among Political Con-
    tributors." In *Religion and American Political Behavior*, ed. Ted G. Jelen. New
    York: Praeger, 233–41.
Guth, James L., John C. Green, Lyman A. Kellstedt, and Corwin E. Smidt. 1994.
    "Onward Christian Soldiers: Religious Interest Group Activists." In *Interest
    Group Politics*, 4th ed., ed. Allan Cigler and Burdett Loomis. Washington, D.C.:
    CQ Press, 55–76.
Guth, James L., John C. Green, Corwin E. Smidt, Lyman A. Kellstedt, and Marga-
    ret Poloma. 1997. *The Bully Pulpit: The Politics of Protestant Clergy*. Lawrence:
    University Press of Kansas.
Hertzke, Allen D. 1993. *Echoes of Discontent: Jesse Jackson, Pat Robertson, and the
    Resurgence of Populism*. Washington, D.C.: Congressional Quarterly Press.
Hook, Janet. 2004. "Initiatives to Ban Gay Marriage Could Help Bush in Key
    States." *Los Angeles Times*, 12 July, A1.
Langenbach, Lisa, and John C. Green. 1992. "Hollow Core: Evangelical Clergy and
    the 1988 Robertson Campaign." *Polity* 25:147–58.
Layman, Geoffrey. 2001. *The Great Divide: Religious and Cultural Conflict in American
    Party Politics*. New York: Columbia University Press.
Liebman, Robert C., and Robert Wuthnow. 1983. *The New Christian Right: Mobili-
    zation and Legitimation*. Hawthorne, N.Y.: Aldine Publishing Co.
Marshall, Paul. 2004. "Fundamentalists & Other Fun People." *Weekly Standard*, 22
    November, 16.
Martin, William. 1996. *With God on Our Side: The Rise of the Religious Right in
    America*. New York: Broadway Books.
Moen, Matthew C. 1992. *The Transformation of the Christian Right*. Tuscaloosa: Uni-
    versity of Alabama Press.
Muirhead, Russell, Nancy L. Rosenblum, Daniel Schlozman, and Francis X. Shen.
    2005. "Religion in the 2004 Presidential Election." In *Divided States of America:
    The Slash and Burn Politics of the 2004 Presidential Election*, ed. Larry Sabato.
    New York: Longman.
Myers, Randy. 2005. "Religious Liberals Urge Activism." *San Jose Mercury News*,
    30 July.
Oldfield, Duane Murray. 1996. *The Right and the Righteous: The Christian Right
    Confronts the Republican Party*. Lanham, Md.: Rowman & Littlefield.
Racheter, Donald P., Lyman A. Kellstedt, and John C. Green. 2003. "Iowa: Crucible
    of the Christian Right." In *The Christian Right in America*, ed. John C. Green,

Mark J. Rozell, and Clyde Wilcox. Washington, D.C.: Georgetown University Press, 121–44.

Rozell, Mark, and Clyde Wilcox. 1996. *Second Coming: The New Christian Right in the Virginia Politics*. Baltimore: Johns Hopkins University Press.

Rozell, Mark J., Clyde Wilcox, and John C. Green. 1998. "Religious Constituencies and Support for the Christian Right in the 1990s." *Social Science Quarterly* 39:815–21.

Smidt, Corwin E., Lyman A. Kellstedt, John C. Green, and James L. Guth. 1994. "The Characteristics of Religious Group Activists: An Interest Group Analysis." In *Christian Political Activism at the Crossroads*, ed. William Stevenson. Lanham, Md.: University Press of America, 133–71.

Watson, Justin. 1997. *The Christian Coalition: Dreams of Restoration, Demands for Recognition*. New York: St. Martin's Press.

Wilcox, Clyde. 1988. "Seeing the Connection: Religion and Politics in the Ohio Moral Majority." *Review of Religious Research*. 30:47–58.

———. 1992. *God's Warriors: The Christian Right in Twentieth Century America*. Baltimore: The Johns Hopkins University Press.

———. 1996. *Onward Christian Soldiers? The Religious Right in American Politics*. Boulder, Colo.: Westview Press.

Wilcox, Clyde, Sharon Linzey, and Ted G. Jelen. 1991. "Reluctant Warriors: Premillenialism and Politics in the Moral Majority." *Journal for the Scientific Study of Religion* 30:245–58.

CHAPTER THREE

Saving Marriage by Banning Marriage

The Christian Right Finds a New Issue in 2004

CLYDE WILCOX, LINDA M. MEROLLA,

AND DAVID BEER

"What you're doing is undermining the whole legal definition, the underpinnings of the institution of the family, and when that goes, everything goes with it, including the stability of the country . . . and the future of Western civilization."

DR. JAMES DOBSON, head of Focus on the Family

"It is the poster issue for the titanic struggle that is . . . going on in our society between those who believe in a Judeo-Christian basis for our culture and those who believe in a neo-pagan, relativist base for our culture."

DR. RICHARD LAND, head of the Ethics and Religious Liberty Commission of the Southern Baptist Convention

ON NOVEMBER 18, 2003, THE MASSACHUSETTS STATE SUPREME Court ruled in *Goodridge et al. v. Department of Public Health* that "barring an individual from the protections, benefits, and obligations of civil marriage solely because that person would marry a person of the same sex violates the Massachusetts constitution." The decision essentially legalized same-sex marriage in Massachusetts. In February 2004, the mayor of San Francisco and officials in several other jurisdictions performed same-sex marriages in highly publicized ceremonies that attracted the attention of a sizable portion of the public. Although state courts later halted these marriages outside of Massachusetts, the legal status of same-sex marriages in California remains uncertain.

For most Americans, the issue of same-sex marriage seemed to burst unexpectedly onto the public agenda. The public had grappled with a series of gay rights issues over the past decade, and public opinion had become remarkably more liberal on each of them (Wilcox et al., in press). Few Americans had thought seriously about same-sex marriage, however—and this "blank slate" presented interest groups with an opportunity to frame the issue for the public. Christian Right groups had long anticipated the emergence of the same-sex marriage issue and had planned for the issue for some time. Movement activists had tested various messages and arguments; wrote papers, pamphlets, and even books on the subject; and were amply prepared to seize the initiative.

Many members of the Christian Right regarded the same-sex marriage issue as the defining battle in the culture wars—more important than other gay rights issues and even more immediately critical than abortion.[1] Some Christian Right activists thought that the United States would be judged in the manner of Sodom and Gomorrah if it allowed same-sex marriage to continue; others believed that the basic fabric of society itself would unravel and heterosexual marriage would collapse as an institution. The issue defined and structured the efforts of the Christian Right in the 2004 election and may have lasting importance for the future of the movement.

Issues play a complex role in social movements. The issue stands of social movement organizations represent their policy agenda—a set of promises to their members and patrons for policies they will enact if they gain access to political power. In most cases, these issues arouse deep passion among activists and supporters, accounting for the intensity of social movement politics.

Yet issues also represent a major resource for the internal maintenance of interest groups. Issues are useful in raising funds through direct-mail letters, telemarketing, and (increasingly) Internet appeals. Issues help social movement organizations recruit new members and turn regular members into activists. Paradoxically, issues are most useful for social movements when they pose seeming crises for movement policy goals. Once movements succeed in influencing policy, the crisis atmosphere is difficult to maintain, rendering an issue less useful in bringing key resources to the movement's organizations.

In 2004, however, after nearly thirty years of activity, the key issue agenda of the Christian Right remained unfulfilled. Although the movement had succeeded in passing two laws that limited abortion rights, for example, one (which defined murder of a pregnant woman as a double homicide in federal murder cases) had little scope, and the other (a ban on "partial birth" abortions) seemed likely to be overturned by the U.S. Supreme Court. In addition, the movement enjoyed some very limited success in education: Many states focused their sex education curriculum on abstinence, and some limited the teaching of evolution in biology classes.

On other sets of issues, including gender equality and gay rights, the movement had suffered major setbacks. Perhaps more important, there was little
evidence of momentum on any of these issues at the national or state level,
nor did evidence exist that the public was gradually being persuaded by the
movement's arguments (Wilcox and Larson 2006).

The same-sex marriage issue was the first new issue with significant
public appeal since the debate over inclusion of gays in the military in early
1993. The same-sex marriage issue presented several opportunities to the
movement. Unlike other issues on the Christian Right agenda, the same-
sex marriage issue attracted majority support in 2004, and in some states
popular opposition to same-sex marriage was overwhelming. The issue
appealed to individuals across religious boundaries that previously had
stymied movement coalition building; conservative Catholics, Mormons,
and even Muslims were committed to preventing gay marriage. The issue
even appealed to African American churches—a constituency that Ralph
Reed had once half-heartedly tried to involve in the Christian Coalition
(Campbell and Larson, in press).

The same-sex marriage issue transformed the Christian Right in several important ways in 2004. First, it rearranged the issue agenda, with
same-sex marriage receiving higher priority than any existing issue in
the minds of many activists. Second, it created ecumenical and interracial
coalitions that had not previously existed. Third, it helped to generate
new state organizations, as well as to invigorate existing ones. Finally, it
stimulated electoral activity in pastors and congregations that previously
had been inactive. These changes generally were healthy for the movement, although it is too soon to say if they will endure.

Taking the Early Offensive: Framing
the Same-Sex Marriage Issue

Christian Right leaders had discussed the same-sex marriage issue as early
as 1990, when legal challenges to Hawaii's marriage law were first filed in
state court. In 1996 a circuit court ruled that the state had no compelling
reason to deny same-sex couples the right to marry. Although the decision
was upheld on appeal to the state's Supreme Court, voters subsequently
passed a constitutional amendment that allowed legislators to ban same-
sex marriage by statute. Christian Right groups were heavily involved in a
March 2000 effort in which California voters enacted by initiative a provision that limited marriage to a union between one man and one woman.[2]

Yet most Americans outside those two states had not paid much attention to the same-sex marriage issue; as a result, the 2003 Massachusetts

court decision presented a new issue. Surveys demonstrated considerable ambivalence within the U.S. public, with majorities opposing same-sex marriage but substantially supporting many of the key legal protections of marriage (Wilcox et al., in press). Many Americans seemed to be uneasy with respect to same-sex marriage, but at the same time they seemed reluctant to discriminate against gays and lesbians. This ambivalence allowed contending political groups to compete to define or "frame" the issue for the public (Gordon, Tadlock, and Popp, in press; Hull 2001; for a more general account of framing gay rights issues, see Brewer 2003a, 2003b).

In 2003–4 gay rights groups were not prepared to mount a vigorous campaign to frame the same-sex marriage issue for voters, for a variety of reasons. In addition, the presidential candidates seemed to be reluctant to take strong positions on the issue; George Bush endorsed a national constitutional amendment to bar same-sex marriage hesitantly and with little apparent enthusiasm, and John Kerry endorsed instead an amendment to the Massachusetts state constitution to bar same-sex marriage.

This situation presented the Christian Right with the opportunity to define the issue for voters. Yet the Christian Right also confronted significant problems with respect to finding a common message among the various groups in the movement. First, some (though clearly not all) Christian Right groups had long demonized gay men and lesbians in direct mail appeals that inspired increased giving among the group's members. They had told their members and donors that gay men and lesbians recruited and abused young children and had used language that implied or, in some cases, openly stated that gays and lesbians belonged in prison.[3] The rhetoric of these groups was offensive to many potential coalition partners, including the Catholic church, which opposed same-sex marriage but had clear teachings about offering respect and dignity to gay men and lesbians. Moreover, such appeals were likely to create a backlash among the general public, which opposed same-sex marriage but also had become far more accepting of gays and lesbians in the preceding decade.

Second, movement groups disagreed about the proper strategy and tactics to combat same-sex marriage. All supported an amendment to the U.S. Constitution that would define marriage as a union between one man and one woman in all states, thereby overriding all state constitutions and laws. Yet the Alliance for Marriage favored a bare-bones amendment that would define marriage as an institution between one man and one woman and would bar the Supreme Court from discovering a right to same-sex marriage in the Constitution but would leave states free to create civil unions and domestic partnerships. Other groups opposed civil unions as proxy marriages and wanted an amendment that would bar them as well. A few groups wished to push for even stronger language that would bar states and cities from providing any benefits to same-sex couples (Cooper-man 2003).

Ultimately, the movement focused mainly on a push to "protect" marriage by barring same-sex couples from marrying. Some groups, such as the Family Research Council, promoted elaborate rationales for why heterosexual marriage was threatened by legal recognition of same-sex couples; others merely sought to stimulate fear of same-sex marriage.[4] In the short run, this issue frame was very successful, although after delibera-tion Americans may find the argument that the institution of marriage is endangered by allowing other Americans to marry is less compelling.

Christian Right groups also sought to define the issue as a case of judi-cial activism, and they used this frame to focus attention on the composi-tion of national and state courts, as well as to prepare their membership for fights over the confirmation of future Bush appointees to the Supreme Court. Again, this depiction proved a powerful short-term frame, although the movement clearly would have reacted no differently if same-sex mar-riages in Massachusetts had been a result of legislative, instead of judicial, action. Indeed, Christian Right leaders responded negatively to the deci-sion by Connecticut's elected officials to legalize civil unions, even though no activist judges were involved. The judicial activism frame led logically to a push to amend state constitutions to preclude "activist liberal judges" from "discovering" a right to same-sex marriage in state constitutions, as well as a similar push for adoption of a national amendment to bar all states from doing so.

In the absence of an alternate frame—for example, a focus on equal-ity that might have been suggested by liberal groups or a spirited defense of same-sex marriage by any prominent Democratic politician—the Christian Right's framing of the same-sex marriage issue dominated the political discourse during 2004. Yet Republicans, leery of the remarkable change in public attitudes regarding gay rights issues over the preceding two decades, were reluctant to fully embrace the national amendment that Christian groups had proposed. Indeed, President Bush announced his support only after considerable pressure from groups such as Concerned Women for America (Hallow 2004). Subsequently, the Bush campaign tersely stated that the president had said all he would say on the topic, although the campaign did use the issue in carefully targeted communi-cations with religious conservative voters.[5] As a result, Bush had spent no political capital when the amendment failed in the U.S. Senate in 2004 (Larson and Wilcox 2005).

Meanwhile, many state activists and organizations promoted amend-ments to state constitutions that would not only define marriage as a union between a man and a woman and deny any constitutional right to same-sex marriage but in some cases would bar civil unions or any contract that conferred any of the benefits of marriage. In 2004 thirteen states passed constitutional amendments: Missouri and Louisiana before November and Arkansas, Georgia, Kentucky, Michigan, Mississippi, North Dakota, Montana, North Dakota, Ohio, Oklahoma, Oregon, and Utah on Election Day.

Most of the states that passed referenda in 2004 were in little actual danger of legalizing same-sex marriage; most were marked by conservative legislatures, conservative courts, and state constitutions that lacked strong equality provisions. In many of these states the outcome of the referenda seemed a foregone conclusion, and liberal groups offered only token opposition. In Ohio, Oregon, and Michigan, however, powerful political forces opposed the amendments, and liberal groups mounted a spirited campaign. In Oregon and Michigan, the amendments passed with less than 60 percent of the popular vote; in Ohio and Utah, the amendments garnered almost two-thirds of the popular vote. In other states, the margin generally was about 3 to 1.

In Ohio the measure passed with 62 percent of the popular vote despite opposition from a broad coalition of Democrats, Republicans, and business, labor, and civic groups that warned that the issue would be detrimental to Ohio's economy and image.[6] Ohio Governor Bob Taft, U.S. Senators Mike DeWine and George Voinovich, Ohio Attorney General Jim Petro, Ohio State University, AARP Ohio, the League of Women Voters of Ohio, and the Ohio AFL-CIO opposed the referendum.[7] Major corporations in the state also opposed the measure, saying that it would be bad for business.[8]

Same-Sex Marriage and the Potential Transformation of the Christian Right

The same-sex marriage issue changed Christian Right rhetoric, fundraising, and activities in 2004, and it retains the potential to more fundamentally transform the movement in the near future. The issue altered the Christian Right's issue agenda, coalition partners, state organizations, and possibly its congregational potential.

The Crucial Battle of the Culture War

Existing organizations made the same-sex issue a high priority in 2004, and they appear to be prepared to continue to do so in the future. Many regarded same-sex marriage as the most important issue facing the country and believed that by acting quickly they could draw a sharp line of state constitutional and statutory law to bar its spread. Most major national groups were active in one way or another, and all claimed some credit for the victory represented by prevailing in the state referenda of 2004.

Focus on the Family—probably the key player in efforts to pass a national constitutional amendment—also aided in some of the state referenda efforts. Focus on the Family worked with other groups to promote the issue through special events such as "Protect Marriage Sunday" on September 19, 2004—cosponsored with Citizens for Community Values, the Family Research Council (FRC), the American Family Association, and others—and the "Mayday for Marriage" rally on the National Mall in Washington, D.C., on October 15, 2004.[9] The organization distributed sample sermons to sympathetic ministers and sent cash contributions to affiliates working in Oregon and Michigan, where polling initially indicated that the amendments might fail (Campbell and Larson, in press). It also participated in broad coalitions such as the Arlington Group and with the Marriage Amendment Project, which included not only Christian Right groups but also denominational bodies and an association of African American pastors (Campbell and Larson, in press).

The FRC also made the issue central to its agenda; it issued policy papers and lobbied Congress on behalf of the federal amendment. The FRC also helped to coordinate coalitions in opposition to same-sex marriage. Concerned Women for America (CWA) issued policy papers as well, and its leaders made many public appearances on television and radio to discuss the issue. CWA also initiated direct mailings on the issue to its members, especially in states where amendments were on the ballot.

Thus, the same-sex marriage issue has become a very high priority for the Christian Right and, as a result, has featured prominently in movement fundraising. For example, the American Center for Law and Justice (ACLJ) mailed twenty-two solicitations referencing the issue in 2004, making same-sex marriage the single most frequently discussed issue in the Center's fundraising. Not surprisingly, the issue was not part of fundraising efforts in 2003.[10] Our inspection of tax records of leading Christian Right groups suggests that the issue did not lead to a marked increase in fundraising, however. Indeed, several prominent groups reported less income in 2004 than they had in 2002.

New Partners, New Possibilities

The same-sex marriage issue offered the Christian Right the opportunity to build bridges with potential supporters that had never fully embraced the Christian Right in the past. The Church of Jesus Christ of Latter-Day

Saints—the Mormons—joined with Christian Right groups to oppose same-sex marriage, as it had in the California referendum a few years earlier (Campbell and Monson, in press). Many prominent Catholic leaders became deeply involved in the effort and may have helped to moderate the rhetoric of the movement. Orthodox Jews and Muslims also joined the marriage coalition. Although Ralph Reed of the Christian Coalition had often spoken of "people of faith" in very inclusive ways, the Christian Right historically had been largely·unable to forge durable coalitions outside the white evangelical community.

Perhaps most significant, several African American pastors joined the effort (Campbell and Larson, in press). Although evidence of potential support for the Christian Right among African Americans had existed during the 1980s and afterwards, the movement previously had made only half-hearted efforts to include blacks (Wilcox 1990). Djupe, Neiheisel, and Sokhey (2004) report that during the 2004 campaign, however, the Ohio Campaign to Protect Marriage contacted 70 percent of black pastors in Columbus; this figure represents a remarkable effort to mobilize diverse racial-religious constituencies.

This unprecedented ecumenical coalition might presage a more inclusive Christian Right movement. The overwhelming Republican orientation of the movement will make any substantial inroads into black churches difficult, but the growing cultural divide between young, devout Catholics and their older counterparts suggests the possibility of future gains among Catholics (for further analysis of the age divide among devout Catholics, see Mockabee, forthcoming).

The State of the States

The same-sex marriage issue led to the formation of several state organizations and might have played a role in the revitalization of others. In most states, coalitions of groups formed special, ad hoc organizations to mount an effective campaign. In Oregon the Defense of Marriage Coalition conducted telephone "push polls" that were designed to move rather than measure public opinion.[11] The coalition had a sophisticated web page and distributed DVDs that were shown in many churches during the petition drive and the campaign.[12] The Ohio Campaign to Protect Marriage reportedly placed 3.3 million phone calls, registered 54,000 new voters, and placed 2.5 million church bulletin inserts in 17,000 churches across the state (Djupe, Neiheisel, and Sokhey 2004).

In Ohio and some other states, Christian Coalition chapters appeared to be revitalized, often with financial support from other organizations or wealthy patrons but little coordination from national headquarters.

State chapters of CWA and affiliates of Focus on the Family also reported increased membership and financial contributions, although there has been no systematic study of these claims. Whether this increase presages a renewed vibrancy of state organizations in the movement is unclear. It is worth noting, however, that organizations that have succeeded in achieving their goal quickly frequently find new goals; in this manner, the infrastructure that was created in these state referenda drives may prove to be a potent new tool for the movement.

From Pews to Precincts: Churches Enter Politics

This infrastructure includes networks of politicized pastors and congregations, some of which had not been active in elections previously. Movement leaders worked hard to reach new churches and pastors, especially in battleground states such as Michigan, Ohio, and Oregon. The Christian Right has long benefited from ties with individual congregations; the Moral Majority held voter registration drives in churches and used megachurches as organizational resources, and the Christian Coalition used evangelical churches to distribute its voter guides (Wilcox and Larson 2006). Although this factor is impossible to quantify, clearly many pastors who previously had avoided talking about elections from the pulpit did so in 2004, and the same-sex marriage issue was a key part of that transition.

In Oregon, for example, the East Hill Foursquare Church in Gresham—the state's largest church, with more than 5,000 members—showed a DVD produced by the Defense of Marriage Coalition at each of its four services during the petition drive to place the amendment on the state ballot.[13] The church registered 375 new voters, and on two Saturdays members of the church fanned out into neighborhoods, where they prayed for voters and knocked on their doors, urging support for the measure.[14] The church usually tries to stay out of the political arena, said Pastor Ray Young, administrator for East Hill. On Measure 36, however, "we felt it was imperative to weigh in," Young said.[15] Some pastors took the issue to the stump. Rod Parsley of the Columbus, Ohio, megachurch World Harvest traveled the state on a "Silent No More" tour (Johnson and Mahoney 2004.)

Although no national data exist regarding the exact number of churches that became involved in politics for the first time, one survey of pastors in Columbus, Ohio, found that same-sex marriage was discussed in 86 percent of churches (Djupe, Neiheisel, and Sokhey 2004). Fully 36 percent of pastors preached on the issue, and nearly half said that Issue 1 prompted discussion. Notably, 9 percent of pastors reported that a church member came out as gay, and 12 percent said that a member of the congregation was struggling with their sexuality—which became, in turn, part of the discussion of same-sex marriage.

Christian Right groups encouraged pastors to become involved. Focus on the Family distributed special mailings to pastors in states where constitutional amendments were on the ballot, encouraging them to preach on the subject and outlining sample sermons. In June 2004 the Alliance Defense Fund (ADF) sent one such letter, titled "Churches, Marriage and Politics: No Time for Silence."[16] The letter encouraged pastors to involve their churches in grassroots organizing in support of bans on same-sex marriage and pledged that the ADF would "spare no effort to ensure that Christians [would] not be silenced in the battle for marriage."[17] The letter addressed fears that sermons on a ballot issue might jeopardize the church's tax-exempt status.[18] Gary S. McCaleb, senior counsel to the ADF, provided an in-depth analysis of case law surrounding this issue, assuring pastors that "churches have broad constitutional rights to express their views on marriage" as outlined in the letter, including the ability to preach about marriage or to allow petitions to be signed by parishioners on church property.[19] The letter requested that any church or pastor questioned in any manner about such actions immediately contact the ADF for assistance.[20]

The letter characterized the dispute over the propriety of same-sex marriage in terms easily understood by members of the American public: as "a great battle [raging] within our nation . . . to determine whether the very foundation of our society—one man and one woman, joined in marriage—will survive."[21] According to the ADF, efforts were occurring "across America," with "citizens . . . fighting to save marriage by advancing pro-marriage legislation at the state and federal level."[22] In contrast to descriptions of activities by the ADF and its allies as based firmly within the majoritarian political process, the letter profiled the organizational efforts of gay marriage advocates as countermajoritarian, against the will of the American citizenry, and even, at times, based in intimidation: "Homosexual activists know that their arguments will fail if they are put squarely before our nation's citizens, and they do all that they can to prevent the issue from ever coming to a vote. Thus, pro-homosexual groups are threatening churches across the nation with the loss of tax-exempt status, and/or they allege that various state political campaign laws were violated, when churches simply preach about marriage or allow petitions on their properties. It is a simple scare tactic, designed to silence Christians."[23]

The letter went on to describe further the "scare tactics" of gay marriage activists through the assertion that such "activists sent out some 80,000 threat letters" to churches in California in 1996, 1998, and 2000 in reference to the gay marriage issue in that state.[24] The letter reassured pastors that they need not fear such threats and pledged legal support in the event of a challenge to the ability of churches to distribute materials and conduct discussions regarding the effort to pass same-sex marriage amendments.[25] The ADF's legal promises may have led some pastors to preach on this topic who might not otherwise have done so.

Of course, it is unclear how many of the pastors and congregations that mobilized on the same-sex marriage issue will continue to participate in broader electoral activity. Christian Right leaders and Republican Party officials now possess a ready resource, however, in the list of pastors who worked on the same-sex marriage issue, and they are likely to attempt to draw these pastors into future campaigns.

Same-Sex Marriage and the 2004 Elections

The reluctance of George Bush and many leading Republicans to firmly advocate a national constitutional amendment and the Democratic ticket's consistent statement of opposition to same-sex marriage made it difficult for Christian Right forces to use the issue effectively in the 2004 election campaign. Yet the Christian Right still attempted to use the issue. The Bush campaign, Republican candidates more generally, and Christian Right groups all sought to portray Republican candidates as the most reliable defenders of traditional marriage and insinuated that Democrats were sympathetic with liberals who were trying to destroy the institution of marriage.[26]

The Bush campaign was happy to let Christian Right groups debate same-sex marriage for him, allowing the president to take the "high road" by avoiding the issue in his carefully scripted road stops. The campaign made sure, however, that surrogates used the issue effectively. In some morally conservative swing states, such as West Virginia, the Republican National Committee mailed letters to homes noting that liberals wanted to allow same-sex marriage (and take away Christians' Bibles to boot!). Carefully targeted phone messages reminded conservative voters that the future of marriage was at stake and that George Bush shared their values.

In addition, several GOP congressional candidates made the issue a central focus of their television advertising (Lucas, in press). In general, the advertising did not attempt to portray Democratic opponents as supporters of same-sex marriage, given that most Democrats also opposed it. Instead, these candidates simply ran strong positional ads that spoke of the depths of their commitment to "defend" marriage (Lucas, in press). In this manner, Republicans used the issue as a subtle values cue, counting on the perception among more religious voters that the GOP was the party of religious values. Thus, by increasing the salience of the issue and reinforcing their support for traditional marriage, they generally did not need to attack Democratic candidates.

Focus on the Family asked candidates for national and state legislatures to pledge support for constitutional amendments barring same-sex marriage and urged voters to base vote decisions on this information. The group distributed sample sermons to pastors that focused on candidate positions on a federal (not state) marriage amendment, thereby implying that Bush was more committed to traditional heterosexual marriage than was John Kerry.[27] Revitalized Christian Coalition chapters in some states distributed voter guides that contrasted candidate positions on the issues—though far fewer than in their heyday of the mid 1990s.

Did the same-sex marriage issue ultimately aid in the reelection of George Bush? In Ohio the amendment succeeded with 62 percent of the vote, whereas Bush carried the state by a scant 118,000 votes. The assumption that associating himself with a popular referendum issue helped Bush in Ohio seems logical. Yet there are reasons to be skeptical of the contention that same-sex marriage was the source of Bush's victory. First, although Bush did very well among white, churchgoing Christian voters, there are many other explanations for these votes. Bush had staked out a consistent, if somewhat vague, prolife position on abortion, for example, whereas John Kerry had an almost perfect prochoice record in the Senate. Bush talked openly and easily about his faith, whereas Kerry was curiously unwilling to talk about religious issues in the campaign, although he had discussed these issues in speeches in previous years (D'Antonio and White 2004).

Moreover, Bush increased his national vote share over his showing in the 2000 election, and that increase was greater in states that did not vote on marriage referenda than in those that did. That is, Bush's margin of victory increased less in states with marriage amendments on the ballot than it did in states without an amendment referendum. Academic studies to date generally have concluded that Bush's victory was more a result of the Iraq war and fears of terrorism than his opposition to same-sex marriage. Abramowitz (2004) concludes that Bush's vote share was no higher than expected for an incumbent running with existing economic conditions and that existing cleavages in the electorate continued in 2004. Abramowitz did not find any boost for Bush in states that held gay marriage referenda, although he did find that Bush did slightly better than expected in states that were directly affected by terrorism. Burden (2004) reports that Bush won by doing better than expected among white and married women, who were affected by domestic security concerns. Like Abramowitz, Burden also concludes that Bush did not do better than expected in states with marriage referenda on the ballot. Similarly, Hillygus and Shields (2005) used data from a large national survey to conclude that values generally, and same-sex marriage in particular, played only a minor role in voting nationwide, whereas partisanship, ideology, attitudes toward the Iraq war and terrorism, and the economy mattered far more.

Of course, several of the key states with marriage referenda were already very supportive of Bush, so a dramatically increased Bush vote share in these states would be highly unlikely. Moreover, the marriage amendment might not have helped Bush in Oklahoma but did help in Ohio and Michigan, for example. Campbell and Monson (in press) examined individual-level and county-level data and concluded that the same-sex marriage issue allowed Bush to win more Catholic votes and to increase turnout among white evangelicals and Catholics.

Our analysis (not shown) suggests that although the same-sex marriage issue did not affect turnout or vote choice nationally, it did have an impact in Ohio. Using data from the National Election Study—a survey of voters and nonvoters nationally—we estimated the effects of support for and opposition to same-sex marriage on turnout, holding constant factors of age, education, income, race, and strength of partisanship. Neither supporters nor opponents of same-sex marriage were more likely to vote than those who volunteered the intermediate position that civil unions but not marriage should be allowed. Next we estimated the effects of same-sex marriage on the presidential vote, holding constant factors of partisanship, ideology, and evaluations of the economy and the war in Iraq. Even with this limited set of independent variables, neither supporters nor opponents voted differently from those in the middle. Additional controls for other demographic variables, religious characteristics, and other policy attitudes such as abortion did not alter this result.

Our analysis of the 2004 Ohio exit poll, however, shows that the same-sex marriage issue did affect votes. The data show that Issue 1 (the state referendum to amend the constitution to bar same-sex marriage) was supported by 80 percent of Republicans, 55 percent of independents, and 43 percent of Democrats.[28] In table 3.1, we show the percentage of Democrats, independents, and Republicans who cast ballots for George Bush, by vote on Issue 1. The data suggest strongly that the same-sex marriage issue moved votes in Ohio. Democrats who voted for the initiative were 12 percent more likely to vote for Bush than those who voted against it, and Republicans who voted for the initiative were 11 percent more likely to also vote for the president than those who voted against the measure. The impact among independents was more striking: Supporters were 37 percent more likely to vote for Bush than those who opposed the measure. The greater impact for same-sex marriage among independents echoes the finding of Abramowitz (1995) in his study of abortion in the 1992

Table 3.1   Ohio Issue 1 and Presidential Voting (% voting for Bush)

Party	For Initiative	Against Initiative
Democrats	16	4
Independents	57	20
Republicans	96	85

Source: Ohio exit poll.

election, but the impact among partisan voters is greater than he found in that study.

On the basis of these data, the issue appears to cut both ways, helping both Bush and Kerry. Approximately 16 percent of Democrats who voted for the initiative cast ballots for Bush, and 15 percent of Republicans who voted for the initiative voted for Kerry. The sizes of these groups were uneven, however: Democrats who cast ballots for the initiative and for Bush constituted about 7 percent of all Ohio voters, whereas Republicans who opposed the initiative and voted for Kerry constituted only 3 percent.

Of course, these defections may be the result of other factors—overall ideology, religious values more generally, or evaluations of the war in Iraq or the war on terror. We estimated a series of logistic regression models predicting presidential vote with various controls and an indicator of their vote on Issue 1. In table 3.2 we present a model with controls for partisanship; ideology; evaluations of how the war in Iraq is going now; evaluation of the Ohio economy; basic demographic variables; dummy variables for Catholics and white, born-again Christians; and frequency of church attendance. We also estimated models with other economic attitudes, including the financial situation of the respondent and evaluation of jobs in their community, and with other measures of attitudes toward the war in Iraq and terrorism. The basic result remains unchanged in all of these models.

The data show that evaluations of the war in Iraq and partisanship were the strongest predictors of a Bush vote in Ohio but that the respondent's vote on Issue 1 was a significant predictor—stronger than general ideology, evaluations of the Ohio economy, and basic demographic and religious variables. Holding everything else constant, respondents who voted for Issue 1 were 2½ times more likely to vote for Bush than other voters. We could not control for attitudes on abortion and other social-moral issues, so some of this effect might be a more general social conservatism. The data strongly suggest, however, that votes moved because of the same-sex marriage referendum in Ohio.

Table 3.2   Multivariate Analysis of Ohio Presidential Voting

Variable	b	Wald
Partisanship	1.59	92.80[a]
Ideology	.57	7.97[a]
Evaluation of Iraq	−1.78	108.34[a]
Evaluation of Ohio economy	−.54	8.91[a]
Married	.08	.11
Black	−.71	2.08
Female	.75	10.25[a]
Age	.04	.60
Income	.09	1.27
Education	.06	.26
Catholic	−.23	.68
White born again	.05	.02
Frequency of attendance	.15	2.14
Issue 1 vote	.92	14.12[a]
N	2042	
Nagelkerke R-square	.81	
Predicted correctly (%):		
Kerry	92	
Bush	93	
Overall	92	

[a]Beta weight significant at .10 level or better.
Source: Ohio exit poll.

The Christian Right and the Future of Same-Sex Marriage

The same-sex marriage issue transformed the Christian Right in 2004, but how lasting those changes will be remains to be seen. The movement is likely to continue to make the issue a priority, for both ideological reasons (activists believe that it is important) and practical ones (the issue is a winning one for them in the short run). Already the movement is pushing for state amendment votes in 2006, and some groups have published sophisticated guides to the politics and procedures of the amendment process in the remaining states.

The ecumenical and interracial coalition that formed over this issue is unlikely to be a harbinger of a more inclusive Christian Right, however. Most African Americans do not share the movement's partisan leanings, its economic and foreign policy agenda, or its views on women's roles and other issues. In other states, black pastors doubtlessly will join efforts to amend state constitutions, but once those amendments are passed, the alliance probably will dissolve.

Yet this issue, combined with the issues raised by the Terry Schiavo case and other issues of shared salience, might help to forge a more viable alliance between conservative Catholics and evangelicals. There are many signs that the longstanding tension between white evangelicals and Catholics is lessening. Evangelicals flocked to Mel Gibson's *The Passion of the Christ*, although it told the story with a distinctively Catholic emphasis. More than two decades of working together in state politics have helped to build personal friendships between many conservative Catholics and conservative evangelicals, and a new, highly salient issue on which the groups see eye to eye may help to strengthen their cooperation.

State and local organizations that were formed and invigorated during the 2004 referenda campaigns seem likely to shrink substantially now that the amendments have passed. Nevertheless, the infrastructure from the 2004 referenda remains in place for political entrepreneurs to use, and at least some of those networks are likely to be called upon in 2006 and 2008. Some groups that formed for the marriage referenda will find new reasons for continuing to exist, by refining their mission or focusing on new issues.

Finally, at least some of the churches that participated in the 2004 referenda campaigns are likely to become more politically involved in future elections, because politics can be exciting, and participating in the future is easier after the first time. Other churches, however, are likely to retreat to the private religious sphere. Whether they do so may be the most important question regarding the lasting impact of the mobilization to "protect" marriage in 2004. If a significant number of pastors shed their reluctance to be politically involved, and if congregations welcome pastoral comments on coming elections, the infrastructure of the Christian Right may be strengthened, even without strengthening the groups themselves.

In the longer term, same-sex marriage might not be a long-term winning issue for the Christian Right. When President Bill Clinton announced his intention in 1993 to allow gays and lesbians to serve openly in the military, the announcement created a firestorm that divided the country; today, however, there is overwhelming approval for allowing gays and lesbians to openly serve. In the early 1990s fewer than one in four Americans favored allowing gays and lesbians to adopt children; today the figure is slightly more than half (Wilcox et al., in press). A similar liberalizing trend is likely to apply to same-sex marriage because increasing numbers of Americans realize that they know a gay man or a lesbian woman, and increasing numbers of Americans do not believe that sexual orientation is a choice.

Of course, much depends on future events. If the U.S. Supreme Court were to overturn the Defense of Marriage Act (DOMA), states could forbid same-sex marriage but would have to recognize those performed in other states, which would mean that any gay or lesbian couple with enough money and time could fly to Massachusetts and marry. At that point, the movement would be likely to mount a massive effort to amend the national constitution—a difficult task. If the Supreme Court upholds DOMA and Massachusetts amends its state constitution to bar same-sex marriage, the issue's momentum is likely to dissipate. If the Supreme Court upholds DOMA but some other states move to legalize civil unions or same-sex marriages, Americans are likely to find the argument that the institution of marriage is threatened by same-sex unions more difficult to accept as they come into contact with happily married gay and lesbian couples. In that case, public opinion seems most likely to liberalize on same-sex marriage, as it has on other gay rights issues.

Notes

1. Although many activists believed that abortion was a more critical problem than same-sex marriage, they had little hope of changing policy immediately and saw no threat that policy would immediately become more liberal. On same-sex marriage, in contrast, many believed that if action were not taken immediately, several states would soon allow same-sex marriage, and the Supreme Court might then overturn the Defense of Marriage Act—meaning that a marriage in Massachusetts must be honored in Texas.

2. Unlike the state constitutional amendments of 2004, the Hawaii amendment did not bar same-sex marriage; it merely allowed the legislature to do so. The California measure affected state law, not the state constitution. In early 2005 the California courts were considering whether the law violated the state's constitution.

3. In 1999 Jerry Falwell publicly apologized to former speechwriter Mel White for fundraising appeals that White maintained had inspired violence against gays and lesbians.

4. For an example of the many policy briefs prepared by Family Research Council, see www.frc.org/get.cfm?i=PL03D1.

5. The Republican National Committee mailed persuasion pieces in West Virginia and other states suggesting that liberals wanted to take away Bibles and allow same-sex marriage. It also ran ads on selected radio stations, which reach targeted audiences. See www.cbsnews.com/stories/2004/09/24/politics/main645393.shtml.

6. See Laura Bischoff, "Ohio Passes Gay Marriage Ban," Cox News Service, 3 November 2004.

7. Ibid.

8. Ibid.

9. See www.ohiomarriage.com/E-News-09172004.htm.

10. These figures are based on our analysis of fundraising appeals in the People for the American Way library.

11. See Bill Graves and Jeff Mapes, "Faith Politics Could Tip Vote," *The Oregonian*, 30 October 2004, D1.

12. See https://defenseofmarriagecoalition.org.

13. See www.ohiomarriage.com/E-News-09172004.htm.

14. Ibid.

15. Ibid.

16. See www.alliancedefensefund.org.

17. "Churches, Marriage and Politics: No Time for Silence," Alliance Defense Fund letter to pastors, p. 4, at www.alliancedefensefund.org. The letter also states, "Homosexual activists' outrageous, intolerant efforts to stop churches from expressing their faith will succeed only if pastors succumb to fear and stand mute when marriage is attacked. But nothing in the law supports these activists' demands, and no pastor should yield to fear. Rather, pastors can (and should) speak clearly regarding moral truth and freely participate in the political processes within the limits set forth by our laws."

18. Ibid.

19. Ibid., 3.

20. Ibid., 2.

21. Ibid., 1.

22. Ibid.

23. Ibid.

24. Ibid.

25. Ibid., 2.

26. One radio ad stated, "There is a line drawn in America today. On one side are the radicals trying to uproot our traditional values and our culture. They're fighting to hijack the institution of marriage, plotting to legalize partial-birth abortion, and working to take God out of the pledge of allegiance and force the worst of Hollywood on the rest of America." The ad asks, "Are you on their side of the line?" before making the plea to "support conservative Republican candidates." See www.cbsnews.com/stories/2004/09/24/politics/main645393.shtml.

27. For a sample, see www.ivotevalues.org/templates/cusivotevaluesorg/details.asp?id=27885&PID=160978&mast=.

28. This percentage includes in the denominator respondents who did not vote on the issue but voted for other offices and issues.

References

Abramowitz, Alan. 1995. "It's Abortion, Stupid: Policy Voting in the 1992 Presidential Election." *Journal of Politics* 57:176–86.

———. 2004. "Terrorism, Gay Marriage, and Incumbency: Explaining the Republican Victory in the 2004 Presidential Election." *The Forum* 2, no. 4: article 3; available at www.bepress.com/forum.

Brewer, Paul. 2003a. "The Shifting Foundations of Public Opinion about Gay
    Rights," *Journal of Politics* 65:1208–20.
———. 2003b. "Values, Political Knowledge, and Public Opinion about Gay Rights:
    A Framing-Based Account." *Public Opinion Quarterly* 67:173–201.
Burden, Barry C. 2004. "An Alternative Account of the 2004 Presidential Election."
    The Forum 2, no. 4: Article 2; available at www.bepress.com/forum.
Campbell, David E., and Carin Larson. In press. "Religious Coalitions For and
    Against Gay Marriage: The Culture War Rages On." In *The Politics of Same-
    Sex Marriage*, ed. Craig Rimmerman and Clyde Wilcox. Chicago: University
    of Chicago Press.
Campbell, David E., and J. Quin Monson. In press. "Dry Kindling: A Political
    Profile of American Mormons." In *From Pews to Polling Places: Political Mobili-
    zation in the American Religious Mosaic*, ed. Matthew Wilson. Washington, D.C.:
    Georgetown University Press.
Cooperman, Alan. 2003. "Opponents of Gay Marriage Divided." *Washington Post*,
    29 November. Available at www.msnbc.com/news/999176.asp.
D'Antonio, William, and John K. White. 2004. "Catholics and the Politics of
    Change: The Presidential Campaigns of Two JFKs." Paper presented at con-
    ference on "Religion and the Presidency," Grand Valley State University,
    Grand Rapids, Mich., 18 November.
Djupe, Paul A., Jake R. Neiheisel, and Anand E. Sokhey. 2004. "Clergy and Contro-
    versy: A Study of Clergy and Gay Rights in Columbus, Ohio." Paper presented
    at annual meeting of Midwest Political Science Association, Chicago.
Gordon, C. Ann, Barry L. Tadlock, and Elizabeth Popp. In press. "Framing the
    Issue of Same-Sex Marriage: Traditional Values versus Equal Rights." In *The
    Politics of Same-Sex Marriage*, ed. Craig Rimmerman and Clyde Wilcox. Chi-
    cago: University of Chicago Press.
Hallow, Ralph Z. 2004. "Evangelicals Frustrated by Bush." *Washington Times*, 20
    February.
Hillygus, D. Sunshine, and Todd G. Shields. 2005. "Moral Issues and Voter Deci-
    sionmaking in the 2004 Presidential Election." *PS: Political Science & Politics*
    38 (2): 201–10.
Hull, Kathleen N. 2001. "The Political Limits of the Rights Frame: The Case of
    Same Sex Marriage in Hawaii." *Social Perspectives* 44:207–32.
Johnson, Alan, and Dennis Mahoney. 2004. "Same-Sex Marriage Ban; Issue 1
    Divides Religious Leaders; While Some Crusade, Others Are Troubled."
    Columbus Dispatch, 30 October, 1C.
Larson, Carin, and Clyde Wilcox. 2005. "The Faith of George W. Bush: The Per-
    sonal, Practical, and Political." Paper presented at conference on "Religion
    and the Presidency," Grand Valley State University, Grand Rapids, Mich., 18
    November.
Lucas, DeWayne. In press. "Same Sex Marriage in Election 2004." In *The Politics of
    Same-Sex Marriage*, ed. Craig Rimmerman and Clyde Wilcox. Chicago: Uni-
    versity of Chicago Press.
Mockabee, Stephen T. Forthcoming. "The Political Behavior of American Catholics:
    Change and Continuity." In *From Pews to Polling Places*, ed. Matthew Wilson.

Wilcox, Clyde. 1990. "Blacks and the New Christian Right: Support for the Moral Majority and Pat Robertson among Washington, D.C. Blacks." *Review of Religious Research*. 32:43–56.

Wilcox, Clyde, and Carin Larson. 2006. *Onward Christian Soldiers? The Religious Right in American Politics*. Boulder, Colo.: Westview Press.

Wilcox, Clyde, Paul Brewer, Shauna Shanes, and Celinda Lake. In press. "Same Sex Marriage and Public Opinion." In *The Politics of Same Sex Marriage*, ed. Craig Rimmerman and Clyde Wilcox. Chicago: University of Chicago Press.

PART TWO

The Key States in the 2004 Election

CHAPTER FOUR

Ohio

The Bible and the Buckeye State

JOHN C. GREEN

OHIO PLAYED A CRUCIAL ROLE IN THE 2004 PRESIDENTIAL ELEC-
tion, providing George W. Bush with the final handful of electoral votes
to return to the White House—secured with a slim 50.8 percent of the
popular vote. The Christian Right was unusually active and visible in the
Buckeye State campaign, waging a successful effort on behalf of Issue 1
(an amendment to the Ohio state constitution banning same-sex marriage)
and working vigorously for Bush's reelection. This chapter describes these
activities and offers some evidence of their impact on the election results
and future politics in the Buckeye State.

The Christian Right's extensive campaign efforts, especially increased
involvement by the evangelical clergy, may have had an impact on Ohio
voters. In any event, evangelical Protestants and other observant Christians were important to Issue 1's large margins and even more crucial to
Bush's narrow win. In this regard, Issue 1 may have made a small but significant contribution to the President's victory. These campaigns appear
to have reinvigorated the Christian Right in Ohio.

A good place to begin is with the special characteristics of the Buckeye
State.

Ohio Politics and the Christian Right

Ohio was important in the 2004 presidential election for the same reason it
has long mattered in presidential politics: Among the large states, it comes
closest to being a microcosm of the nation as a whole.[1] Indeed, nearly all

of the important voting blocs and interests are well represented within its boundaries. Ohio has eight major metropolitan areas, each composed of declining central cities, a wide variety of stable suburbs, and rapidly growing exurbs. In addition, large portions of the state are rural, dotted with small cities and towns. Each of these "city states" and "country provinces" has its own mix of economic interests, media outlets, and political values.

Religion is a central part of this diversity. Ohio closely resembles the nation in terms of religious affiliation. Evangelical Protestants are the largest religious tradition, accounting for about one-quarter of the adult population, and the full range of evangelicals inhabit the state—including Southern Baptists, Pentecostals, Amish, independent fundamentalists, non-denominational megachurches, and everything in between. Mainline Protestants also are common, making up a little less than one-fifth of the adult population, with significant representation of the all the major denominations, from the United Methodists to the United Church of Christ. White Protestants dominate rural and suburban areas. African American Protestants are concentrated in the big cities, making up a little less than one-tenth of the adult population. Roman Catholics are the second-largest religious group overall (and the single largest denomination), at just under one-quarter of the population, and are most common in urban areas. The remaining groups also have a metropolitan focus. A full range of other Christian is also churches present, including Eastern Orthodox, the Church of Jesus Christ of Latter-Day Saints (Mormons), and Unitarian Universalists. Finally, Jews, Muslims, and other non-Christians are found in about the same relative numbers as in the nation as a whole. About one-sixth of adult population has no religious affiliation.

We should not be surprised that religious groups have been part of the fabric of Ohio politics since the origin of the state, closely following national patterns. A good example was the New Deal era, when Ohio Democrats were largely an alliance of Catholics, Jews, and evangelical Protestants, while the Ohio GOP was the party of the Protestant mainline (Knepper 1989). In this regard, the antecedents of the contemporary Christian Right appeared in Buckeye State politics throughout the twentieth century. For instance, the anticommunist movement of the 1950s and 1960s was active in the state, reinforcing the right-wing factions in the GOP on an array of issues. Such conservatism often appealed to Democratic religious constituencies, which is one reason Ohio voted a bit more Republican than Democratic over the past century, despite its social and political diversity (Curtin 1996).

The contemporary Christian Right has been present in Ohio from the beginning of the movement in the late 1970s. This presence included a state chapter of the Moral Majority in the 1980s (Wilcox 1988), state and county affiliates of the Christian Coalition in the 1990s (Berkowitz and Green 1997), and several profamily organizations by the beginning of the twenty-first century (Putnam 2001). The state's diversity has set limits on the influence of the Christian Right, however. As a consequence, the movement's activism was channeled largely through the strong Republican party organizations, where its demands were aggregated with those of other constituencies (Conger and Green 2002).

This process substantially checked the Christian Right's direct political impact—a frustrating experience for its activists. Yet participating in this broader party coalition produced some rewards. For example, it connected the movement to the party machinery, slowly moving the Republican coalition in a conservative direction. It also produced some influence over policy once Republicans took control of state government in the early 1990s. These changes included a state ban on late-term abortions (subsequently struck down by the federal courts), an experimental school vouchers program (which the U.S. Supreme Court upheld), and opposition to the expansion of gambling (the defeat of progambling ballot initiatives). By 2004 the movement was poised to play a more active and visible role in politics.

In short, the Christian Right's experience in Ohio closely paralleled its experience at the national level (Green, Rozell, and Wilcox 2003).

Issue 1: The Ohio Marriage Amendment

Opposition to same-sex marriage has been important to the Christian Right from its inception, but the topic became a central concern in response to the gay rights movement in the 1990s (Green 2000). This shift helped produced the Defense of Marriage Act (DOMA) enacted at the federal level (and signed into law by President Clinton in 1996) and similar statutes in about three dozen states. Ohio did not pass a DOMA during this period, however. Republican legislative leaders argued that such legislation was not necessary, given existing state and federal law; moreover, moderate Republicans and the business community opposed it.

The situation changed suddenly when the Massachusetts supreme court legalized same-sex marriage in November 2003. Under intense pressure from Christian conservatives, the Ohio General Assembly quickly passed a DOMA, and moderate Republican Governor Bob Taft signed it into law in early February 2004. The Ohio DOMA was judged to be one of the strictest in the country, effectively outlawing civil unions as well same-sex marriage (Theis 2003). Christian Right leaders were not satisfied with simply passing a DOMA, however; they proposed putting its strictures into the state constitution.

There were two reasons for this strategy. First, the movement feared that "activist" courts would undermine the law. As one Ohio leader said, "We cannot trust marriage to Ohio's court system. Acting on their own personal bias, contrary to the will of the people, Ohio's Supreme Court could declare our DOMA unconstitutional" (Citizens for Community Values 2004). This position certainly was plausible from the point of view of Christian Rightists, given the actions of courts around the country and in the Buckeye State. Indeed, Ohio courts had refused to declare unconstitutional a city ordinance setting up a domestic partnership "registry" (a symbol with no legal status). In addition, there was good reason to believe that a majority of Ohioans would support the amendment if it were on the ballot (McCullough 2004).

Second, this approach was part of a national "amendment" strategy that included changing the U.S. Constitution (with the Federal Marriage Amendment) and state constitutions (such amendments were proposed and passed in thirteen states in 2004, and more were planned for the future). The amendment strategy, in turn, was part of a broader "judicial" strategy to change the personnel and direction of the courts. These strategies dovetailed with the movement's desire to help President Bush and other Republicans win the election because continued Republican control of the federal government was essential to most of these goals. The Christian Right clearly was aware of the potential impact of the state marriage amendments on the presidential vote, as were many other political actors and observers (Schlesinger 2004). Movement leaders considered this possibility less as a way to reelect Bush, however, than as a means of forcing Republicans to give the issue priority.[2]

Shortly after passage of Ohio's DOMA, movement leaders asked the General Assembly to put a marriage amendment on the November 2004 ballot. Legislative leaders demurred, partly because the GOP was divided on its policy and political implications. Many disagreed with the approach, and others feared a backlash if the party were perceived as intolerant. There also were logistical problems. The effort would have required a three-fifths vote of both houses of the legislature (as opposed to the simple majority required to pass DOMA), as well as a lengthy legislative process.

Once the Christian Right realized that the legislature would not act, the movement organized a petition drive to put the measure on the ballot directly. This task was daunting. State law required collection of signatures of registered voters equal to 10 percent of the votes cast in the previous gubernatorial election; in addition, the signature total had to equal 5 percent of the gubernatorial vote in forty-four of Ohio's eight-eight counties. This requirement amounted to 323,000 signatures to be collected by August 3,

2004 (if the first deadline were met, additional signatures could be submitted by September 17, 2004, to supplement the original submission).

Formally, the petition drive was undertaken by the "Ohio Campaign to Protect Marriage," but the chief sponsor was Citizens for Community Values (CCV)—a free-standing state "family research council" that was part of the Focus on the Family network of organizations. Founded in 1983, CCV had long advocated for "profamily" issues in Ohio, and its leader, Phil Burress, was part of the movement's national leadership (Dao 2004). CCV received considerable assistance from Focus on the Family Action and an array of national Christian Right groups, and it worked closely with other Ohio Christian Rightists. Although some Ohio Republicans, such as Secretary of State Ken Blackwell, supported the effort, on the whole Ohio Republicans neither helped nor hindered the petition drive (Williams 2004). The national Republican party and the Bush campaign adopted a similar posture (Achenbach 2004), although behind the scenes, campaign officials may have encouraged it.

Events spurred the Ohio petition drive forward, including the first (legal) same-sex marriages in Massachusetts and the granting of (illegal) marriage licenses to same-sex couples in San Francisco. Perhaps the most important episode was the defeat of the Federal Marriage Amendment in the U.S. Senate in July 2004. Although at the time this defeat was widely interpreted as a setback, it unleashed a wave of Christian Right activism, including in the Buckeye State (Cooperman and Edsall 2004). Roughly ninety days after it began, the petition drive submitted more than 400,000 signatures on the August 3rd deadline. A little more than 280,000 were judged valid, and the measure qualified in 71 counties; an additional 155,000 signatures were submitted by the September 17 deadline, of which 73,000 were valid (for a total of 350,000 valid signatures). To put these figures in perspective, the total number of raw signatures collected by the marriage amendment backers collected was larger than the 500,000 vote increase Bush received in Ohio between 2000 and 2004 general elections. The number of valid signatures was almost three times as large as Bush's winning margin of 118,000 in the 2004 general election.

The petition drive was undertaken in large part by volunteers, who accounted for 79 percent of the petition circulators. These volunteers appeared to be drawn extensively from the CCV and Focus on the Family members in the state (estimated at 50,000 and 78,000, respectively). Many of these volunteers worked through churches—most of which were white evangelical congregations, although some black Protestant churches were active as well. Nondenominational, Southern Baptist, and Assembly of God congregations were especially involved. The volunteers were supplemented by paid circulators, who accounted for 21 percent of the total. Drawn from 19 different states, these paid circulators received an average of $1.50 per signature from CCV. Although the signatures came from all 88 counties, they were concentrated in counties where Bush had done well in 2000 and where evangelical Protestants were most numerous.[3]

The marriage amendment cleared all legal challenges in late September 2004 and officially became state Issue 1, with the following ballot language:

> Be it Resolved by the People of the State of Ohio:
>   That the Constitution of the State of Ohio be amended by adopting a section to be Designated as Section 11 of Article XV thereof, to read as follows:

> Article XV
> Section 11. Only a union between one man and one woman may be a marriage valid in or recognized by this state and its political subdivisions. This state and its political subdivisions shall not create or recognize a legal status for relationships or unmarried couples that intends to approximate the design, qualities, significance, or effect of marriage.

Like the Ohio DOMA, Issue 1 was regarded as the strictest of the marriage amendments on state ballots in 2004 because it banned civil unions as well as same-sex marriages (Hotakainen 2004; Theis 2004). Roughly 150 days after the petition drive was launched—and a scant month before the general election—the campaign to pass Issue 1 began in earnest.

The Fall Campaign

CCV reportedly spent a total of $3.5 million on the Issue 1 campaign, including the costs of petitioning and the general election campaign.[4] Much of the funding came from Focus on the Family Action, a new political arm of Focus on the Family (Gorski 2005), although some money was raised by CCV and from individual donors in Ohio. State campaign finance records show that the Ohio Campaign to Protect Marriage spent $1.2 million in the general election, including $1.1 million in "in-kind contributions" from CCV and Focus on the Family.

The Issue 1 campaign was extensive: It involved $600,000 in television advertising, several hundred thousand dollars for radio ads, direct mail, yard signs, and get-out-the-vote (GOTV) efforts. The campaign reported registering 54,000 voters, making 3.3 million telephone calls, and targeting 850,000 supporters. In addition, the campaign sent 2.5 million church-bulletin inserts to 17,000 congregations (essentially all Christian houses of worship in Ohio). The inserts were simple affairs that quoted the New Testament: "For this cause shall a man leave father and mother, and shall cleave to his wife: and the two shall become one flesh" (Matthew 10:5). It also noted, "As Christians, we must firmly plant in our hearts and minds that marriage—as the lifelong, monogamous relationship between one man and one woman—is a Divine, eternal truth." The campaign also contacted a subset of 10,000 churches twice each by telephone in the runup to Election Day and sponsored numerous rallies. The most prominent rally was the September 19, 2004, "Marriage Sunday"—a "simulcast" of national Christian Right leaders in which many Ohio churches participated.

This focus on churches was a central feature of the campaign. There were ten briefings of clergy throughout the state. Hundreds of thousands of dollars were spent on this effort by other national groups, such as the Alliance for Marriage, Let Freedom Ring, Americans United to Preserve Marriage, and the National Clergy Council. Many of these groups joined with Focus on the Family to send churches literature and GOTV materials (one example was a DVD with a spot by Jim Caviezel, who played Jesus in Mel Gibson's *The Passion of the Christ*). Prominent Christian Right litigating groups, such as the American Center for Law and Justice and the Alliance Defense Fund, provided legal advice on how clergy could discuss the issue with their congregations. Some evangelical denominations (especially the Southern Baptist Convention and the Assemblies of God) emphasized Issue 1, as did Christian broadcasters throughout the state.

There is considerable evidence that Ohio clergy were unusually active and vocal in the 2004 campaign. Indeed, long-time Christian Right activists in the state were stunned by the level of pastoral interest and response to Issue 1. Previous attempts at using clergy as building blocs of movement organizations had met with only limited success (Guth 1996). The most common form of activity was sermons on traditional marriage, voter registration drives, and urging parishioners to vote. This activity was the most common among the evangelical clergy, especially those who were not strong partisans (see Djupe, Neiheisel, and Sokhey 2005). In addition, churches and clergy spoke out on the topic. The Roman Catholic Church formally endorsed Issue 1, as did groups of black Protestant ministers; the usually apolitical Eastern Orthodox and Amish communities were active on Issue 1 (Tinsley 2004; Briggs 2004; Johnson 2004a).

The opposition to Issue 1 was led by "Ohioans Protecting the Constitution," which spent a total of $900,000 against the initiative. This group was joined by liberal clergy, especially in Mainline Protestant churches, who spoke out vigorously against the measure (Garrett 2004). Liberal religious groups such as the Unitarian Universalists, Reform Jews, and minority clergy joined with gay rights groups in campaigning against the measure (Johnson and Mahoney 2004). Prominent Democratic leaders strongly opposed Issue 1, and they were joined by a "Who's Who" of top Republican officeholders in the state, including Governor Bob Taft, Attorney General Jim Petro, and U.S. Senators George Voinovich and Mike DeWine. This GOP opposition balanced support from other Republican officeholders, such as Secretary of State Blackwell (who supported Issue 1 in radio spots and telephone messages), Treasurer Joe Deters, and Auditor Betty Montgomery (Johnson 2004b).

Beyond Issue 1, the Christian Right was active in the 2004 presidential campaign. For example, the Ohio Christian Coalition implemented its voter guide program, distributing 2 million voter guides in congregations. The guides endorsed Issue 1 and indicated that President Bush and Republican congressional and state legislative candidates were generally superior to their Democratic rivals on issues such as the Federal Marriage Amendment, banning partial-birth abortion, protecting the Ten Commandments, and keeping "Under God" in the Pledge of Allegiance—as well as opposition to gun control and increased taxes. Other groups, such as Concerned Women for American, Ohio Right to Life, and local Christian Right groups, also were active at the grassroots.

Many of the these activities were reinforced by broader voter mobilization efforts, ranging from the "I Vote Values" campaign—a voter registration program—to letters from prominent evangelical leaders, such as Pastor Rick Warren, the author of the best-selling *A Purpose Driven Life*. In addition, there was considerable activity on behalf of Bush by conservative Catholics, Jews, and black Protestants. For example, one flyer proclaimed, "Vote Catholic—Not Kerry," and in an ad sponsored by the Republican Jewish Coalition a Jewish Democratic woman from Cleveland was quoted, "I feel safe with President Bush."

The Christian Right activist corps in Ohio certainly was energized in 2004 and may have been substantially larger than in recent elections. Although there are no firm numbers, a reasonable estimate is that several thousand movement activists worked hard on the campaign through various venues. One such venue was the Bush campaign and an extraordinary grassroots organization created by the Ohio Republican Party. All told, this highly integrated effort involved some 85,000 volunteers. Some Christian Right activists already were part of the Republican organization; others were recruited through the "team leaders" program, one division of which focused on "values." The key to this organization was highly detailed "microtargeting" and personal contact with voters (Bai 2004; Kirkpatrick 2004b).

Despite its ambivalent view of Issue 1, the Bush campaign aggressively courted Christian conservatives in Ohio. This effort was central to the campaign's "base mobilization" strategy and Karl Rove's goal of turning out an additional 4 million evangelicals nationwide. The campaign cast a much wider net, however, actively pursuing traditional Catholics, conservative Mainline Protestants, and black Protestants. Ohio campaign officials claimed to have identified about 750,000 "social conservatives" who were pro-Bush but had not gone to the polls in 2000 and set up a statewide network to mobilize them. A co-chair of the Ohio Bush campaign articulated the campaign's message: "The President has demonstrated in his three and a half years in office a commitment to the same concerns: moral values and protection of the family" (Drew 2004).

One element of this statewide network was voter registration. The Ohio GOP had ten staff members designated to conduct voter registration in congregations, and the party actively sought church directories for this purpose—an effort that was controversial in the national media, though much less so at the grassroots in Ohio (Kirkpatrick 2004a). Indeed, many such efforts were well under way in many localities before the program was officially initiated (Cooperman and Edsall 2004). Another element of the campaign was automated telephone calls featuring religious figures such as Rev. Franklin Graham and Christian singer Michael K. Smith.

Another tactic was direct mail targeted at "values" voters. One of the best-known pieces featured a country church with a white steeple, a nuclear family, and the legend "Protect Life, Strengthen Families, Defend Marriage" on one side and "If you believe in these values, then we would ask for your vote for our Republican team." Another piece showed photogenic children at play and the caption, "Their future hangs in the balance. . . . They are counting on you to PROTECT LIFE . . . PROTECT MARRIAGE . . . PROTECT FAMILIES." The fine print noted that "liberal Democrats" opposed banning partial-birth abortion, the Federal Marriage Amendment, and the Unborn Victims of Violence Act (a federal law inspired by the Laci Peterson murder). As one analyst noted, "The message would not have been any clearer if it had quoted the Bible" (Farhi and Williams 2004). Finally, President Bush consistently emphasized the "values" issue during his extensive campaign visits to the Buckeye State.

Democrats did not entirely concede the "values" terrain to the Republicans. Senator Kerry and his vice presidential nominee, John Edwards, often spoke about "values" as well. One Kerry mailer identified him as "A Man of Faith and Hope." A piece from the Ohio Democratic Party proclaimed, "John Kerry Shares Our Values" and quoted the Senator: "I believe that those of us guided by faith have to live out our faith. . . . If you believe in the teachings of Jesus Christ, and I do, then you believe that you have some responsibility to other people. . . . I don't think that our policies in the last years have lived up to the values that we ought to be living up to." The piece then claimed that Kerry "truly promotes life" and that "Bush has failed to promote life. Under his watch abortion rates have increased."

Liberal religious activists made this kind of argument on Kerry's behalf. The Progressive Faith Media brought liberal Evangelical and mainline Protestants to campaign in Ohio. A more extensive effort was made to rally Kerry's fellow Catholics, conducted by Catholics for Political Responsibility, Catholics for the Common Good, and Pax Christi. This effort included radio spots, newspaper ads, and leaflets for congregations. These efforts were directed at countering pro-Bush Catholic advertising. Similar efforts occurred in the Jewish and black Protestant communities.

The Election Results

Determining the impact of political activity on the vote is difficult under any circumstances, and the 2004 Ohio campaign presents a special challenge because of the intensity of the contest, where a total of about $150 million was spent to influence the outcome (Mockabee et al. 2005). What we can do is look for clues of the effects of this effort in the election results.

On Election Day, Issue 1 passed with 62 percent of the vote. Almost 5.4 million Ohioans cast votes on the measure—470,000 more than voted for President Bush, who won Ohio with 50.8 percent of the popular vote. Indeed, the number of Issue 1 ballots was just 200,000 less than the total presidential vote (5.4 versus 5.6 million), and both totals were substantially greater than the number of presidential ballots cast in Ohio in 2000 (4.7 million). Issue 1 passed in 87 of 88 counties, though it did best in rural and exurban areas. Bush increased his vote by about 500,000 over his 2000 total (from 2.3 million to 2.8 million), while John Kerry gained 550,000 votes over Al Gore's 2000 performance (from 2.2 million to 2.7 million). Bush won by 118,000 votes—50,000 fewer than in 2000.[5] Overall, turnout increased to 72 percent of registered voters.

Table 4.1 reports Ohio exit poll data on Issue 1 and the presidential vote, broken down by key religious groups: the major religious traditions, with the largest groups divided by weekly worship attendance. Although most of the voters in these categories voted for Issue 1, there were important differences among them. Evangelical Protestants were the biggest backers of the marriage amendment—more than four-fifths of voters in this group supported the measure—with weekly church attendees a bit stronger than their less observant co-religionists. In descending order, Catholics, black Protestants, and mainline Protestants also voted for Issue 1. Note, how-

Table 4.1 Ohio Religious Groups, Issue 1, and Bush Vote in 2004 (%)

Religious Group	Issue 1 Yes	Presidential Bush
Evangelical Protestant		
Weekly worship attender	88	82
Less than weekly	82	64
Mainline Protestant		
Weekly worship attender	61	56
Less than weekly	51	45
Black Protestant		
Weekly worship attender	70	23
Less than weekly	53	12
Roman Catholic		
Weekly worship attender	71	65
Less than weekly	56	47
Other Christians	63	49
Other Faiths	39	20
Unaffiliated	34	30
All	**62**	**51**

Source: 2004 General Election National Election Pool, Ohio.

ever, the larger division by worship attendance, the measure won by slim majorities among the less-than-weekly attenders. The combined category of "Other Christians" also backed the amendment solidly (Mormons, Eastern Orthodox, and so forth). The only two categories that did not give majority support to Issue 1 were "Unaffiliated" voters and the combined category of "Other Faiths" (Jews, Muslims, and so forth). Overall, evangelicals provided more than half of all Issue 1 votes, and weekly attending Christians provided three-quarters of the measure's votes.

The presidential vote shows a similar pattern but with markedly lower levels of support for Bush. Weekly attending evangelicals were most supportive of the president; more than four-fifths of these voters cast their ballots for Bush. Note, however, that the Bush vote dropped below two-thirds for less observant evangelicals. This pattern appeared among the other large Christian groups in a more dramatic fashion. For example, weekly attending Catholics gave Bush almost two-thirds of their votes, whereas a majority of less observant Catholics voted for Kerry. A similar pattern held for mainline Protestants but at an even lower level, and the "Other Christians" divided their vote almost evenly. Although Bush received more than one-fifth of the votes of weekly attending black Protestants—a dramatic change from 2000—Kerry won these categories by large majorities, as he did with "Other Faiths" and the "Unaffiliated." Overall, evangelicals accounted for more than one-third of the Bush vote, and weekly attending Christians were a slight majority of his supporters.

These figures are very revealing. The prime targets of Christian Right and GOP mobilization, evangelicals and other observant Christians, were important to the success of Issue 1 and even more crucial to the narrow Bush victory. Thus, the Christian Right's extensive mobilization efforts may have affected the election results; likewise, liberal religious activists may have had some effect on their less numerous constituents. By all accounts, the mobilization of evangelicals was especially effective (see Rowland 2004; Finkel 2004; Langfitt 2004; and Dolan and Langfitt 2004 for excellent descriptions of evangelical mobilization in Ohio.)

By the same token, support for Issue 1 was broad and diverse; passage of the measure represented a signal policy victory. Likewise, Bush's reelection depended on a broader coalition of voters, not just Christian conservatives. The latter point is worth illustrating further: Four-fifths of Bush's voters backed Issue 1, but one-fifth did not. If Bush had not had support from the latter, John Kerry probably would be in the White House. Likewise, two-fifths of the Kerry vote also voted for Issue 1—and if this group had been slightly larger, he might well have won the election.[6]

This last point can be illustrated by looking at the relationship between "moral values" and votes. Although just 22 percent of Ohio exit poll respondents said "moral values" was the most important issue to their vote (ranked second behind the economy and jobs), among those who voted for both Bush and Issue 1, 40 percent chose moral values, with terrorism the next most important issue. Bush voters who did not support Issue 1 were more likely to pick economic or foreign policy items. Kerry voters gave top priority to the economy and jobs whether they backed Issue 1 or not.

Given the large size of the Issue 1 vote and the small margin in the presidential contest, the former may have affected the latter enough to make a difference to the close outcome. Analyses of the 2004 exit poll data reveal that Issue 1 had a positive impact on the vote even when other factors were controlled (see chapter 3 of this book for a detailed model of the impact of Issue 1 on the Bush vote). These findings suggest that on balance Issue 1 benefited Bush and Republicans. Interestingly, similar results obtained for U.S. Senator George Voinovich's vote; he was reelected by a large margin although he publicly opposed Issue 1. Taken together, these findings suggest that Issue 1 helped the GOP overall.

Table 4.2 presents the results of two analyses that investigate this possibility further. The first column is an analysis of the county-level vote for Bush.[7] A measure of partisanship (the 2000 county-level vote for Bush) is the strongest independent predictor of the Bush vote, followed by the Issue 1 vote. The evangelical and low-income populations mattered as well, though to a much smaller extent. Applying the coefficient for the Issue 1 vote to the raw vote totals produces an estimate of approximately 200,000 extra votes for Bush from Issue 1 supporters.[8]

Of course, such an estimate must be assessed with caution. For instance, the direction of causality is unclear: Perhaps Bush supporters voted for Issue 1, not the other way around. On the other hand, these figures also may underestimate the impact of Issue 1 because partisanship and other factors have been taken into account. In any event, such an impact could have arisen from two sources: support for Issue 1 among Bush voters mobilized for other reasons and an increased turnout among Issue 1 supporters.

The second column in table 4.2 addresses turnout with an analysis of Bush's net gain over 2000, also using county-level vote data.[9] As before, the 2000 Bush vote was a strong predictor of gains in 2004, suggesting that Bush made the greatest gains in Republican areas—a conclusion that is reinforced by the negative impact of the low-income population (concentrated in Democratic counties). The evangelical Protestant population also was positively associated with net Bush gains (although the level of statistical significance is lower). Note, however, that the Issue 1 vote was the strongest independent predictor of increased support for Bush.

Applying the coefficient for the Issue 1 vote to the raw vote totals produces an estimate of a net gain of 38,000 votes for Bush. This figure implies that Bush obtained 98,000 new votes from Issue 1 backers and Kerry gained 60,000. Combined with the previous estimate of 200,000 new Bush voters, these figures suggest that about half of this gain was about evenly divided between Bush voters mobilized for other reasons who voted for Issue 1 and increased turnout by Issue 1 supporters.[10] If these figures are correct, then Issue 1 contributed to the Bush victory but was not by itself the primary cause (see Shapiro 2004; Kirkpatrick 2004c).

Some additional data support these estimates. A comparison of the 2000 and 2004 Ohio exit polls shows that the 2004 electorate contained almost 5 percent more self-identified Republicans (40.2 percent to 35.3 percent) and almost 4 percent more self-identified conservatives (33.3 percent to 29.5 percent) than in 2000. A similar change occurred for religion: White Protestants were almost 5 percent more common in 2004 than in

Table 4.2   Issue 1 and the Ohio Presidential Vote, 2004

	2004 Vote by County	
Vote	Bush Vote	Net Bush Gain
2000 Bush Vote	.62[a]	.31[a]
Issue 1 Vote	.32[a]	.40[a]
Evangelical Protestants	.09[a]	.13[b]
Low-income population	-.21[a]	-.27[a]
Adjusted R^2	.92	.58

[a]Beta weight significant at .05 level or better.
[b]Beta weight significant at .10 level or better.
Note: See text and notes for details of the analysis.

2000 (46.6 to 41.8 percent). In addition, an October 14–17, 2004, ABC News poll of likely voters in Ohio found that 4 percent rated Issue 1 as the most important topic on the ballot. These differences are modest, to be sure, but consistent with the foregoing analysis.[11]

2004 and Beyond

In 2004 the Christian Right was unusually active and visible in the Buckeye State. The centerpiece of this effort was Issue 1, which was among the strictest marriage amendments in the country and part of a national strategy to oppose same-sex marriage. Its passage by a large margin in a high-turnout election was a signal policy victory for the Christian Right. The movement's campaign efforts, especially increased involvement by evangelical clergy, probably had an impact on voters. In any event, evangelical Protestants and other observant Christians were important to the marriage amendment's large margin of victory and even more critical to Bush's narrow reelection. In this regard, Issue 1 may have made a small contribution to the president's victory.

One immediate effect of this activism has been reinvigoration of the Christian Right in Ohio—again paralleling the movement's national experience. Phil Burress of CCV has pledged to build on the Issue 1 campaign (Dao 2004), and one of the key players in that campaign, Rev. Rod Parsley, has similar goals for his Center for Moral Clarity (Hallett 2005), dubbed "Reformation Ohio." A new organization is the Ohio Restoration Project, headed by Rev. Russell Johnson, which is part of a national effort to recruit and organize "Patriot Pastors" (Page 2005). These new efforts rely on pastors as building blocks of movement organizations—a new version of an old idea that has enjoyed only limited long-term success in the past.

The outline of this approach is evident in the initial goals of the Ohio Restoration Project:[12]

Create, fund, and operate a public information program for pastors and the Christian community with five goals:

1. Bring to the forefront issues that are relevant to the Christian community and provide candidates a forum to specifically address these issues that dramatically impact the family including such matters as: Marriage, Right to Life, Educational Choice, Taxes, Employment, and other Value Issues.

2. Information >> Inspiration >> Mobilization of pastors. "Patriot Pastors" appreciate the stewardship of our citizenship and understand the window of opportunity that God is providing. Patriot Pastors will pray, inform, and equip the Christian community to be engaged in the 2006 elections. Each Patriot Pastor will seek God's wisdom as they:

   - Provide our Ohio pro-family forums with 100 intercessors who will join in an Ohio network of E-Prayer to pray at a moment's notice.
   - These "Minutemen of Prayer" will enable 100,000 faithful to intercede at a moment's notice via e-mail.
   - Provide our Ohio pro-family forums with the addresses of 200 new faithful citizens who want to be equipped and able to make a difference in their congressional district.
   - Register at least 300 new voters able to shine a light for Godly candidates in the 2006 election cycle.

3. By the close of the 2006 election cycle we would like see 2,000 Ohio Patriot Pastors who understand the sacred trust of this moment in history and who are mobilized to make a difference.

   - Provide 100,000 new e-mail supporters who serve as E-Prayer Intercessors.
   - Provide 200,000 new addresses of supporters to our Ohio pro-family forums.
   - Register 300,000 new "Values Voters" through "Stewardship of our Citizenship" Sundays between March 2005 and October 2006.

4. Involve our Patriot Pastors in an Ohio for Jesus Rally at Nationwide Arena hosting 30,000 supporters of the Ohio Pro-Family Forum in the winter of 2006. At this time we would like to invite Franklin Graham and Rod Parsley to speak as we honor James Dobson, Ken Blackwell, Tony Perkins, and Phil Burress for their contribution to the cause of Christ and their stand for Biblical family values.

5. Increase "Values Voter" turnout in 2006 from 22 percent to 35 percent in 2006.

These goals are ambitious, and one would hardly be surprised if the movement fell short of achieving them. Yet many of these goals are no more daunting than the Issue 1 campaign. To the extent that the Ohio Restoration Project achieves these goals, it could change the role of the Christian Right in Buckeye State politics. An early test of this new emphasis will come in the 2006 gubernatorial elections; the candidates will include Secretary of State Ken Blackwell—one of the few Republican officeholders who actively supported Issue 1.

Notes

1. For a good description of Ohio's diversity, see "The Five Ohios," *Cleveland Plain Dealer*, 10 December 2004 (www.cleveland.com/fiveohios).

2. There was a similar debate in Ohio about a ballot initiative to legalize gambling. Democrats strongly feared that such an amendment would increase the turnout of conservative Christians as well.

3. These statistics came from a random sample of Issue 1 petition circulators collected by the author from official state records.

4. The statistics presented in this section are from Ohio campaign finance records, the author's interviews with Christian Right and other activists, and campaign materials collected during the 2004 campaign. See Hull (2004) and Djupe, Neiheisel, and Sokhey (2005) for additional details.

5. Kerry's 50,000-vote gain could be attributed to the absence of Ralph Nader on the 2004 Ohio ballot (Green 2004).

6. Other scholars also found that Issue 1 helped the Republicans in Ohio, including Donavan, Tolbert, and Smith (2005); Campbell and Monson (2005); and Rausch (2005). McAdams and Weisberg (2006) found less support for the impact of gay marriage in Ohio but a strong impact of "moral values."

7. This analysis employed ordinary least squares (OLS) regression, using county-level vote data. The dependent variable was the Bush vote, expressed as a percent of registered voters in the county. The dependent variables were as follows: the 2000 Bush vote by county, expressed as a percentage of registered voters; evangelicals as a percentage of the adult population, estimated from the Glenmary Research Center 2000 Census of Religious Congregations and Membership in the United States (contact author for details); low income voters (annual family income of $29,000 or less) as a percentage of the population; and the county-level Issue 1 vote as a percentage of registered voters by county.

8. This figure was estimated by taking the b coefficient and standard error from the OLS regression and applying it to the raw vote totals. The 219,000 vote figure is

the estimate at the middle of the confidence interval; the high estimate was 240,000 and the low estimate was 178,000.

9. This analysis was identical to the preceding analysis, except that the dependent variable was the net Bush gain in voters from 2000 to 2004, expressed as a percentage of registered voters at the county level.

10. This figure was estimated by taking the b coefficient and standard error from the OLS regression and applying it to the raw vote totals. The 38,000 vote figure is the estimate at the middle of the confidence interval; the high estimate was 41,000 and the low estimate was 31,000. Because this figure is a net figure, it is the result of the net gain in Bush votes minus the net gain in Kerry votes over 2000. An assumption of a 62 to 38 percent split in the new votes produces the estimate of 98,000 new Bush votes and 60,000 new Kerry votes.

11. Four percent of the 2004 presidential vote was 224,000, and if we assume that Bush received 93 percent of these new Republican votes, the result is 208,000 new Bush votes. The poll was ABC News Poll #2004-970: Ohio Politics and Elections.

12. These materials are from the Ohio Restoration Project in December 2005; see http://ohiorestorationproject.com/.

References

Achenbach, Joel. 2004. "Whose Values Won the Election?" *Washington Post Weekly Edition*, November, 10–11.

Bai, Matt. 2004 "The Multilevel Marketing of the President." *New York Times Magazine*, 25 April, 43.

Berkowitz, Laura, and John C. Green. 1997. "Charting the Coalition: The Local Chapters of the Ohio Christian Coalition." In *Sojourners in the Wilderness: The Christian Right in Comparative Perspective*, ed. Corwin E. Smidt and James M. Penning. Lanham, Md.: Rowman & Littlefield, 57–74.

Briggs, David. 2004. "Same-sex Marriage Is No. 1 in Minds of Religious Groups." *Cleveland Plain Dealer*, 29 October, A12.

Campbell, David E., and J. Quin Monson. 2005. "The Religion Card: Gay Marriage and the 2004 Presidential Election." Paper presented at annual meeting of American Political Science Association, Washington, D.C., September 1–4.

Citizens for Community Values. 2004. "Petition Drive a Must!" *Citizens' Courier*, June.

Conger, Kimberly H., and John C. Green. 2002. "The Christian Right in the States: 2000." *Campaigns and Elections* 23 (1): 58–60, 64–65.

Cooperman, Alan, and Thomas B. Edsall. 2004. "Onward, Christian Soldiers." *Washington Post Weekly Edition*, 15–21 November, 12–13.

Curtin, Michael E. 1996. *Ohio Politics Almanac*. Kent, Ohio: Kent State University Press.

Dao, James. 2004. "Flush with Victory, Grass-roots Crusader against Same-sex Marriage Thinks Big." *New York Times*, 26 November.

Djupe, Paul A., Jake R. Neiheisel, and Anand E. Sokhey. 2005. "Clergy and Controversy: A Study of Clergy and Gay Rights in Columbus, Ohio." Paper presented at annual meeting of Midwest Political Science Association, Chicago,
April 7–10.

Dolan, Matthew, and Frank Langfitt. 2004. "The Morality Factor." *Baltimore Sun*,
7 November.

Donovan, Todd, Caroline Tolbert, and Daniel Smith. 2005. "Do State-Level Ballot
Initiates Affect Presidential Elections? Gay Marriage and the 2004 Election."
Paper presented at annual meeting of American Political Science Association,
Washington, D.C., September 1–4.

Drew, James. 2004. "Faith and Values May Decide the Election." *Toledo Blade*, 11
July.

Farhi, Paul, and Vanessa Williams. 2004. "Politics and Pulpits Combine to Sway
Swing-State Voters." *Washington Post*, 25 October, A7.

Finkel, David. 2004. "'It's a Victory for People Like Us': Bush Emphasis on Values
Drew Ohio Evangelicals." *Washington Post*, 5 November, A3.

Garrett, Amanda. 2004. "Clergy Rally against Banning Gay Marriage." *Cleveland
Plain Dealer*, 20 October.

Green, John C. 2000. "Antigay: Varieties of Opposition to Gay Rights." In *The
Politics of Gay Rights*, ed. Craig Rimmerman, Kenneth D. Wald, and Clyde
Wilcox. Chicago: University of Chicago Press, 121–38.

———. 2004. "Ohio: The Heart of It All." December 10. Available at www.bepress.
com/forum/vol2/iss3/art3.

Green, John C., Mark J. Rozell, and Clyde Wilcox. 2003. "The Christian Right's
Long Political March." In *The Christian Right in America*, ed. John C. Green,
Mark J. Rozell, and Clyde Wilcox. Washington, D.C.: Georgetown University
Press, 1–20.

Gorski, Eric. 2005. "Focus Is on Politics for Nonprofits." *Denver Post*, 3 June, A1.

Guth, James L. 1996. "The Politics of the Christian Right." In *Religion and the Culture Wars: Dispatches from the Front*, ed. John C. Green, James L. Guth, Corwin
E. Smidt, and Lyman A. Kellstedt. New York: Rowman & Littlefield, 7–29.

Hallett, Joe. 2005. "Churches Flexing Political Muscle." *Columbus Dispatch*, 11
April, 1a.

Hotakainen, Rob. 2004. "Marriage Issue Could Swing Ohio." Kansas City *Star
Tribune*, 20 June, A1.

Hull, Dana. 2004. "Gay Marriage Votes Drive Conservative Voters, Help Bush."
Knight Ridder Newspapers, 3 November.

Johnson, Alan. 2004a. "Plain Power." *Columbus Dispatch*, 20 September.

———. 2004b. "Twenty in GOP Backing Issue 1." *Columbus Dispatch*, 20 October.

Johnson, Alan, and Dennis Mahoney. 2004. "Issue 1 Divides Religious Leaders."
Columbus Dispatch, 30 October.

Kirkpatrick, David. 2004a. "GOP Seeking Congregations for Bush Effort." *New
York Times*, 3 June.

———. 2004b. "Churches See an Election Role and Spread the Word on Bush."
New York Times, 9 August.

————. 2004c. "Gay Marriage Becomes a Swing Issue with Pull." *New York Times*, 14 August.

Knepper, George W. 1989. *Ohio and Its People*. Kent, Ohio: Kent State University Press.

Langfitt, Frank. 2004. "Banning Gay Marriage." *Baltimore Sun*, 16 October, 1a.

McAdams, Erin S., and Herbert F. Weisberg. 2006. "Moral Values in the 2004 Ohio Presidential Election." Paper presented at Wartime Election Conference, Columbus, Ohio, January 12–15.

McCullough, Amy. 2004. "Group Pushes Anti-Gay Amendment." *Gannett New Service*, 27 April.

Mockabee, Stephen, Michael Margolis, Stephen Brooks, Rick Farmer, and John C. Green. 2005. "The 2004 Ohio U.S. Presidential Race." In *Dancing without Partners*, ed. David B. Magleby, J. Quin Monson, and Kelly D. Patterson. Provo, Utah: Brigham Young University: Center for the Study of Elections and Democracy.

Page, Susan. 2005. "Shaping Politics from the Pulpit." *USA Today*, 4 August.

Putnam, Bard C. 2001. "Pressing toward the Mark: Ohio Christian Coalition Revisited." Unpublished masters paper, University of Akron.

Rausch, John David. 2005. "Morality and Locality: The Political Context of Marriage Definition." Paper presented at annual meeting of American Political Science Association, Washington, D.C., September 1–4.

Rowland, Darrel. 2004. "Mixed on War, Evangelicals Back Bush." *Columbus Dispatch*, 2 October.

Schlesinger, Jacob M. 2004. "As Gay Marriage Roils the States, the Right May Gain." *Wall Street Journal*, 5 May, 1.

Shapiro, Walter. 2004. "Presidential Election May Have Hinged on One Issue: Issue 1." *USA Today*, 5 November, 6A.

Theis, Sandy. 2003. "Gay-Marriage Battle Moves into Ohio." *Cleveland Plain Dealer*, 7 December, H1.

————. 2004. "Group Wants Constitutional Ban on Gay Marriage." *Cleveland Plain Dealer*, 24 October, T51.

Tinsley, Jesse. 2004. "Ministers Raise Voices in Support of Issue 1." *Cleveland Plain Dealer*, 12 October.

Wilcox, Clyde. 1988. "Seeing the Connection: Religion and Politics in the Ohio Moral Majority." *Review of Religious Research* 30:47–58.

Williams, Vanessa. 2004. "Ohio Gay Marriage Initiative Roils Skeptics." *Washington Post*, 10 May, A5.

CHAPTER FIVE

Michigan

A War on the Home Front?

JAMES M. PENNING AND CORWIN E. SMIDT

FOLLOWING THE 2004 U.S. PRESIDENTIAL ELECTION, MANY ANALYSTS concluded that conservative Christians associated with the Christian Right contributed in important ways to President Bush's reelection (Finley 2004; Riley 2004; Hitt 2004).[1] Exit polls revealed that about one-fifth of American voters selected "moral values" as the most important issue in casting their vote—outpacing even the war in Iraq and the economy.[2] Among these "moral values" voters, Bush won an overwhelming 80 percent.

Christian Right leaders were quick to claim credit for the electoral success of Bush and the Republican Party. Roberta Coombs, president of the Christian Coalition of America, asserted that "Christian evangelicals made the major difference once again this year" (AFP 2004). Other analysts, however, issued a word of caution, attributing Bush's success to a variety of factors. Political scientist James Q. Wilson suggested that "one can make a good case that the economy or the war in Iraq were just as important as morality" in deciding the 2004 presidential election (Wilson 2004). Still others argued Bush's victory reflected weakness in his opponent, John Kerry. *Detroit Free Press* columnist Dawson Bell, for example, argued that Kerry was "too lame, too liberal, [and] too unlovable" (Bell 2004b).

In any case, the 2004 Bush campaign clearly made every effort to mobilize conservative Christian voters. The GOP worked diligently "to stay abreast of the Christian Right and consulted with the movement's leaders in weekly conference calls" (Cooperman and Edsall 2004). In addition, GOP operatives spent considerable effort at the grassroots level to mobilize pastors and congregants who were concerned about issues such as abortion, gay rights, gambling, and pornography (Riley 2004; Ostling 2004; O'Donnell 2004).

Some observers have suggested that these "cultural" issues were even more important than the efforts of party organizations in mobilizing Christian Right voters. Particularly important, in this view, was the fact that in 2004 eleven states had proposals to ban same-sex marriages on the ballot. According to Roberta Coombs of the Christian Coalition, "There is no doubt that because four radical left-wing Massachusetts judges ruled that homosexual marriages are constitutional last year, there was a conservative backlash which played a major role in the election outcome" (AFP 2004).

Nonetheless, one must be cautious in making sweeping claims about increased Christian Right turnout because exit polls do not permit direct comparison between evangelical turnout in 2000 and 2004. In 2000 voters were asked, "Do you consider yourself part of the conservative Christian political movement, also known as the religious right?" In 2004, however, this question was changed to "Would you describe yourself as a born-again or evangelical Christian?" The latter wording probably taps a larger pool of voters and seems likely to produce larger estimates of Christian Right turnout. Nonetheless, as *Washington Post* reporters Alan Cooperman and Thomas Edsall note, we at least have solid evidence that "the percentage of voters who said that they attend church more than once a week grew from 14 to 16 percent, a significant difference in an election decided by three percentage points." In addition, Cooperman and Edsall note that "the percent of the electorate that believes that abortion should be 'illegal in all cases' grew from 13 to 16 percent. These voters backed Bush by 77 percent to 22 percent" (Cooperman and Edsall 2004).

In view of conflicting assertions, analyzing the Christian Right's role in the 2004 election is important. Toward that end, this chapter examines the Christian Right in Michigan, focusing in particular on three key factors: the social, economic, and political context or ecology within which the Christian Right in Michigan operates; the major organizations and groups associated with the Christian Right in Michigan; and the political activities and impact of Christian Right organizations in the 2004 election.

Although focusing on a single state entails the usual problems of external validity, it has the advantage of permitting a more nuanced analysis. In addition, there are three more specific reasons for focusing on Michigan. First, Michigan is a relatively large, politically competitive state that was "targeted" by both the Bush and Kerry campaigns in 2004. Preelection polls revealed that either candidate could carry Michigan, and both candidates made repeated visits to the state, spending considerable money seeking to mobilize the state's voters (Christoff 2004). Second, Michigan contains a large number of political groups associated with the Christian Right—groups that at times have played important roles in state politics (Penning and Smidt 2000; Smidt and Penning 1995, 1997, 2003). Finally, the 2004 Michigan ballot contained two proposals to amend the state constitution that were of particular interest to Christian Right voters. Proposal 1 required voter approval of new casino gambling, and Proposal 2 outlawed same-sex marriage.[3]

The Context of Michigan Politics

The term "Christian Right" refers to a variety of individuals and groups rooted largely, though not exclusively, in the Protestant tradition and committed to the advancement of culturally conservative values.[4] In Michigan, as in other states, the Christian Right is not a static phenomenon; it has changed considerably over time. Indeed, one can fairly argue that, like the Christian Right in Virginia (Rozell and Wilcox 1996), the Christian Right in Michigan has evolved from a disorganized social movement into a set of organized interest groups and factions within the state's Republican Party.

These Christian Right interest groups operate within a socioeconomic context or ecology that shapes and conditions their behavior. Previous analysis (Smidt and Penning 2003) has demonstrated that this context is characterized by considerable diversity. In addition, the Christian Right in Michigan operates within a political environment characterized by high levels of partisan conflict and highly professional governmental institutions. In this complex environment, the most successful Christian Right groups are those that have the organizational resources and political skills necessary to make their voices heard over the cacophony created by multiple competing interest groups and political parties.

Christian Right Organizations in Michigan

The Christian Right in Michigan is organizationally fragmented; no single group or organization fully represents the movement. In part this fragmentation reflects the fact that, in an organizational sense, the Christian Right in the state developed only recently. With the exception of Right-to-Life of Michigan (RTLM), institutionalization of the Christian Right is still incomplete, and not all of the state's Christian Right groups are healthy and politically effective.

Right-to-Life of Michigan (RTLM)

Begun in the late 1960s, RTLM is one of Michigan's most powerful interest groups—well led, well focused, well financed, and well organized. Indeed, the *Detroit News* has suggested that RTLM "now rivals organized labor as a power on the state's political landscape" (Cain 1997). Of course, one might argue that because RTLM accepts support from all sympathizers, regardless of religious affiliation, it is only marginally a "Christian Right" organization. Yet because RTLM's supporter base consists, to a large degree, of conservative evangelical Protestants and Roman Catholics, one could argue that it can be fairly included in a discussion of Christian Right organizations in Michigan.

RTLM's power in Michigan is demonstrated, in the first place, by its considerable support among top officials, including a majority of members of the state legislature. As one might expect, the group's influence is particularly great in the state GOP. Indeed, not since Governor Milliken's 1978 campaign has a prochoice Republican been nominated for governor. Recently RTLM has successfully blocked the efforts of prochoice candidates seeking GOP endorsement at statewide conventions.

A second indicator of RTLM's political muscle is its ability to help elect candidates in general elections. According to Barb Listing, head of RTLM, "People vote on a variety of issues. Ours is one they feel strongly about. If there is a difference between candidates on the abortion issue, we can make a difference; if abortion is the only difference we can make a bigger difference" (Cain 1997). The existence of term limits in Michigan seems to have increased RTLM's success rate, particularly in state legislative elections. According to *Grand Rapids Press* reporters Sara Scott and Barton Deiters, "Term limits, which first began to have a significant impact in the House in 1996, have had a tremendous effect on Right to Life's strength." They note that before term limits were implemented only a minority of members of the Michigan's 110-member State House of Representatives supported RTLM, whereas since term limits were implemented, nearly two-thirds do so. In addition, in recent elections RTLM has enjoyed more than a 75 percent success rate among candidates it has endorsed (Scott and Dieters 2001).

A third indicator of RTLM's political effectiveness is its ability to influence public policy. RTLM has successfully developed voter initiatives to ban tax-paid abortions for poor women (1988) and to require parental consent for minors seeking abortions (1990). In addition, RTLM has been so successful in working with the Michigan legislature that *Detroit Free Press* reporter Brian Dickerson argues that "the Legislature is practically a wholly owned subsidiary of Right to Life" (Dickerson 2000). In the 1999–2000 session alone, members of the Michigan legislature introduced sixty-six bills—the most ever—that made the "watch list" of prochoice activists (Scott and Dieters 2001) and passed twenty-three measures dealing with abortion and family planning, many of them intended to limit the numbers of abortions (Heinlein 2000). RTLM succeeded in blocking proposed legislation that would have permitted advanced nurse practitioners to dispense prescription drugs (including the abortion drug RU-486) without physician supervision. In December 2000 RTLM succeeded in persuading the legislature to outlaw coverage of abortions as part of basic health plans, instead requiring coverage to be offered as an option, at additional cost (Heinlein 2000).

Several factors help to explain the success of RTLM. First, RTLM is among the best-organized Christian Right interests in the state.[5] In addition to benefiting from its solid organization, RTLM also has benefited from a long period of stable, skilled leadership from its president, Barb Listing—a woman with excellent political instincts, outstanding organizational skills, and a high degree of commitment to her cause. Finally, RTLM's political clout reflects the sheer numbers as well as the commitment of its political supporters. Although a spokesman for Planned Parenthood of Michigan argues that RTLM's success derives primarily from organization and money, Pamela Sherstad, a staff member at RTLM headquarters, asserts that the reason for RTLM's success is that "the majority of the electorate is anti-abortion" (Scott and Dieters 2001).

Michigan Family Forum

Another relatively strong Christian Right organization is the Michigan Family Forum (MFF). Headquartered in Lansing, MFF was founded in April 1990 as a nonprofit research and education organization with 501(c)3 Internal Revenue Service (IRS) status. As a 501(c)3 organization, MFF must abide by IRS regulations that prohibit it from devoting a "substantial part of its activities" to influencing legislation. Consequently, in contrast to RTLM, MFF does not hire lobbyists or sponsor a political action committee (PAC).

MFF was established to function as a "family policy council" associated with the national group Focus on the Family, founded by Dr. James Dobson, a psychologist whose radio program is aired on more than 1,450 radio stations nationwide. However, MFF is neither legally nor financially tied to the national Focus on the Family organization, which is a parachurch organization headquartered in Colorado Springs that seeks to promote traditional family values based on biblical teachings. The links are more psychological than structural.

MFF advocates efforts to limit the size and scope of government. Its literature asserts that government cannot solve all of our culture's problems and should not try to do so. Instead, MFF contends that our problems need attention and input from all facets of society—strong families, active churches, and civic organizations—with each playing its appropriate role (see www.mfforum.com/about.html). MFF does tend to favor government activity in support of a profamily legislative agenda, however, including support for "strengthening marriage, promoting fatherhood, protecting children, and honoring elders" (see www.michiganfamily.org/board.htm). Toward those ends, MFF has endorsed the repeal of no-fault divorce laws, abstinence-based sex education, school choice, regulation of the display of obscenity, and traditional definitions of marriage.

By its own admission, MFF began as a disorganized and unfocused group, with diffuse policy goals and an unsophisticated approach to Michigan politics. Over the past decade, however, the group has developed a complex organizational structure and honed its political skills. According to MFF, "Since Michigan Family Forum opened its doors in April of 1990, its focus has evolved and sharpened with increased experience in the governmental process" (see www.mfforum.com/about.html). Today, MFF has a full-time staff of four persons, including an executive director, a director of research and public policy, a Michigan Prayer Network/board assistant, and a communications director. MFF's five-member executive board meets monthly to set policy and review operations, and a larger advisory board meets semiannually to provide vision. Furthermore, MFF has established a Research and Public Policy Department and a Community Impact Department; the latter provides training for MFF supporters (at regional meetings) and oversees several organizations, including the Physician's Resource Council and the Clergy Network, that aim at mobilizing specific groups of professionals. In addition, MFF sponsors the Michigan Prayer Network to work for the success of MFF's objectives.

MFF communicates with supporters in a variety of ways, including distributing printed materials, publishing an e-mail newsletter, and providing e-mail "alerts" concerning pending legislation pertaining to marriage and families. In election years, MFF publishes voter guides to help supporters evaluate candidates for local, state, and national offices. In 1998, for example, MFF distributed more than 1 million guides for the fall election—twice the 500,000 voter guides it distributed in 1996. MFF relies heavily on a network of volunteers, carefully coordinating its work with clergy and churches. In 2004 MFF placed greater emphasis on electronic communication than ever before; it developed one of Michigan's most sophisticated online voter guides, which permitted voters to select particular counties and access information, including MFF endorsement information, on virtually all federal and state candidates.

American Family Association of Michigan

Although MFF is arguably Michigan's leading profamily organization, several other groups pursue overlapping agendas. One is the Michigan chapter of the American Family Association (AFA). In recent years, AFA of Michigan has played an increasingly visible role in state politics, opposing gay rights initiatives across the state. In addition, AFA of Michigan opposes pornography, "radical" environmentalists, and speech codes (see www.afamichigan.org).

Much of the publicity AFA of Michigan has received, particularly with respect to the controversial area of gay rights, is attributable to the energetic leadership of its current president, Gary Glenn. Headquartered in Midland, Glenn has aggressively attacked what AFA labels the "homosexual agenda" and has vigorously opposed proposals to permit gays to head Boy Scout troops, as well as sexual nondiscrimination ordinances proposed by various cities across Michigan. Not surprisingly, AFA of Michigan's top priority in the 2004 election was passage of Proposal 2, and the group worked hard on its behalf. In early July, Glenn helped deliver thirty-five boxes of Proposal 2 petitions to the Secretary of State's office in Lansing (O'Donnell 2004). In addition, Glenn participated in several debates with opponents of the proposal (Jarema 2004).

Citizens for Traditional Values

Based in Lansing, Citizens for Traditional Values (CTV) traces its origins to Rev. Pat Robertson's 1988 presidential campaign. CTV was organized in 1986 as the Michigan Committee for Freedom and promptly became involved in supporting Robertson's campaign. Shortly after Robertson's defeat, his forces largely withdrew from the state, leaving the organization confused and deeply in debt. At that time, the board of directors decided to ask James Muffett, former director of Robertson's Vermont campaign, to head their organization. Muffett acted quickly and decisively to eliminate the organization's $500,000 debt. In 1994 the group filed as a 401(c)4 organization, and a year later it adopted its current name, Citizens for Traditional Values.

Under Muffett's leadership, four governing principles guide CTV activities: "preserving the influence of faith and family as the great foundation of American freedom embodied in our Judeo-Christian heritage"; "protecting our God-given right to life, from conception through every state of life"; "promoting a free enterprise philosophy of government which includes freedom from excessive taxation and government regulation"; and "providing the means by which parents can obtain educational freedom and strive for academic excellence in the instruction of their children. Ultimate responsibility for a child's education lies with the parents" (CTV 1997). To a large degree, these principles parallel those of MFF, although CTV tends to take a more explicitly free-market approach to economic issues and to give higher priority to economic policy. Like MFF, CTV has adopted a broad agenda, encouraging citizens to question candidates for public office on a wide variety of issues relating to "faith and family," the "proper role of government," and "education" (CTV 1997, 1–2).

Recognizing that pursuing such a broad policy agenda can dilute group resources and blunt its focus, CTV recently narrowed its focus. Nonetheless, it continues to urge its supporters to "take a stand for our Judeo-Christian values" on a broad array of policy issues, including abortion, creationism, crime, education, health care, gun control, seniors, taxes, displaying the Ten Commandments, and welfare reform (see www.ctvmichigan.org). In so doing, CTV has enjoyed considerable success. Indeed, former Michigan Lieutenant Governor Dick Posthumus has called CTV "the most underrated political organization in Michigan in relation to the amount of impact generated" (www.ctvmichigan.org).

Over time, CTV has developed a complex organizational structure, though not as complex as those of RTLM or MFF. In seeking its own identity, CTV chose not to become a mass-based organization with a high profile. Instead, according to Muffett, CTV chose to adopt a "servant" rather than a "confrontational" mode (Smidt and Penning 1997). To that end, CTV refuses to identify itself with any national organization; instead, it remains an independent organization, governed by a six- to eight-person board of directors, focusing primarily on state elections and policy.

In 1993 CTV created the Foundation for Traditional Values (FTV), a 501(c)3 tax-exempt, nonprofit organization, to serve as its educational arm. FTV, which shares a building with CTV, publishes its own newsletter, *Liberty Lamp*, giving special attention to education issues. FTV sponsors an annual Student Statesmanship Institute and distributes a variety of educational books, tapes, and other materials. FTV maintains a website that provides information concerning group positions on issues and government action.

CTV has established a separate PAC to assist candidates in targeted legislative districts. Endorsed candidates must share CTV values, including "support for: the sanctity of life, Judeo-Christian standards of morality in public policy, educational and academic freedom for parents and schools [and] a free enterprise philosophy minimizing governmental control over families and business." CTV also considers a variety of other matters, however, such as personal character, incumbency, electability, district demographics, other endorsements, "fire in the belly," and the opinions of consultants (see www.ctvmichigan.org).

In 2004 CTV endorsed one candidate for federal office: President Bush. At the state level, CTV chose to endorse only a limited number of judges, candidates for university boards, and members of the state House of Representatives. CTV's decision to target only a limited number of races no doubt is a product of resource limitations. Compared with RTLM or even MFF, CTV is exceedingly small. CTV and FTV combined have a staff of approximately ten people, including clerical workers, and an annual budget of less than $350,000.

Christian Coalition of Michigan

The Christian Coalition of Michigan (CCM) is exceedingly weak across the entire state, demonstrating little ability to mobilize volunteers or influence elections. To the frustration of national leaders, CCM has tended to remain organizationally independent of the national organization. In practice, this structure has meant that its president and board of directors have felt relatively free to pursue their own agendas—agendas that have changed with each change in CCM leadership. Although this flexibility has permitted CCM to concentrate on certain state-specific issues, such as the actions of the Michigan State Board of Education, at times it also has hindered efforts to present a clear and consistent message to Michigan voters and has generated considerable tension both within CCM and between CCM and the national organization. A major division involves conflict between "purists" who have sought to hold the Christian Coalition to a conservative social agenda and "pragmatists," who are more willing to compromise with political opponents.

Recently, Jack Horton, former state representative and county commissioner from the Grand Rapids area, has served as temporary CCM president. The organization largely exists in name only, however. In nonelection years, for example, CCM maintains no paid staff. The organization maintains an exceedingly small mailing list of 10,000 persons, although it claims a larger contributor list of approximately 55,000. CCM has attempted to organize on a county basis across the state but has had minimal success in generating broad grassroots appeal. Horton asserts, "For all practical purposes, the Christian Coalition in Michigan is nonexistent" (Zagaroli 1999).

The Christian Right in Recent Michigan Elections

The Christian Right in Michigan, then, is composed of a variety of organizations with varying degrees of political strength, different organizational structures, and diverse objectives. Clearly, however, over time the Christian Right in Michigan has institutionalized, developing from a disorganized social movement into several political organizations that have the potential to play important roles in Michigan elections. To assess the electoral activity and effectiveness of the Christian Right in the 2004

Michigan election, we must seek to clearly identify and specific the characteristics of Christian Right supporters in the state.

Identifying Christian Right Supporters

Although membership in particular organizations associated with the Christian Right can be ascertained relatively directly, determining the members of a social movement within the mass public is much more difficult. Movements, by definition, are dynamic in nature and amorphous in structure. The best available data concerning "membership" in the Christian Right among Michigan voters are those drawn from 2000 exit polls. The 2000 exit poll asked voters whether they considered themselves "part of the conservative Christian movement, also known as the religious right," whereas the 2004 exit poll simply asked voters whether considered themselves "born-again, evangelical Christians." Because there is a certain degree of overlap between the two categories, however, table 5.1 compares the characteristics of "Christian Right" voters in with those of "white, born-again, evangelical Christian" voters in 2004.

As table 5.1 makes clear, Christian Right voters and white evangelical Christian voters constitute a sizable, though far from dominant, bloc of voters in the state of Michigan; as 15 percent of Michigan voters in the 2000 election and 17 percent in the 2004 election can be so classified.[6] Generally speaking, both categories of voters comprise relatively high percentages of voters living in small towns and suburbs, as well as Republicans and conservatives. Although members of the Christian Right constituted a relatively high proportion of voters with lower levels of education in 2000, that was not the case among born-again evangelicals in 2004. Nor do Christian Right voters in 2000 or born-again evangelical voters in 2004 appear to exhibit any major "gender gap" within their ranks.

The Christian Right in Recent Elections

Table 5.2 reveals that self-identified Christian Right supporters in Michigan are far from neutral observers in presidential elections. Exit poll data reveal that in the 1996 election, two-thirds of Christian Right members recalled supporting the Republican candidate, Bob Dole, and only 28 percent recalled supporting the Democratic candidate, Bill Clinton. Yet Clinton easily carried the state because 63 percent of non–Christian Right voters voted for him.

Although members of the Christian Right strongly supported Dole in 1996, they were even more supportive of Republican presidential candidate George W. Bush and incumbent Republican Senator Spencer Abra-

Table 5.1   Social and Demographic Location of White Christian Right Voters and White Born-Again Evangelical Voters in Michigan, 2000 and 2004 (%)

Demographic	2000 Christian Right	2004 Born-Again Evangelical
% of Michigan voters	15	17
Gender		
Male	16	17
Female	14	17
Age		
18–29	17	15
30–44	15	15
45–59	15	17
60+	14	20
Education		
High school or less	19	17
Some college	16	16
College graduate	13	21
Some postgraduate	9	17
Size of residence		
City over 50,000	10	9
Suburbs	17	19
Small city/rural	18	20
Party identification		
Democrat	8	3
Independent/other	10	11
Republican	29	40

Sources: Voter News Service exit poll data, Michigan, 2000; Edison/Mitofsky exit poll data, 2004.

ham in 2000. Both Bush and Abraham garnered more than three-quarters of the votes cast by members of the Christian Right in Michigan, while their opponents attracted majority support among non–Christian Right voters (57 percent for Democratic presidential candidate Al Gore and 56 percent for Democratic senatorial candidate Debbie Stabenow). Given the fact that Gore carried the state and Stabenow narrowly defeated the GOP incumbent, Senator Abraham, it is clear that the Christian Right clearly did not provide the margin of victory needed in the state for either Bush or Abraham. Approximately 25 percent of the votes cast for Bush

Table 5.2 Voting Behavior of White Christian Right Members in Michigan, 1996–2004 (%)

Voting Behavior	Non–Christian Right	Christian Right
Presidential vote in 1996		
Clinton	63	28
Dole	27	67
Perot	10	5
Presidential vote in 2000		
Gore	57	21
Bush	41	77
Nader	2	2
Senate vote in 2000		
Stabenow (D)	56	22
Abraham (R)	44	78
Presidential vote in 2004[a]		
Kerry	60	8
Bush	39	92
Nader	1	0

[a]"Christian Right" data for 2004 reflect votes cast by "white, born-again, evangelical" respondents.
Sources: Voter News Service exit poll data, Michigan, 2000; Edison/Mitofsky exit poll data, 2004.

and Abraham in the Michigan election were delivered by Christian Right voters (data not shown). Thus, although the Christian Right in Michigan appears to have provided an important base for GOP candidates running in statewide elections, the support of Christian Right voters was far from sufficient to ensure statewide electoral victory.

Despite these Democratic victories at the statewide level in 2000, the Republican party in Michigan won control of both houses of the state legislature. The Christian Right also has been relatively successful in targeting local races (Penning and Smidt 2000). It also has been active in state party organizational activities. Nonetheless, although the Christian Right may have found a "home" in the Michigan Republican party, the party is far broader in terms of its composition and representation than that of the Christian Right. The Christian Right plays an important, but not necessarily determining, role within party politics.

The 2004 election in Michigan involved races for a host of local, state, and national offices, as well as contests over two ballot proposals. When the election was over, the Christian Right's record was mixed, at best. On one hand, the Christian Right failed in its efforts to carry the state for Bush; John Kerry narrowly won the state with 51 percent of the popular vote. In addition, the GOP contingent in Michigan's 110-member state House of Representatives shrank from sixty-six seats to fifty-eight—a less than salutary result for the largely Republican Christian Right. On the other hand, the GOP retained its nine seats in the Michigan congressional delegation.

Because most of the legislative seats at the state and federal levels were relatively "safe," most media and voter attention was focused on two controversial ballot proposals and the hotly contested presidential race. These two ballot proposals, both of which were supported by members of the Christian Right, won handily: Proposal 1, limiting the expansion of gambling, received 58 percent of the votes cast statewide, and Proposal 2, outlawing same-sex marriage, received 59 percent of the vote.

Hence, our primary focus in this chapter also is on the ballot proposals and the presidential race. Both ballot proposals (especially Proposal 2) and the presidential election generated a tremendous amount of political activity on the part of the "soldiers" of the Christian Right—activity so fierce that it may be appropriate to label the 2004 election as something of a "war on the home front." The stakes were high, and Christian Right organizations mobilized their members as never before.

The Battle over Proposal 1

The 2004 election year in Michigan began with the People's Choice Initiative, a successful effort by RTLM and supporters to override Governor Granholm's veto of antiabortion legislation. Although the People's Choice Initiative occurred early in the year (January–March) and did not involve a November electoral contest, the campaign energized groups such as RTLM and CTV, providing them with a "head start" on fall electoral activities. On the other hand, the conflict also helped to mobilize organizations on the political left. The Michigan Chapter of the American Civil Liberties Union (ACLU), for example, expressed outrage at the People's Choice Initiative and vowed to challenge its success in court (ACLU of Michigan 2004).

Like the People's Choice Initiative, the battle over Proposal 1 began with controversy in Lansing. In 2002 backers of Proposal 1 tried, unsuccessfully, to get the Michigan legislature to consider a constitutional amendment that would require a vote by the people of Michigan for all new gaming in the state (Bodipo-Memba 2004). In 2003 the Michigan legislature, seeking to find ways to assist the state's faltering horse-racing industry and ease the state's budget crunch, considered a proposal to permit state racetracks to establish "racinos"—racetrack casinos with electronic gaming facilities, including slot machines. The fact that the proposal stalled in the legislature because the House and Senate passed different bills was scant comfort to gambling opponents because the racino measure was just a conference committee away from approval (Heinlein 2004). As a result, in 2004 racino opponents circulated petitions to get an antigambling proposal on the ballot, collecting more than 440,000 signatures (Bodipo-Memba 2004).[7]

As written, Proposal 1 exempted virtually all Indian gaming, as well as three Detroit casinos, from its provisions. Instead, the proposal required both statewide and local approval for any expansion of electronic gaming and table games such as blackjack (Luke 2004a).[8] Because Proposal 1 included a retroactive enforcement provision (to January 1, 2004), it effectively killed any prospective legislative vote on racinos.

Like the proverbial Baptist-bootlegger coalition of Appalachia, the political coalitions generated by the Proposal 1 contest proved to be exceedingly strange. One part of the pro–Proposal 1 coalition included business interests, which were concerned that any expansion of gaming would harm the workforce and draw business away from traditional merchants. Helping to lead the charge was a PAC consisting of many of western Michigan's top business leaders. Calling itself "23 is enough" (after the total number of casinos in Michigan), the group, headed by prominent businessman Mike Jandernoa, worked diligently in concert with like-minded groups such as the Detroit Chamber of Commerce to support the proposal. A second group of proponents consisted of existing gaming interests (essentially the three Detroit casinos plus Indian tribes operating casinos), which regarded the proposal as a way to protect their economic self-interest by, in effect, limiting competition (Bell 2004a). Indeed, Indian tribes proved to be the foremost financial backers of Proposal 1.

These two groups of economic interests were joined, however, by traditional social conservatives, who opposed any expansion of gambling on moral grounds. Among the most active Christian Right groups supporting Proposal 1 were the MFF and CTV. Both of these groups endorsed the proposal and helped to ensure its inclusion on the fall ballot. Bill Ballenger, editor of the widely read periodical *Inside Michigan Politics*, concluded that the pro–Proposal 1 forces represented an alliance of "casinos and the religious Mafia of West Michigan" (Ballenger 2004).

Several prominent Michigan politicians also backed Proposal 1, although for varying reasons. Detroit Mayor Kwame Kilpatrick, for example, regarded the proposal as a means to protect Detroit's gaming industry. A large group of West Michigan Republicans, including former Lieutenant Governor Dick Posthumus and eleven conservative state legislators, also endorsed the proposal, primarily on moral grounds (*Grand Rapids Press* 2004b).

Opponents of Proposal 1 also formed an exceedingly unusual alliance. One category of opponents included economic interests fearing a loss of business. As one might expect, horse racing interests were in the forefront of the opposition. A variety of other economic interests, many of them concerned about economic losses or possible reductions in state revenues resulting from restrictions placed on the state lottery, also got involved. These actors included an unusual coalition of groups such as the Michigan Farm Bureau, the Michigan Teamsters Union, the Bowling Centers Association of Michigan, and the Michigan Milk Producers (*Grand Rapids Press* 2004b).

Perhaps the most unusual alliance opposing Proposal 1 linked Michigan's Democratic governor, Jennifer Granholm; the Republican Speaker of the House, Rick Johnson; and various education interests in Michigan, including the Michigan Association of School Boards, the Michigan Education Association, and the Michigan Parent/Teacher/Student Association. Each of these interests expressed concern over educational funding in the state relating to Proposal 1's restrictions on the Michigan lottery. Each year the Michigan lottery generates approximately $600 million for education (approximately 5 percent of total state and local education spending), and education backers were concerned that restrictions on new lottery games might limit state revenues. Indeed, Governor Granholm and Speaker Johnson were so concerned about Proposal 1 that they took the usual step of sponsoring joint antiproposal television and radio advertisements.

The battle over Proposal 1 proved to be exceedingly expensive; by October 23, a week before the election, a total of $19.4 million had been spent by groups supporting and opposing Proposal 1. Most of the money came from procasino economic interests, including $6.5 million from the Saginaw Chippewa Indian Tribe and $5 million from the MGM Grand Detroit casino. On the other hand, Hazel Park Raceway contributed $1.3 million and Northville Downs contributed $1 million to defeat the proposal (Luke 2004c).

Because of a lack of available data, assessing the precise impact of the Christian Right on Proposal 1 is difficult. Some useful data are available, however, from a *Detroit News* tracking poll conducted a week before the general election. These data are reported in tables 5.3 and 5.4.

As table 5.3 demonstrates, support for Proposal 1 was not uniform across religious traditions. Protestants tended to be most supportive; nearly two-thirds indicated that they planned to vote for the proposal. On the other hand, only a minority of Catholics (47 percent) supported the proposal. Support for the proposal among those with other religions (56

Table 5.3 Religion and Public Opinion on Ballot Proposals in Michigan, 2004 (%)

Ballot Proposal	Protestant	Catholic	Other	None
Proposal 1				
Yes	64	47	56	50
No	38	53	44	50
Proposal 2				
Yes	70	70	59	48
No	30	30	41	52

Source: Detroit News tracking poll by Mitchell Research & Company, October 18–24, 2004.
Note: Don't Know/Refused responses excluded.

percent) and no religion (50 percent) fell somewhere between the Protestant and Catholic groups.

Moreover, an examination of support for Proposal 1 by church attendance shows a close connection. For example, whereas 66 percent of voters attending church "more than once per week" supported Proposal 1, only 50 percent of those who "never" attend supported Proposal 1.

These data suggest that members of the Christian Right tended to give strong support to Proposal 1. Certainly, support tended to be relatively high among Protestants and among frequent church attendees. Thus, Christian Right voters probably provided a solid base of support for Proposal 1. Nevertheless, given that Proposal 1 passed by a substantial margin and that non–Christian Right groups also tended to support the proposal, we

Table 5.4 Church Attendance and Public Opinion on Ballot Proposals in Michigan, 2004 (%)

Ballot Proposal	More than Once/Week	Once/Week	Once or Twice/Month	A Few Times/Year	Never
Proposal 1					
Yes	66	59	51	57	50
No	34	41	49	43	50
Proposal 2					
Yes	89	78	61	58	38
No	11	22	39	45	62

Source: Detroit News tracking poll by Mitchell Research & Company, October 18–24, 2004.
Note: Don't Know/Refused responses excluded.

cannot conclude that the Christian Right was the only factor facilitating the success of Proposal 1. Three additional factors also mattered. First, the proposal tapped into growing voter unease over the growth of gambling in the state. In addition, proponents tended to be better funded than their opposition, enabling supporters to dominate the airwaves. Finally, supporters were able to successfully frame the debate in terms of voter choice rather than gambling, arguing that Proposal 1 was provoter (choice) rather than necessarily antigambling. This "rights" language had broad appeal among Michigan voters.

The Battle over Proposal 2

The battle over Proposal 1 was only a skirmish compared to the conflict over Proposal 2—an anti–gay marriage constitutional amendment that divided people along cultural lines and split religious denominations and traditional political alliances. In November 2004, Michigan was one of eleven states with an anti–gay marriage amendment on the ballot. Although the wording of the state proposals varied, they passed handily in all eleven states, with majorities ranging from 86 percent (Mississippi) to 57 percent (Oregon). Although Michigan voters' 59 percent approval of Proposal 1 was solid, only the election in Oregon produced a lower percentage of support.[9]

Prior to 2004 Michigan's legislature had passed legislation banning gay marriages in the state. Backers of the ban wanted to secure this ban, however, by including it in the Michigan constitution (Meehan 2004c). The legislature was unable, however, to muster the two-thirds majority in each house required to place an amendment proposal on the ballot. As a result, in 2004 prominent supporters of CTV, including former Michigan State Representative Harold Voorhees, formed a separate organization, Citizens for the Protection of Marriage, to gather signatures to place a "marriage" amendment on the November ballot. The new group began its campaign in April, placing local coordinators in all eighty-three Michigan counties and recruiting hundreds of volunteers to work on the campaign (Martin 2004b). Between April and July, the group, headed by longtime Republican and conservative activist Marlene Elwell, collected more than 500,000 signatures—far more than required to put the measure (which was later labeled Proposal 2) on the ballot (Branson 2004).

A partisan division on the Michigan Board of Canvassers, however, threatened to derail the proposal before voters were given their say. The Board split 2–2, with the two Democratic members suggesting that Proposal 2 was substantively problematical and the two Republican members arguing that the petitioners had fulfilled all of the procedural requirements to put the measure on the fall ballot (Emery and Luke 2004). Ultimately the courts backed the Republicans' position and ordered the proposal placed on the fall ballot.

The precise wording of Proposal 2 suggests that its initiators were seeking a comprehensive ban on gay marriage in the state: "The proposal would amend the state constitution to provide that the union of one man and one woman in marriage shall be the only agreement recognized as marriage or similar union for any purpose." Critics charged that the proposal's sweeping language not only would ban gay marriage but that it also would ban civil unions between gay partners and threaten employer benefits to same-sex households (Mask 2004). Proponents, however, labeled such charges "scare tactics."

Prior to the election, analysts disagreed over the impact of Proposal 2 on both voter turnout and the presidential race. A nationwide poll, conducted in spring 2004, suggested that "gay marriage is a more powerful social issue for voters than either abortion or gun control" (Associated Press 2004). According to Bill Rustem of Public Sector Consultants in Lansing, the gay marriage proposal seemed likely to help President Bush and the Michigan GOP. According to Rustem, the "bloc most fired up by the issue seems to be conservative, fundamentalist Christians, a group that votes heavily Republican" (Roelofs 2004). Some Democrats also saw the issue that way, arguing that Proposal 2 was "a ploy by right-wing church and political groups to get out the vote for President George W. Bush, a strong supporter of a federal constitutional amendment banning same-sex marriages" (Meehan 2004c). According to veteran reporter Peter Luke, "Democrats fear that [the] amendment will draw to the polls large numbers of evangelical Christians who otherwise might stay home. And while they're at the polls, they will vote for George W. Bush" (Luke 2004b).

Others, however, suggested that Proposal 2 would have little impact on either turnout or the general election. Ed Sarpolis, a Lansing-based pollster and consultant, asserted, "This is already a high interest election. . . . I haven't heard anybody say 'I'm voting because of Proposal 2'" (Hornbeck and Cain 2004). Similarly, reporter Peter Luke argued, "It's unclear just how angry Michigan voters are about gay marriage in Massachusetts and thus feel compelled to erect constitutional armor against it here" (Luke 2004b).

Sarpolis and Luke may have underestimated the passions aroused by Proposal 2. Indeed, so powerful was the issue that it helped cement a very unusual alliance between white evangelical Protestants, African American Protestants, and Roman Catholics throughout the state. The initial impetus for the proposal came from white Protestants associated with such Christian Right organizations as AFA, CTV, and MFF. Throughout the campaign, such groups continued to play a major role. Although some Proposal 2 supporters used fiery, homophobic language (Morrison 2004), most evangelical supporters of the proposal adopted a more moderate position, arguing that the proposal was "profamily" rather than "antigay." Kristina Hemphill, a spokesperson for Citizens for the Protection of Marriage, asserted that "our message all along has focused simply on the definition of marriage, the union of one man and one woman, and that strong marriages produce strong families and keep our nation strong" (Emery 2004). To promote this position, Hemphill's organization sponsored a statewide television and radio blitz in major metropolitan areas. In addition, the group distributed 1 million flyers at protestant churches throughout Michigan (Montemurri and Bello 2004).

Throughout the campaign, Proposal 2 received considerable support from white evangelical clergy, particularly clergy heading independent, fundamentalist congregations. For example, Rev. John Munro, pastor of a nondenominational church in Kalamazoo, asserted, "We believe in a Christian marriage right from creation is between a man and a woman" (Meehan 2004a). In addition, however, Proposal 2 received strong support from African American clergy: "Detroit's influential black pastors, historically liberal and Democratic voters on social justice issues, want Proposal 2 to pass, reflecting the African American community's traditional values about marriage. They find themselves in unique agreement with the conservative, Republican-oriented Michigan Family Forum and Family Research Council" (Montemurri and Bello 2004). For example, the influential Council of Baptist Pastors in Detroit and Vicinity voted overwhelmingly to support Proposal 2 (Montemurri and Bello 2004). Similarly, Rev. Levon Yuille of Ypsilanti, head of the National Black Pro-Life Congress, endorsed Proposal 2 and worked closely with AFA's Gary Glenn to collect signatures for Proposal 2 (O'Donnell 2004).

White evangelical Protestants and African Americans were joined in supporting Proposal 2 by leaders of the Catholic church. Indeed, Catholics contributed nearly $700,000 of the more than $1 million spent in support of Proposal 2. The proposal was endorsed by the Michigan Catholic Conference (MCC), and virtually every diocese in Michigan made a substantial contribution. In an October 15 mailing to 500,000 Catholic households in Michigan, MCC asserted, "Defining marriage as the union of one man and one woman does not diminish others' rights" (*Grand Rapids Press* 2004a). At the direction of Detroit Cardinal Adam Maida, the diocese of Grand Rapids contributed $106,000, Lansing dioceses contributed $133,500, and the Detroit diocese contributed $270,000 (Meehan 2004a; Martin 2004a). In addition, Cardinal Maida helped create a pro–Proposal 2 video to be shown in Catholic churches across the state. Other major funding for the proposal (a total of $310,000) came from conservative evangelicals in West Michigan, including the prominent DeVos family (Harmon 2004).

Opposition to Proposal 2 came, in part, from "secular," human rights organizations such as the ACLU, economic groups such as labor unions (which were concerned about possible interference with collective bargaining), and government organizations such as the Jackson Human Rights Commission and the Michigan Civil Rights Commission. After the Michigan Civil Rights Commission voted 5–2 to oppose Proposal 2, Commission Vice-Chairman Mark Bernstein of Ann Arbor, who proposed the resolution, urged voters "to forcefully reject this hateful, unnecessary, redundant, ambiguous, disgraceful, shameful proposal" (Chandler 2004). Perhaps the leading secular organization opposing Proposal 2, however, was a group labeling itself the Coalition for a Fair Michigan, which spent more than $300,000 on the campaign. In addition, the anti–Proposal 2 campaign received substantial support from gay and lesbian groups such as the Triangle Foundation. The Washington-based Human Rights Campaign, a gay/lesbian/transgender advocacy group, contributed $175,000 to the cause, and individuals and other gay rights groups added another $128,000 (Emery 2004).

Religious groups—particularly those representing mainline Protestant denominations—also opposed Proposal 2. The bishops of all four Episcopalian dioceses in Michigan, for example, came out against the proposal (Harr 2004). So did a coalition of 125 ministers calling themselves the Concerned Clergy of West Michigan. This group ran ads and billboards calling Proposal 2 "unequal, unfair, and unjust" (Honey 2004).

Fortunately, available data are more complete with respect to Proposal 2 than with respect to Proposal 1.[10] Table 5.3 demonstrates that there was considerable similarity in opinions regarding Proposal 2 among Protestants and Catholics: Preelection tracking polls indicated that 70 percent of each group supported the proposal. This similarity is particularly striking in view of the considerable differences between the two groups (discussed above) with respect to Proposal 1. Persons with "other" religious traditions gave less support (59 percent) to Proposal 2, and only a minority of those with no religion supported the measure.

Tracking poll data, reported in table 5.4, reveal that there was a clear, monotonic relationship between church attendance and support for Proposal 2. Whereas 89 percent of respondents who reported that they attend church "more than once a week" supported the proposal, that support declined consistently along with church attendance—reaching a low point of 38 percent support among respondents who reported that they "never" attend church. Although these findings parallel those for Proposal 1, the pattern is even more consistent for Proposal 1.

CNN exit poll data, reported in table 5.5, comport well with these tracking poll findings. The CNN data reveal that both Protestant and Catholic voters strongly supported Proposal 2—giving it 66 percent and 62 percent support, respectively. In contrast, only 14 percent of Jewish voters supported the measure. Similarly, exit polls reveal that whereas 88 percent of white, conservative Protestants supported Proposal 2, only 53 percent of other voters did so. Moreover, whereas 80 percent of "white, born-again Christians" supported Proposal 2, only a slight majority (52 percent) of other voters did so.

As with the tracking polls, exit polls demonstrate a strong relationship between church attendance and support for Proposal 2 (data not shown). Whereas 82 percent of respondents attending church "more than once a

Table 5.5   Vote on Proposal 2 (Gay Marriage) by Religious Variables: Michigan, 2004 (%)

Variables	Yes on Proposal 2	No on Proposal 2
Religious Tradition		
Protestant (53%)	66	34
Catholic (29%)	62	38
Jewish (2%)	14	86
White, Conservative Protestant		
Yes (17%)	88	12
No (83%)	53	47
White, Evangelical, Born-Again		
Yes (25%)	80	20
No (75%)	52	48
Church Attendance		
More than once/week (16%)	82	18
Weekly (28%)	69	31
Monthly (13%)	58	42
A few times/year (29%)	48	52
Never (13%)	35	65
Religion and Attendance		
Protestant/weekly (16%)	74	26
Protestant less often (16%)	55	45
Catholic/weekly (14%)	73	27
Catholic less often (14%)	52	48
All others (37%)	52	48

Source: CNN.com Election 2004.

week" supported Proposal 2, only 35 percent of those who "never" attend church supported the proposal. Indeed, religiosity appears to be a crucial factor in explaining both Protestant and Catholic support for Proposal 2: Approximately three-quarters of "weekly attenders" in each group supported the proposal, but only slightly more than half of the infrequent attenders in each group supported the proposal. Indeed, the level of support for Proposal 2 given by infrequently attending Protestants and Catholics approximated that given by "all others."

The data presented here suggest that the Christian Right gave considerable support to the movement for Proposal 2. Indeed, one can argue fairly that the Christian Right, along with cultural conservatives in the Catholic and African American communities, provided a firm base of support for Proposal 2. Yet given that Proposal 2, like Proposal 1, passed by a wide margin and that a majority of voters who are not white, conservative Protestants also supported Proposal 2, one cannot conclude that the Christian Right was solely responsible for the outcome.

The Presidential Election

In 2004 the Christian Right worked diligently not only on behalf of the two ballot proposals but also on behalf of the GOP ticket more generally. President Bush received particularly enthusiastic support. As Bush campaign spokesman John Truscott remarked, "It's unprecedented. There's more outreach than we've ever seen before by the conservative religious groups" (Montemurri and Bello 2004). Given that John Kerry won the state in 2004, one can hardly argue that this effort determined the outcome of the presidential race. Nevertheless, this effort at least may have narrowed the gap between the two candidates and may have had some impact on "down ticket" races such as those for the ballot proposals.

To clarify the role of the Christian Right in the presidential election, table 5.6 presents relationships between religious variables and voting behavior. The table reveals that President Bush did well among Protestants, winning 54 percent of their votes. He also received nearly half (49 percent) of Catholic votes in 2004. On the other hand, Bush received less than one-third of the votes of voters in the "Jewish," "other," or "none" categories.

Bush did particularly well among voters who identified themselves as "white, conservative, Protestant," winning an overwhelming 92 percent of their votes. He also did well among voters in the "white, evangelical, born-again" category, winning 71 percent of their votes. Indeed, one could fairly label these two overlapping categories of voters as constituting Bush's core

Table 5.6   Presidential Vote by Religious Variables: Michigan, 2004 (%)

Variable	Bush	Kerry	Nader
Religion			
Protestant (53%)	54	45	0
Catholic (29%)	49	50	0
Jewish (2%)	22	71	a
Other (6%)	32	66	3
None (10%)	26	69	1
White, Conservative, Protestant			
Yes (17%)	92	8	a
No (83%)	39	59	1
White, Evangelical, Born-Again			
Yes (24%)	71	29	0
No (76%)	41	58	1
Church Attendance			
More than weekly (15%)	58	40	a
Weekly (27%)	55	44	1
Monthly (13%)	47	53	1
A few times a year (29%)	42	57	1
Never (13%)	32	64	2
Religion and Attendance			
Protestant/weekly (16%)	64	34	1
Protestant/less often (15%)	51	48	0
Catholic/weekly (14%)	49	50	0
Catholic/less often (14%)	49	50	1
All others	38	60	1

Sources: CNN.com Election 2004; exit poll data.
[a]Represents a statistically insignificant number of voters.

constituency in the state. Unfortunately for Bush, however, neither category accounted for more than one-quarter of the state's electorate.

As with the two ballot proposals, there was a strong, monotonic relationship between church attendance and voting behavior: Frequent attenders were far more supportive of Bush than infrequent attenders or nonattenders. Whereas 58 percent of persons attending church "more than weekly" voted for Bush, only 32 percent of those who "never" attend church voted for Bush. Looking at the combination of religion and attendance, attendance clearly matters most among Protestant voters. Whereas nearly two-thirds of Protestants who attend church weekly voted for Bush, only a slight majority of Protestants who attend church less often voted for Bush. Among Catholics, however, church attendance mattered little; "weekly" and "less often" attenders gave Bush equal support (49 percent).

Conclusion

Over the past two decades, a variety of Christian Right groups have formed in Michigan in an effort to promote a culturally conservative agenda. Although these groups differ considerably in terms of objectives, size, organization, and political effectiveness, the general pattern followed by the Christian Right in Michigan has entailed transformation from a disorganized social movement toward formation of organized groups or party factions.

The Christian Right in Michigan constitutes a powerful, though not a dominant, political force. Several factors help to account for the political success of Christian Right organizations in Michigan. First, over time the Christian Right has found a home in the Republican Party, where it now constitutes a major party faction. That wasn't always the case. In the contest for the 1988 Republican presidential nomination, for example, supporters of Rev. Pat Robertson threw the Michigan GOP into chaos with their aggressive efforts on his behalf, producing a split between Robertson's Christian Right supporters and more moderate supporters of George H. W. Bush (Smidt and Penning 1997).

A second factor contributing to the growth and success of the Christian Right in Michigan involves the impact of events at the national level. A variety of events, including U.S. Supreme Court decisions (e.g., on prayer and Bible reading in schools) and social turmoil surrounding the Vietnam War prompted social conservatives to engage more directly in political activity. In addition, the presidential campaigns of "born-again" presidential candidates such as Jimmy Carter, Pat Robertson, and George W. Bush have helped to generate enthusiasm among the faithful and have provided them with opportunities to hone their political skills. The administration of President Ronald Reagan also may have played a role in encouraging Christian Right activity. Not only was President Reagan openly sympathetic to the Christian Right (in word if not always in deed), but his policy of devolving power and responsibility to the states and localities may have provided Christian Right organizations with the incentive required to organize effectively at the grassroots level.

A third reason for the success of the Christian Right has been the growing political sophistication of at least some of its constituent organizations. This sophistication is evident, for example, in the choice of issue agendas. Groups such as RTLM have focused their resources very effectively on a relatively narrow set of political issues, thereby maximizing their impact on those issues. Other groups have used different tactics to allocate scarce resources, targeting a limited number of key electoral contests rather than spreading their resources more broadly. In addition, most of the successful Christian Right organizations have learned to coordinate their activities with those of other groups that share their objectives. In the 2004 election, for example, conservative white Protestants were able to make common cause with both African Americans and Catholics in the effort to pass Proposal 2.

A final reason for the continuing success of Michigan's Christian Right organizations concerns changing political rhetoric. To a large extent, the Christian Right has replaced its earlier language of moralism with the language of liberalism (Moen 1997). Rather than framing public policy issues in moralistic, sectarian terms, the Christian Right has recast many of its arguments in terms of the language of rights, freedom, and equality that is associated with liberal democratic thought. This approach was evident in the 2004 discussion of Proposal 1—which was sold to voters as a "voters' rights" proposal rather than a proposal on the morality of gaming.

On the other hand, the Christian Right in Michigan is far from all-powerful. One factor limiting its influence is internal conflict. As the Christian Right has institutionalized, transforming itself from a social movement to a more formally organized set of interest groups, internal disputes have arisen, pitting purists against pragmatists. In the more successful organizations, including RTLM and CTV, strong leadership and a sense of mission have helped resolve such conflicts or at least minimize their deleterious impact. In other organizations, however—most notably CCM—internal divisions (as well as conflict between state and national organizations) have seriously weakened the organization and limited its political impact.

A second factor limiting the clout of Michigan's Christian Right is its political immaturity, which manifested particularly in the early years of the movement. Although Christian Right organizations in the state have grown in political sophistication, the earlier lack of political sophistication led some groups to make crucial tactical errors. Perhaps most problematic has been the attempt of some groups to pursue an exceedingly broad policy agenda, thereby diluting their resources and, perhaps, engendering more internal conflict than was necessary.

Finally, the Christian Right in Michigan has been limited by group countermobilization. Groups such as Planned Parenthood and the ACLU, for example, have sought to counter the activities of RTLM. The anti-gay activities of AFA of Michigan have fostered a considerable amount of opposition from both state and national gay organizations. Perhaps most interesting, the political activities of "Christian Right" clergy have prompted clergy on the "left" to countermobilize.

The 2004 election in Michigan illustrates this view of the Christian Right as powerful but not dominant in state politics. On one hand, the Christian Right could not carry the state for President George W. Bush. Although "moral values" voters provided an important base of support for Bush and may even have narrowed Kerry's margin over Bush, economic issues proved to be even more important than moral issues in Michigan. On the other hand, when moral issues became *the* issue on which voters were focusing—as was the case with Proposal 1 and (especially) Proposal 2—the Christian Right was able to achieve considerable success. Although both proposals might have passed without the support of the Christian Right, there is little doubt that the margin of victory would have been narrower.

In the 2006 and 2008 elections, the Christian Right in Michigan is likely to continue to exert a significant, though limited, impact on politics and policy. To be politically successful, the movement will have to balance the tension between purists and pragmatists. It also will have to continue to develop its political skills. Furthermore, as a distinct minority in state politics, it will have to work cooperatively with like-minded citizens and organizations to achieve its policy objectives.

Notes

1. This chapter relies heavily on Penning (2005).

2. In part these findings may be an artifact of question wording. According to the Pew Research Center, when voters were presented with a close-ended "most important issue" question, "moral values" came out on top, but when they were presented with an open-ended question, other issues, including the war in Iraq, trumped moral values (Lester 2004).

3. Data are drawn from several sources. Some data are drawn from a variety of published reports, including academic analyses and newspaper accounts of the 2004 election. Other data are drawn from interviews with key members of Christian Right organizations in Michigan. Finally, the chapter uses exit poll data from the 2000 and 2004 presidential elections in Michigan.

4. This section relies heavily on Smidt and Penning (2003). Over time, the movement has gone by various different names. In the 1970s the term favored by the media and leaders such as Rev. Jerry Falwell was the "religious right." More recently, the most common term has been the "Christian Right." Yet some members of the media and leaders of the Christian Right have expressed a preference for terms such as "evangelical Christian" or "conservative Christian" (Noah 2004). In this chapter we use the term Christian Right because it is more specific than the broader term "evangelical Christian."

5. RTLM is structured as a 501(c)4 organization for most purposes. Hence, under IRS regulations it is permitted to function as an advocacy group, lobbying government officials to achieve its policy ends. Under 501(c)4 regulations, however, contributions to the organization are not tax deductible. As a result, RTLM also has established three legally separate 501(c)3 organizations. These three organizations—an Education Fund, a Legal Defense Fund, and an Endowment Fund—are legally required to avoid direct lobbying of government officials. Their primary focus is "educational," and contributions to these three organizations are tax deductible.

6. Christian Right voters in 2000 were operationally defined as white voters who willingly classified themselves as "part of the conservative Christian political movement, also known as the religious right." Using the same operational definition with 1996 exit poll data, 15 percent of Michigan voters in 1996 could be classified as part of the Christian Right—the same percentage as that in 2000. In 2004 Christian Right voters were defined as white, born-again, evangelical Christians.

7. The anticasino movement in Michigan was sparked by growing voter unease over the rapid growth of legal gaming in the state. Whereas in the early 1980s the only gaming officially permitted in the state involved church "bingo" and "casino" nights, by 2004 the state arguably had become the gaming capital of the Midwest, not only sponsoring a state lottery but also sanctioning three non-Indian casinos in Detroit and twenty Indian casinos throughout the state. More Indian casinos were on the drawing board. Although federal law restricts voter control over Indian gaming, it does not restrict such control over non-Indian gaming.

8. The official language of Proposal 1 was as follows: "No law enacted after January 1, 2004, that authorizes any form of gambling shall be effective, nor after January 1, 2004, shall any new state Lottery games utilizing table games or player operated mechanical or electronic devices be established, without the approval of a majority of electors voting in a statewide general election and a majority of electors voting in the township or city where gambling will take place. This section shall not apply to gambling in up to three casinos in the City of Detroit or to Indian tribal gaming."

9. The percentages of voters supporting anti–gay marriage amendments were as follows: Arkansas, 75 percent; Georgia, 76 percent; Kentucky, 75 percent; Michigan, 59 percent; Mississippi, 86 percent; Montana, 67 percent; North Dakota, 73 percent; Ohio, 72 percent; Oklahoma, 76 percent; Oregon, 57 percent; and Utah, 66 percent.

10. Both preelection tracking polls and exit polls included questions pertaining to Proposal 2.

References

Note: Website references were accurate as of time of writing; websites change over time, however, so URLs listed may not be up to date.

Agence France Press (AFP). 2004. "US Christian Right Exultant after Bush Re-Election." 22 November. Available at www.religionnewsblog.com/9261-.html (accessed February 5, 2006).

American Civil Liberties Union (ACLU) of Michigan. 2004. "ACLU Will Again Challenge Abortion Ban." Press release, June 9. Available at www.aclumich. org/modules.php?name=News&file=article&sid=359 (access July 6, 2004).

Associated Press. 2004. "Poll: Gay Marriage Is Big Voter Issue." March 1. Available at www.foxnews.com/story/0,2933,112897,00.html (accessed October 20, 2004).

Ballenger, Bill. 2004. "The 2004 Michigan Election." Paper presented at annual meeting of Michigan Conference of Political Scientists, October 16, Mt. Pleasant.

Bell, Dawson. 2004a. "Campaign to Limit Gambling Gets Boost." *Detroit Free Press.* Available at www.freep.com/cgi-bin/forms/printerfriendly.pl (accessed July 2, 2004).

———. 2004b. "Why Kerry Lost: Too Lame, Too Liberal, Too Unlovable." *Detroit Free Press*, 8 November.

Bodipo-Memba, Alejandro. 2004. "Poll: Michigan Voters Want a Say on Gaming." *Detroit Free Press*, 5 October.

Branson, David. 2004. "Initiative Calls for Ban on Gay Marriages." *Michigan Daily*, 15 April.

Cain, Charlie. 1997. "Right to Life: In 25 Years, Michigan's Group Gains Enough Political Clout to Rival Unions." *Detroit News*, 2 March.

Chandler, Greg. 2004. "State Civil Rights Panel Calls Prop 2 'Hateful.'" *Grand Rapids Press*, 26 October.

Christoff, Chris. 2004. "Election in Michigan: Economy and War Swing State Support for Kerry." *Detroit Free Press*, 3 November.

Citizens for Traditional Values (CTV). 1997. *A Voice for Your Values.* Lansing, Mich.: Citizens for Traditional Values.

Cooperman, Alan, and Thomas B. Edsall. 2004. "Evangelicals Say They Led Charge for the GOP." *Washington Post*, 8 November. Available at www.washingtonpost. com/ac2/wp-dyn/A32793-2004Nov7?language=printer.

Dickerson, Brian. 2000. "Abortion Foes Scoring Quiet, Key Victories." *Detroit Free Press*, 8 December.

Emery, Sharon, and Peter Luke. 2004. "Same-Sex Marriage Ban, Nader Kept Off the Ballot." *Grand Rapids Press*, 24 August, A1.

Emery, Shirley. 2004. "TV Ads Target Gay Marriage Issue." Booth Newspapers. Available at www.mlive.com/search/index.ss?/base/news-5/109891500032330. xml?news/state... (accessed October 29, 2004).

Finley, Nolan. 2004. "Evangelical Voters Won't Back Off on Gay Rights, Abortion." *Detroit News*, 7 November.

Grand Rapids Press. 2004a. "Donation by Diocese to Fight Gay Marriage Irks Some Catholics." *Grand Rapids Press.* Available at www.mlive.com/printer/printer/ ssf?base/news-17/109880239571720.xml (accessed October 26, 2004).

———. 2004b. "Proposal 1 Bedfellows." *Grand Rapids Press.* Available at www. mlive.com/search/index.ssf?base/news-0/109800879986870.xml?grpress?n... (accessed October 18, 2004).

Harmon, Steven. 2004. "Local Giving Fuels Anti-Gay Marriage Drive." *Grand Rapids Press*, 23 October.

Harr, Monetta L. 2004. "A Political Pulpit." *Jackson Citizen Patriot*. Available at www.
     mlive.com/search/index.ssf?/base/news-0/1098720301248440.xml?jacitpat?n...
     (accessed October 25, 2004).

Heinlein, Gary. 2000. "Abortion Limits a Signature away from Law." *Detroit News*,
     20 December.

———. 2004. "Legislator Pushes for Racino Proposal." *Detroit News*, 24 October
     25.

Hitt, Greg. 2004. "Evangelical Christians Set Their Agenda." *Wall Street Journal*,
     11 November, A4.

Honey, Charles. 2004. "The Right Proposal? Constitutional Amendment on Gay
     Marriage Splits Faithful." *Grand Rapids Press*, 16 October.

Hornbeck, Mark, and Charlie Cain. 2004. "Culture Clash May Swing Michigan
     Vote." *Detroit News*, 17 October 18.

Jarema, Morgan. 2004. "Gay Marriage Debate Reveals Sharp Division." *Grand
     Rapids Press*, 13 October, C1.

Lester, Will. 2004. "Poll Wording Influenced Responses." Associated Press, 12
     November.

Luke, Peter. 2004a. "Battle over Prop 1 Brings Kids and Dogs into the Fray."
     Booth Newspapers. Available at www.mlive.com/search/inex.ssf?/base/news-
     5/1097187001253490.xml?news/stat... (accessed October 23, 2004).

———. 2004b. "Gay Marriage Ban Won't Draw Voters." *Grand Rapids Press*, 15
     August, A19.

———. 2004c. "Groups Report $19.4 Million in Support, Opposition to Proposal
     1." Booth Newspapers. Available at www.mlive.com/search/index.ssf?/base/
     news-5/1098484806295050.xml?news/stat... (accessed October 23, 2004).

Martin, Tim. 2004a. "Catholic Church Donations Boost Gay Marriage Ban Cam-
     paign." *Detroit News*. Available at www.detnews.com/2004/politics/0410/09/
     politics-298232.htm (accessed October 9, 2004).

———. 2004b. "Gay Marriage Opponents Target November Ballot." Associ-
     ated Press. Available at www.mlive.com/printer/printer.ssf?/base/news-
     16/108905845729670.xml?aponline (accessed July 6 2004).

Mask, Theresa. 2004. "Gays Fear Marriage Ban Will End Benefits." *Detroit Free
     Press*, 22 October.

Meehan, Chris. 2004a. "Church Money for Prop 2 Passage Irks Some." *Kal-
     amazoo Gazette*. Available at www.mlive.search/index.ssf?/base/news-11/
     109897690327070 (accessed October 29, 2004).

———. 2004b. "Differing Pastors Plan Gay-Marriage Discussion." *Kalama-
     zoo Gazette*. Available at www.mlive.com/search/index.ssf?/base/news-0/
     1097922199300620.xml?kzgazette... (accessed October 29, 2004).

———. 2004c. "Marriage Proposal a Fight over Values." *Kalamazoo Gazette*. Avail-
     able at www.mlive.com/searc/index.ssf?/base/news-11/1098613527195070.
     xml?kzgazett... (accessed October 29, 2004).

Moen, Matthew. 1997. "The Changing Nature of Christian Right Activism:
     1970s–1990s." In *Sojourners in the Wilderness: The Christian Right in Compara-
     tive Perspectives*, ed. C. Smidt and J. M. Penning. Lanham, Md.: Rowman and
     Littlefield.

Montemurri, Patricia. 2004. "Catholics Split Statewide over Moral Choices." *Detroit Free Press*, 25 October 25.

Montemurri, Patricia, and Marisol Bello. 2004. "Proposal 2: Marriage Ban Divides, Unites Religions." *Detroit Free Press*, 21 October 30.

Morrison, Gary W. 2004. "TV Evangelist Warns Christians to Vote." *Grand Rapids Press*, 23 October, B7.

Noah, Timothy. 2004. "Why You Can't Call Them 'the Christian right.'" *Slate Magazine*. Available at www.slate.com/toolbar.aspx?action=print&id=2109370.

O'Donnell, Catherine. 2004. "Pastor Helps Lead Fight for Proposal." *Ann Arbor News*. Available at www.mlive.com/search/index.ssf?/base/news-o/10987156525700.xml?aanews?NE... (accessed October 28, 2004).

Ostling, Richard. 2004. "Ideology on the Line." *Grand Rapids Press*, 13 October, A10.

Penning, James M. 2005. "A War on the Home Front? The Christian Right in the 2004 Michigan Election." Paper presented at annual meeting of Southern Political Science Association, January 6–8, New Orleans.

Penning, James M., and Corwin E. Smidt. 2000. "Michigan: The 'Right Stuff.'" In *Prayers in the Precincts: The Christian Right in the 1998 Elections*, ed. John C. Green, Mark J. Rozell, and Clyde Wilcox. Washington, D.C.: Georgetown University Press, 163–86.

Riley, Rochelle. 2004. "Democrats Get a Lesson in Morality." *Detroit Free Press*, 4 November.

Roelofs, Ted. 2004. "Gay Marriage Vote May Tip Michigan for President." *Grand Rapids Press*, 3 July, A1.

Rozell, Mark J., and Clyde Wilcox. 1996. *Second Coming: The New Christian Right in Virginia Politics*. Baltimore: Johns Hopkins University Press.

Scott, Sara, and Barton Dieters. 2001. "Abortion Still Prime Legislative Target." *Grand Rapids Press*, 16 July, A1.

Smidt, Corwin E., and James M. Penning. 1995. "Michigan: Veering to the Right?" In *God at the Grassroots: The Christian Right in the 1994 Elections*, ed. Mark J. Rozell and Clyde Wilcox. Lanham, Md.: Rowman & Littlefield, 147–68.

———. 1997. "Michigan: Veering to the Left?" In *God at the Grass Roots: The Christian Right in the 1996 Elections*, ed. Mark J. Rozell and Clyde Wilcox. Lanham, Md.: Rowman & Littlefield, 115–34.

———. 2003. "The Christian Right's Mixed Success in Michigan." In *The Christian Right in American Politics: Marching to the Millennium*, ed. John Green, Mark J. Rozell, and Clyde Wilcox. Washington, D.C.: Georgetown University Press, 101–20.

Wilson, James Q. 2004. "Why Did Kerry Lose? (Answer: It Wasn't 'Values.')." *Wall Street Journal*, 8 November, A14.

Zagaroli, Lisa. 1999. "Michigan Is a Priority, Christian Coalition Says." *Detroit News*, 14 October.

CHAPTER SIX

Iowa

In the Heart of Bush Country

KIMBERLY H. CONGER AND DONALD RACHETER

ALL OVER THE COUNTRY, CHRISTIAN RIGHT LEADERS TOOK CREDIT for the reelection of President George W. Bush in 2004. Evangelical Protestants, the primary constituency of the Christian Right, certainly turned out in higher numbers than in 2000. Movement leaders further point to the importance of "values" to voters as evidence that they have been right all along (Rosin 2005, 117). They say Americans want a return to traditional, religious values, and these voices finally have been heard definitively on Election Day. As with any monocausal explanation of political events, however, the reality of the situation is far more complex. That complexity is amply demonstrated in Iowa's change from "blue state" to "red state."

Iowa has long been considered a state where the Christian Right has considerable impact on state and Republican politics. Beginning with Pat Robertson's surprise success in the Republican straw poll of 1987, the movement in Iowa has regularly drawn practical and motivated activists and has seen its power and influence grow and solidify in the state's Republican Party. The campaign of 2004 was no different in this regard. George W. Bush's faith and commitment to conservative Christian issue positions, combined with an unprecedented "get out the vote" effort on the part of the Republican party, consolidated Christian Right efforts and contributed to Bush's victory.

Politics in Iowa

The caucuses have been a defining factor in Iowa politics since 1972. Many observers point to their importance and believe that the caucuses give Iowa politics a significant grassroots element that is missing in other states. Not only are party candidates chosen in the caucuses; so is the party leadership. This structure gives practically anyone with the time and motivation the ability to make an impact in the political arena.

Iowa historically has had significant party competition. Both parties are strong and well organized, and although four of the state's five congressional districts are represented by Republicans, the governor is a Democrat and the state Senate is evenly divided. Perhaps most telling is the state's choice of senators. Tom Harkin, one of the most liberal Democrats in the U.S. Senate, has served as Iowa's senator since 1984. Chuck Grassley, a conservative, has been in the Senate since 1980. This divided representation demonstrates the closeness of the parties that characterizes state politics. Observers say that there really is no part of the state where one party has a lock on every office.

Although there clearly is some regional aspect to state politics—with the western part of the state leaning more Republican and the eastern part of the state leaning more to the Democrats—the importance of local issues tends to blunt the impact of party identification. The importance of local politics cannot be overstated in Iowa politics. The rural character of much of the state makes the role of the local politician much more important than it has become in more suburbanized states. Candidates win state and local races in Iowa by knowing their constituents personally. Voters expect personal campaign contacts, and if they recognize the candidate from the local Elks lodge, all the better. Personal trust is more important than party loyalty. The current state legislature reflects this dynamic.

Although Iowa's caucus system and prominent rural identity give it a unique flavor, the state certainly does not exist in a vacuum. Religiously and socially, it shares characteristics of its neighbors in the upper Midwest. Mainline churches predominate, with the United Methodists claiming the highest membership (Glenmary Research Center 2000). These mainline churches are more conservative theologically and socially, however, than those on either coast. These more conservative churches have higher percentages of "traditionalist" believers who are more orthodox in their beliefs and practices and are significantly more Republican. Catholics are a significant force, primarily in northeastern Iowa. Evangelicals are present, though in lower numbers than in many other Midwestern states.

On social issues Iowans tend to be fairly conservative, but they also are largely unwilling for government to impose standards of behavior on people. As in many states, economic issues recently have come to dominate Iowa politics. A regional economic downturn put further stress on a state that has been dealing with a farm income crisis since the mid-1980s. Population losses and reduced tax revenue have significantly affected the state government's ability to satisfy its fiscal responsibilities.

The 2004 elections in Iowa represent a continuation of political trends of preceding elections, particularly after the terrorist attacks of September 11, 2001. Winds of change are in the air, however, particularly for the Republicans, and we may look back at 2004 as the prelude to significant changes in 2006 and 2008. Iowa became a "red state" in 2004. President George W. Bush won the state with a 10,000-vote margin. Although this margin is larger than the 4,000-vote margin by which Al Gore won in 2000, the race for president was very close, and Iowa was the last state to certify its popular vote tally. Iowa remained a swing state throughout the election season, and the defeat of several prominent Republicans from the state legislature demonstrates the closely divided nature of partisanship in Iowa. The story of the 2004 election, however, for both the Christian Right and the Republican Party, really starts much earlier.

The Christian Right and Republicans in Iowa

Since at least the early 1980s, the Christian Right has sought influence and impact in Iowa's Republican Party. In the early years, the moderates who controlled the party fought hard to keep Christian Right supporters out of positions of power. Observers say that the moderates really believed that the movement was going to be a short-lived phenomenon that would eventually lose its momentum. Two decades later, Christian Right activists have unopposed control of the state party organization as well as many county and local organizations. Whereas once one saw articles in the *Des Moines Register* about the conflict caused in the Republican Party by the "outside forces" of the Christian Right, now the accepted wisdom is that the Christian Right *is* the Republican Party in Iowa. Observers of all stripes, however, are quick to note that these Christian Right activists are not the "nut-cases" of old. They are sophisticated political players who are well versed in strategy and compromise. Their policies and goals do not attract the attention or criticism that earlier Christian Right activists did—both because of their ubiquity in the current party and because of their moderation.

The important Christian Right organizations in the state remain the same as in 2000 (Racheter, Kellstedt, and Green 2003). The Iowa Christian Coalition, Iowa Right to Life, Iowans for Life, and the Iowa Family Policy Center are the most vital. Most observers regard the past four years as a time of continuity in the Christian Right movement in the state. The leadership in most of these organizations has remained the same, and their connections with each other remain strong. The Christian Coalition, in particular, has sought to increase its scope over the past four years. The organization was racked with scandal and dissention early in the 2000 election cycle, but new leadership has significantly improved the organization's fundraising capabilities and has used those resources in significant voter education campaigns and lobbying. Many observers regard Steve Scheffler, the leader of the Christian Coalition and a member of the Republican State Central Committee, as the linchpin of the movement; he has been involved in most of the important Christian Right issues and organizations since his mobilization into politics during the Robertson campaign in 1988.

As in many states, however, the Christian Right's primary strength is its friendship networks of supporters and activists. The activists know each other from a variety of political and social campaigns; they are invited to the same dinners and serve as members on the boards of the same organizations. These relationships form the bedrock on which their power in the Republican Party is based. Many of these people, including the current chair of the Republican Party, got their start in politics in the Robertson campaign and have moved from issue to issue over the past 20 years.

The 2000 election had been a defeat for conservatives in Iowa. Republicans believed that the close outcome of the final presidential tally showed that with a little more effort, they could have put Iowa in the win column for President Bush. This belief, combined with the reduced amount of evangelical Protestant turnout nationally, primed both the Republican party in Iowa and the national Republican party to make significant changes to the campaign in Iowa for 2004. Although the personnel largely were the same—with the same core people in charge of the state convention and the nominating committee for the national convention—a conscious decision was made to make significant tactical changes. Probably the most important change was the massive "get-out-the-vote" effort. Using the 2002 congressional elections as a "dry run," both the state Republican Party and the Republican National Committee (RNC) and Bush operatives in Iowa coordinated unprecedented efforts to get Republicans—primarily conservatives—to the polls. Some unique circumstances, however, made that appeal effective for conservatives in 2004 in ways that make generalization to other election cycles difficult.

One of the problems Christian Right activists usually face is a lack of strategic coherence; this challenge is never more obvious than during a presidential primary campaign. The fault lines in the Christian Right movement—primarily between ideological purists and political pragmatists—make themselves felt most in these contests. In a place such as Iowa, where candidates spend a significant amount of their early time and money, candidates who will not eventually make it to Super Tuesday still appear to have a shot. Hence, supporters of the Christian Right divide among potentially sympathetic candidates before the Iowa caucuses. This splintering has had an impact on the ability of the winning candidate to attract the losing candidate's supporters in the general election. In many cases, supporters of a losing candidate fail to support the nominee with the same enthusiasm or refuse to support him at all. This clearly was the case in 1988 and 2000, when more than one strong and visible member of Christian conservative organizations ran for president.

President George W. Bush's campaign for a second term solved these problems in several ways and kept both the Christian Right and conservative Republicans more generally from the infighting that has plagued them in the past. The Republicans were careful to make sure that the president had no primary challenger in the 2004 cycle. This strategy worked largely because Bush is a demonstrably evangelical Protestant Christian himself, so the conservative Christian part of the Republican coalition was happy and even eager to support him. This lack of a challenger allowed for an uneventful Republican caucus season in Iowa—a situation that had not occurred in 20 years. As a result, Republicans were able to guard their strength for the general election contest in the fall. A unified Christian Right constituency and a unified party allowed Republicans to play to their strength and focus on turning out conservative voters.

This development is interesting both in Iowa and nationally. A focus on motivating the base voters creates a very different campaign atmosphere than a focus on wooing moderate voters. Conservative Christians all over the country responded to this environment, feeling that the president not only sympathized with their issue positions but would make them a priority in his second term. For the first time in a decade, conservative Christians were convinced that their votes might actually make a difference. Although the Christian Right may not have made a definitive difference for President Bush in Iowa or other states, a unified movement clearly makes the goal of a unified Republican party more achievable and activist recruitment much easier.

Will This Campaign Never End?

The general election in Iowa was a long one, however—much longer than anyone expected. Usually the focus of presidential candidates strays elsewhere after the end of caucus season. With the country so equally divided, however, even Iowa's seven electoral votes became important late in the election. In addition, preelection polls in the state remained so close that the two major presidential candidates' numbers were indistinguishable until the end of the campaign. The result was one of the longest campaign seasons in the state's history; both major candidates and their representatives visited Iowa regularly throughout the fall. The long campaign kept the political focus of the state on the presidential race, so less attention was paid to state and local-level elections that would have taken center stage otherwise. The long campaign also kept grassroots activists in both parties mobilized, motivated, and working until the very end.

As in much of the country, the story of the 2004 presidential election in Iowa was as much about the Kerry campaign losing the race as it was about Bush winning. Democrats in general and the Kerry campaign in particular expended extraordinary amounts of effort and money in Iowa. They were going door to door as early as June identifying Democrat and Democrat-leaning voters and laying the groundwork to get those voters to vote absentee. There also was a strong push to make sure that every eligible person was registered to vote. The New Voters Project concentrated on getting younger voters registered, particularly on college campuses around the state. The project registered almost 37,000 new voters in the state (www.newvotersproject.org/iowa). Democrats' focus on registration paid off. By the registration deadline, the Iowa secretary of state announced that 95 percent of the eligible population was registered to vote in the state (www.sos.state.ia.us/press/04/2004_10_25.html).

Several Democratic strategies to increase voter turnout, however, caused controversies that may have helped Republicans on Election Day. There were several problems and significant controversy concerning absentee ballots and early voting in the state. Although fault and posturing occurred on both sides of the partisan divide, the result was that Democrats probably did not gain the advantage they were hoping for from these voting methods. There also were several campaign appearances by prominent music and film celebrities that may have backfired. Although entertainers such as Leonardo DiCaprio and Jon Bon Jovi drew large crowds, their endorsements may not have helped Democrat turnout. Conversely, that strong show of support for John Kerry from Hollywood seemed to cement many conservatives' fears that their values would not be represented by the Democratic ticket. Several observers noted that these visits were a rallying point for conservative mobilization because Iowans did not want people from California telling them what to do.

Overall, although the state had not voted for a Republican presidential candidate since Ronald Reagan, John Kerry faced an uphill battle with undecided voters in Iowa. A hotly contested caucus and primary season left many Democrats feeling that Kerry was not progressive enough, which likely reduced their enthusiasm in November. Kerry also suffered from the perception that he was cold, somewhat detached, and, at the least, very much a New Englander. None of these characteristics played well in Iowa's rural heartland.

The extent of Republican efforts in the presidential campaign was extraordinary. Although Republican activists and supporters of all stripes worked with and for the Bush campaign, mobilization and activity by the Christian Right movement clearly was a factor in the Bush campaign's success in Iowa. We believe that this movement involvement was so pronounced both because President Bust was such an attractive candidate and because the Bush campaign set about to both mobilize and organize conservative Christians in the service of the campaign. Although this situation certainly occurred at the national level, as demonstrated by the Bush campaign's early request for supporters to send in church directories, observers believe that the effort was monumentally successful in Iowa.

The role of the Republican "72-hour campaign" across the country cannot be overemphasized; observers regard it as the key to the Republican Party's success in 2004. Observers believe that the structure of the 72-hour effort in Iowa gave focus and direction to what typically has been a diffuse effort by Christian Right activists to make an impact at election time. This effort demonstrated the ability of Republicans in Iowa and the Bush campaign to turn out not only Christian Right activists but conservatives in general in a coordinated, concerted effort.

As in many election years, the presidential race sat at the pinnacle of each party's efforts, but the organizations made significant efforts on behalf of party candidates all over the state. Republicans in 2004 copied earlier Democrat efforts at producing more coherent and synchronized party lists. Party activists went door to door with personal digital assistants (PDAs) checking information and making get-out-the-vote contacts that were relayed back to a central database at the end of each day. The Republicans especially began to use the mobility of cellular phones for their phone banks, which allowed much greater flexibility and the ability to respond quickly to events with calls to voters in targeted areas. Although television advertising remained important—largely in the presidential race—observers believe that the 2004 campaign in both parties signified a return to the "ground war" philosophy of campaigning. This approach creates a much stronger focus on grassroots efforts—a strategy that works well in small, rural, and politically attentive Iowa.

Many Christian Right activists in Iowa worked through the Republican Party to find, register, and turn out their fellows to vote for President Bush and the rest of the Republican ticket in Iowa in 2004. There also were additional efforts made outside the party, however, by groups such as the Iowa Christian Coalition, that were targeted toward their membership and members' friends and coparishioners. Meetings were held at churches to register voters, explain the political process, and motivate people to participate in the caucuses and conventions and to vote. Evidence also suggests that some efforts by individual Christian Right organizations made an impact through their voter guides and voter contacts. The Christian Coalition produced more voter guides than ever before and was able to include several state legislative races and ballot issues on some of their guides. Iowa Right to Life published candidate questionnaires for all office levels on its website.

The 2004 presidential race clearly was a victory for Republicans and conservatives in Iowa. The organizational and strategic advances made by the party significantly increased turnout in areas that strongly supported the president. These strategies enabled all conservative activists, religious or not, to be extraordinarily effective. Conservative Christians unquestionably played a part in the victory through their mobilization and excitement about President Bush. Yet the perceived influence of the movement in the election and the Republican Party may have more to do with the individuals involved and their personal connections to each other than with any of the traditional Christian Right organizations.

Analysis of voting returns supports this assessment. Evangelical Protestants were the only religious grouping in Iowa to give President Bush a majority of their votes. Although evangelicals in Iowa voted for the president by a lower margin than their compatriots in other states, more than 68 percent of them found him to be more consistent with their views than John Kerry (see table 6.1). Evangelicals make up almost 30 percent of the total population in the state, and their high turnout may have provided the margin of victory for the Bush campaign—regardless of whether those voters were mobilized by Christian Right efforts or the more general focus on conservative Republican turnout.

The Christian Right in State-Level Races

The success of the Republican Party and the Bush campaign in turning Iowa into a "red state" in 2004 was not entirely mirrored in races down the ballot. All five of Iowa's members of Congress were reelected with little difficulty. Most important to the Christian Right was Steve King, a Republican from the conservative district that spans the western part of the state from top to bottom. King is widely regarded as one of the most conservative members of the House, and he serves as a rallying point for much of the conservative activity, Christian or otherwise, in the state. He faced no primary challenger and retained his seat with a 26 percent margin

Table 6.1   2004 Iowa Vote by Religious Tradition

Religious Tradition	State Population	Bush Vote	Kerry Vote
		%	
Evangelical Protestant	29.5	68.1	31.9
Mainline Protestant	29.5	46.0	54.0
Catholic	23.6	46.7	53.3
Other Christians	5.3	48.4	51.6
Other faiths	3.8	25.8	74.2
Unaffiliated	8.2	26.0	74.0
TOTAL	100.0		

Source: National Election Pool.

of victory. Republicans believe that their challenge to the single Democrat member, Leonard Boswell, failed because the Republican candidate ran too far to the middle. Republican success in the presidential race and failure in this congressional race added credence to the strategy of focusing on the party's core constituencies. This move can only increase the power and visibility of the Christian Right in the state.

The Iowa general assembly went into the 2004 election with a small Republican majority; it came out evenly divided. In the Senate, Republicans lost four seats to drop into a 25–25 tie with Democrats. Several of the most conservative members were defeated—including Ken Veenstra, the leading conservative Christian, who was defeated in his primary race. In the House, Republicans lost three seats but retained a majority, 51–49. Thus, with a Democrat governor but a congressional delegation that is almost entirely Republican, the state's elective offices are closely divided. Many observers believe that this state of affairs more accurately reflects the citizens of Iowa than the recent Republican majorities. It does indicate, however, an anomaly in the largely successful Republican turnout strategy.

How, then, did President Bush win and Republicans down the ballot have difficulty? Part of the answer lies in the unusually strong focus on the presidential campaign, at the expense of the state races. Perhaps most important, however, President Bush won with high turnout in western Iowa, where Republicans held on to all of their state legislative seats. High margins in these districts, while increasing the state's overall total for President Bush, did not translate into Republican wins in more Democratic-leaning districts in eastern Iowa. More generally, most observers agree that the Democrats simply did a better job of candidate recruitment than the Republicans. They were able to convince several people to run who were well-known and well-regarded in their hometowns; many were firefighters and police officers, according to one observer. Based on Iowans' preference for representatives they personally know and trust, this strategy paid off in several districts. Furthermore, for the first time in history the Democrats raised more money than the Republicans. This money, channeled primarily through Governor Vilsack's political action committee, made the difference in a few key races that brought the Democrats back into contention in the state legislature.

Looking at these results—particularly the Christian Right identity of several of the prominent Republican losers—one might assume that it signals a backlash against the Christian Right in Iowa. Most observers, however, do not believe that to be the case, for several reasons. First, and probably most important, these losses are widely attributed to personality and campaign issues, not to ideology. The Democrats targeted particular legislators because they were vulnerable, not because they were conservative Christians. The Democrats' success in recruiting strong challengers clearly helped them as well. Primary losses for Christian Right supporters seemed to exhibit the same characteristics. Furthermore, Republican moderates have no real political identity in Iowa today. There is no evidence of a challenge being mounted against the near-total control that conservatives have had in the state's Republican party for the past several years. Moreover, the most prominent of the Christian Right losers was replaced in the primary election by a person who was arguably even more conservative. Thus, the conservative hegemony, bolstered by Christian Right leaders, seems to be solid, at least at the grassroots level and in the state Republican party. The Republican leadership in the state legislature, however, seems to be another matter.

Iowa's evenly divided state legislature has some significant implications for the role of the Christian Right in state politics. Most important is the apparent rift between the Republican leadership in the state legislature and the grassroots activists who are in charge of the Republican party organization. Whereas the legislative leadership believes that their moderateness correctly reflects Republican voters in Iowa, many party and grassroots activists believe that the leaders' long tenure in the legislature has made them too attentive to the needs of the government and less attuned to the conservatism of most Republicans in Iowa. This divide is likely to become greater as power-sharing in the Senate will moderate Republicans' voting records even more. This growing rift is at least partly responsible for the lack of success that conservative Republicans and the Christian Right have had in enacting their policy positions into state law.

Issues and Policy in the 2004 Elections

Like voters in many states, Iowans identified "moral values" as the primary motivation for their votes for President Bush (NEP 2004). The war in Iraq, terrorism, and the economy also were deemed important. Again, however, there seemed to be a difference between the presidential campaign and the campaign for state and local offices. Economic issues appear to have dominated the races for the state legislature; the promised economic recovery has come slowly to Iowa. A controversial state fund to increase new business growth in Iowa became the focus of debate as candidates sought to demonstrate to voters their commitment to economic growth in the state. Observers further suggest that voters were looking for a legislature that would get things done, beyond any other partisan considerations. Proposed tax increases by Governor Vilsack and proposed tax cuts, regulatory relief, and tort reform by the Republicans affected many voters' decisions. These issues, however, operated more often as reinforcement for supporting one's existing party than for switching to the opposition.

Iowa did not have a definition of marriage referendum on the ballot in the fall, as did eleven other states. This issue, however, already had been a controversy in the state in the early spring of 2004, when a state judge "reached out" to grant a divorce to a gay couple rather than denying the request. The judge was up for retention election under Iowa's merit system of judicial selection, and an unusual campaign was mounted to get conservative Christians to vote against him solely for this decision. He was reelected, but by a lower margin than is typical in Iowa judicial elections.

Seeking to extend a marriage definition law already in place in the state, the Iowa legislature considered an amendment to the state's constitution defining marriage as a union between one man and one woman. This proposed amendment was defeated, in what was perceived at the time to be a significant setback for conservative Republicans. Further reflection, however, showed that the issue was another case in which the legislative leadership and Republican activists had differing agendas. Senate Republicans merely wanted to get a vote on the amendment on record to use it against Democratic incumbents in the fall. They apparently put no real political capital into getting it passed, and it was defeated by one vote; four Republicans voted against it. Although several of these legislators were consistently prochoice, the others probably could have been convinced to approve the amendment if the leadership had put its full power behind it. Because state polling suggests that nearly 65 percent of the population supports the traditional definition of marriage (www.picosearch.com/cgi-bin/ts.pl), Christian Right activists point to this situation as evidence that the Republican legislative leadership is out of step with grassroots Republicans in the state. This perception certainly spurred efforts by Christian Right activists to be involved in the issue, but the impact of this activity in the fall legislative election is unclear. Certainly this defeat added to the sense of threat that the Christian Right feels and thus, if nothing else, bolstered President Bush's election margin.

To the extent that issues made a difference in the 2004 elections in Iowa at all levels, they were not necessarily unique to the conservative Christian perspective. Iraq and the war on terror were important to many voters, conservative and otherwise, and the uneven economy has affected people of every partisan stripe. The importance of "moral values" issues is somewhat unclear. Although much was made of this factor in the days following the election, the voters who identified "moral values" as an important issue may have attached different meanings to the question in the exit polling. In Iowa, 22 percent of voters thought moral issues were most important, but 20 percent though Iraq and the economy were most important, and 18 percent listed terrorism as most important. Clearly many issues were on the minds of voters when they went to the polls on Election Day. Conservatives have distinct views on these issues, but Christian Right views may not have had an impact beyond the general conservatism expressed by most Republicans and Bush voters in the state.

The Impact of the Christian Right on Iowa Politics

Clearly the primary impact of the Christian Right in Iowa is through Republican party politics. The movement's influence is felt, but is not necessarily decisive, in other realms of politics in the state. Based on the skills and experience of Christian Right leadership in the state, the Republican party has served as an important avenue of coordination and political integration for activists. The party organization at all levels is filled with Christian Right activists who got their start in movement issues such as abortion or in the presidential campaigns of figures such as Pat Robertson. Observers believe that these activists have mellowed their strategies over time, if not their policy positions.

The Republican state central committee is an interesting case in point. By most observers' count, about two-thirds of the committee's seventeen members are identifiable as Christian Right supporters, whether by policy position or group affiliation. Although this percentage represents a significant level of influence exerted by the movement— perhaps greater than in most states—it actually reflects a reduction in influence from five years previously. Why has the movement's influence decreased? Most observers agree that the Christian Right movement feels very comfortable with its position in the Republican party in Iowa. Although elections may still represent challenges in mobilizing conservative Christian voters, the party itself is solidly controlled by Christian Right activists. This level of control has allowed the movement to be less concerned with people who are perceived to be Republican moderates gaining seats on the state central committee. Members of the movement are confident that their policy positions will win the day. The weakness of moderates in the Republican party in general adds to this perception of control.

One of the most interesting developments has been the growth of the perception of "conservatives" rather than "the Christian Right" in the party. Our sense is that conservative Christians in many ways are trying to move away from older perceptions of the movement as militant, uncompromising, and embarrassingly vocal. This trend has caused many of them to desire to be known simply as conservatives, without the baggage of the Christian Right label. This trend also is evident in the focus of many conservative Christians on economic issues. These issues are not the moral imperatives of the social realm—though some activists may want to portray them that way. Economic issues push activists to use the language of the market and finance, not the Bible and moral requirements. This shift has functionally and literally moderated many Christian Right activists. Most telling is a growing perception that there are a large number of people involved in Republican politics who are conservatives and happen to be Christians and who are motivated by conservative but not necessarily religious policy positions.

Although these distinctions make a difference in the Republican party and in the movement itself, they do not seem to register with many observers of state politics. The 2000 survey of movement influence on Republican politics (Conger and Green 2002) puts Iowa near the top of all states in terms of Christian Right influence. The survey is based on the observations of people from across the political spectrum, so clearly the party is perceived to be controlled by the movement. The ease of access to Iowa's political system through the caucuses and the close division of partisanship in the state make the state a place where political activism is attractive to the Christian Right. Members of the movement feel the threat of their policy positions losing in close races, but they also have the hope of winning those races through well-organized political activity. These factors contribute to the sustained level of impact that the Christian Right continues to have in Iowa politics at all levels.

Conservative Christians' impact on politics in Iowa can be felt in less tangible ways as well. The advent of Christian Right strength in Iowa arguably has increased, in significant ways, the role and impact of conservatives in general. Moreover, Christian Right activity has spurred the advent of groups that oppose the movement's policies and strategies. Most important is the Iowa Interfaith Alliance, a chapter of the national organization of the same name. This group seeks to put a more progressive face on religious involvement in the state. Yet opposition groups largely support Democratic efforts to keep politics from being too conservative in the state; they usually do not have significant impact on their own.

One development has been the advent of a group called Democrats for Life. In late October 2004, just before the election, an Iowa chapter of the national group was formed by Bill Gluba, a Democratic candidate for Congress in northeastern Iowa. Although this group's impact on the abortion stance of the Democrat party in Iowa remains to be seen, the growing call for Democrats to make room for prolifers in their ranks may have great consequence for Republicans and Christian Right activists both in Iowa and around the country. For twenty years, prolife voters really have had only one choice; in many ways the abortion issue has driven the Christian Right movement and the polarization of the two main parties on social issues. A Democratic party with a softer stance on the issue might pull some newly minted Republicans back to a party that may fit their economic interests more closely.

Conclusion

The Christian Right movement is an entrenched part of the political story in Iowa. Christian Right activists have taken advantage of the political opportunity structure in the state and wield almost unchallenged control of the Republican party. Although their direct impact on policy may be hard to trace, the movement clearly has had a significant effect on the way the Republican party sees itself and how it operates in the state. Most observers acknowledge the motivation of having President Bush on the ballot in 2004, and forward-looking conservative Christian activists are aware that the next presidential candidate may not support the movement's goals to the same degree. Some see the governor's race in 2006 as having the potential to foster ideological conflict in the party. We wonder, however, if the lack of real disagreement suggests that this conflict may be more about strategy and degree than about real differences in opinion. Over time, demographic and economic changes may be a more significant threat to the movement's hold on the party. Republicans have to fight for every victory in a state that tends to be closely divided in partisanship. Increases in urbanization and lack of job growth in the state may challenge Republicans' ability to win statewide races, regardless of the version of conservatism to which they declare allegiance. Strong rural conservatism in the western part of the state, however, seems to suggest that win or lose, Republicans will keep their conservative Christian character for the foreseeable future.

Although Iowa became a presidential "red state" in 2004, whether it will remain so in the long term is unclear. The Christian Right certainly will be part of that effort, but political reality in the state may make it difficult for Republicans to hold on to the victory they have fought so hard to achieve.

References

Conger, Kimberly H., and John C. Green. 2002. "Spreading Out and Digging In: Christian Conservatives and State Republican Parties." *Campaigns and Elections* 23, no. 1 (February): 58–65.

Glenmary Research Center. 2000. "Religious Congregations and Membership in the United States." Iowa American Religious Data Archive. Available at www.thearda.com (accessed March 15, 2005).

National Election Pool (NEP). 2004. *National Election Pool General Election Exit Polls 2004* [computer file]. ICPSR version. Somerville, N.J., and Ann Arbor, Mich.: Edison Media Research NY and Mitofsky International.

Racheter, Donald P., Lyman Kellstedt, and John C. Green. 2003. "Iowa: Crucible of the Christian Right." In *The Christian Right in American Politics: Marching to the Millenium*, ed. John C. Green, Mark Rozell, and Clyde Wilcox. Washington, D.C.: Georgetown University Press, 121–44.

Rosin, Hannah. 2005. "Beyond Belief." *The Atlantic Monthly* 295, no. 1 (January/February): 117–20.

CHAPTER SEVEN

Minnesota

Battleground Politics in a New Setting

CHRISTOPHER P. GILBERT

IN 2004 MINNESOTA JOINED THE SET OF CONTEMPORARY PRESI-
dential election battleground states, playing host to a lengthy, intense,
and often bitter campaign. The eventual narrow victory of Senator John
Kerry over President George W. Bush—keeping Minnesota in the Democratic column for the eighth consecutive presidential race—should not
obscure the implications of Minnesota's shift to partisan parity in the past
decade. The Christian Right has played a major role in driving this shift,
and its influence in state politics virtually guarantees that Minnesota will
remain a polarized battleground in future election cycles for local, state,
and national offices.

This chapter traces the recent history of the Christian Right in Minnesota and the parallel rise of the state Republican party to parity status
with the Democratic-Farmer-Labor Party (DFL),[1] focusing especially on the
2004 campaign as an indicator of the strengths and limitations that Christian
Right political groups and activists have within Minnesota politics.

High Hopes

Republicans approached the 2004 presidential contest in Minnesota with
high expectations, fueled by recent results. In the 2000 presidential election, Democratic nominee Al Gore defeated George W. Bush by just 2.5
percentage points (58,607 votes)—the closest Minnesota presidential
election result since 1984 (Gilbert and Peterson 2003, 181). Moreover,
in November 2002 Republicans reclaimed the governorship behind state

Table 7.1   Minnesota State Legislature Party Representation and Presidential Voting, 1986–2002

Year	State House Dem. Seats	Repub. Seats	Margin	State Senate Dem. Seats	Repub. Seats	Margin	Presidential Election Dem. %	Repub. %	Margin
1986	83	51	D +32	47	20	D +27			
1988	81	53	D +28				52.9	45.9	D +7
1990	80	54	D +26	46	21	D +25			
1992	87	47	D +40				43.5	31.9	D +12
1994	71	63	D +8	43	24	D +19			
1996	70	64	D +6				51.1	35.0	D +16
1998	63	71	R +8	42	24	D +18			
2000	65	69	R +4				47.9	45.5	D +2
2002	53	81	R +28	35	31	D +4			

Notes: State House has 134 seats; State Senate has 67 seats. Third-party seats and votes are excluded; thus, seat totals may not add to full size of either body, and presidential vote percentages do not add to 100.
Source: Compiled by 2004 Elections Project, Center for the Study of Politics, Humphrey Institute of Public Affairs, University of Minnesota.

House Majority Leader Tim Pawlenty, in the process extending their state House majority from four seats to twenty-eight seats (see table 7.1). Together with a narrow victory by former St. Paul mayor Norm Coleman in his U.S. Senate race against Walter Mondale,[2] Minnesota Republicans saw 2002 as a sign of more success to come. They believed that 2004 offered a tremendous opportunity to extend their electoral winning streak to the presidential level.

The optimism of Minnesota Republicans was well founded because all electoral trends in Minnesota since the late 1980s have clearly favored Republicans. As table 7.1 indicates, the DFL grip on the state House declined dramatically in the mid-1990s, leading to a shift in partisan control in 1998. Although the DFL remains in the majority in the state Senate, its advantage has shrunk to just four seats after the 2002 elections. Table 7.1 also suggests that in 2000 Minnesota's presidential electorate essentially caught up to the partisan shifts already under way in state legislative elections. Even in an era of candidate-centered elections and split partisanship, that any state's voters would continue to favor one party so heavily at the presidential level while electing large numbers of the other party to the state legislature seems unlikely. The strong Republican showing in 2002 clearly built on the momentum generated from the 2000 election cycle.

The Christian Right in Recent Minnesota Politics

The Christian Right has been a critical factor underlying the increasing success of Republicans in Minnesota. Spearheaded by groups opposed to legal abortion, Christian Right influence in Minnesota emerged in the early 1980s and gained effective control over the state Republican party leadership by 1994. Although opinions differ about whether the Christian Right is an overall benefit or hindrance to the image of the Republican party in Minnesota, there is no question that Christian Right groups and voters are a critical component of the state Republican electoral coalition.

The 1994 election remains both a high point and a cautionary tale in considering the Christian Right's importance in Minnesota politics (for a longer discussion see Gilbert and Peterson 1995). During the tumultuous 1994 primary campaign, Republicans endorsed a former state legislator who was closely associated with prolife causes over the sitting Republican governor. Although the incumbent eventually won both the primary and the general election with ease, the endorsement process demonstrated just how eager Christian Right activists were to move the state GOP toward their own priorities. Moreover, the Republicans also gained sixteen seats in the 1994 state House, winning a majority of total votes cast for the state House in the process and setting the stage for gaining majority status in 1998 (Gilbert and Peterson 2000, 217). Nevertheless, the defeat of the Christian Right's chosen standard-bearer by a two-to-one margin in the September 1994 primary was a sobering reality check; candidates closely associated by voters with the Christian Right would continue to have difficulties winning statewide elections through the 1990s and into the early twenty-first century (Gilbert and Peterson 2003, 182–83).

The locus of Christian Right influence in Minnesota politics, especially within the state Republican party, comprises two groups: Minnesota Citizens Concerned for Life (MCCL) and the Minnesota Family Council (MFC). MCCL was founded in 1968 to counter efforts to liberalize Minnesota abortion laws. After the 1973 *Roe v. Wade* decision permitting legal abortion in the United States, MCCL became the state affiliate of the National Right to Life Committee. It has since developed into a grassroots organization with 225 local chapters and a claimed membership of 67,000 (www.mccl.org). MCCL spearheads all efforts to narrow access to abortion, moving some issue to the legislative agenda nearly every year since the Roe decision (Elazar, Gray, and Spano 1999, 143). The group also has expanded its agenda to cover euthanasia and same-sex marriage, although abortion remains its core interest and mobilizing issue.

Closely allied with MCCL, the MFC describes itself as "the largest nonprofit, nonpartisan, pro-family organization in the state" (www.mfc.org).

Like its national parent group, the Family Research Council, the MFC works principally in five areas: combating the secular and liberal media; presenting profamily news and information; lobbying the legislature on public policy issues; building grassroots support for profamily legislation; and supporting lawsuits on profamily causes through the Northstar Legal Center. Led by director Tom Prichard, a frequent commentator in the Twin Cities media, the MFC has come to focus in particular on passing a state constitutional amendment banning same-sex marriage. To the extent possible, it supports Republican candidates and officeholders and lobbies at the state capitol through grassroots and grasstops efforts.

The dominance of MCCL and the MFC in Minnesota has impeded the growth of other Christian Right organizations, such as the Christian Coalition (Gilbert and Peterson 2003, 173). One other significant barrier to Christian Right groups in general, in terms of framing issues and winning legislative and electoral contests, is the presence of an active, public alternative to conservative evangelical Christian descriptions of salient political issues. That is, Minnesota also has a Christian Center and Christian Left, so casting political issues in religious terms is not left solely to evangelical and Republican voices.

Stemming from Minnesota's moralist political subculture, with "a commitment to using community power to intervene in private activities for the good or well-being of the polity" (Elazar, Gray, and Spano 1999, 206), moral and prophetic voices in Minnesota politics stem from several social justice organizations. The most prominent is the Joint Religious Legislative Coalition (JRLC). Founded in 1971 as the first interfaith public interest lobby group in the United States (including Protestant, Catholic, Jewish, Muslim, and Orthodox members), the JRLC sponsors a lobbying day early in each state legislative session; informs a network of 7,000 members to contact legislators and local officials about issues of interest; and publishes studies on a wide range of social justice issues (www.jrlc.org). Large individual denominations such as the Evangelical Lutheran Church in America also have ready access to state lawmakers because of their size and distribution throughout the state. Thus, in contrast to other states, where evangelical Protestant denominations have gained numerical superiority over fading mainline churches, the traditional Protestant mainline is alive and well in Minnesota, and its religiously based social activism creates a sharp contrast with evangelical-inspired political messages.

The 2004 Presidential Campaign in Minnesota

From the outset of the 2004 presidential campaign, both major parties obviously considered Minnesota to be in play. Although Minnesota essentially sits out the nomination contest—party caucuses in early March take a straw poll, but no delegates are officially selected until state party conventions in June, well after presidential nominations generally are determined—the state's ten electoral votes and its proximity to Iowa meant that leading contenders visited the state early and often. By Election Day, the presidential and vice presidential candidates had made eighteen visits to the state (Pomper 2005, 55); the candidates' spouses and family members accounted for several more visits.

Given Minnesota's recent electoral history and its three decades of Democratic victories in presidential races, John Kerry was perceived as the frontrunner, and poll data supported the view that President Bush would have to close a gap to claim the state in November. A March 2004 poll by the state's largest newspaper, the Minneapolis *Star-Tribune*, gave presumptive nominee Kerry a 50 percent to 38 percent lead over Bush and further indicated the continuing concerns Minnesotans expressed about the war in Iraq and the president's domestic policies (Von Sternberg 2004a).

Concerns over presidential job performance were not the only hurdle the Bush–Cheney campaign faced. The March *Star-Tribune* poll found that born-again Minnesotans favored Bush over Kerry by just 48 percent to 39 percent; many evangelicals wondered if the president's agenda included their concerns about poverty and social justice (Allen 2004). The unease of more moderate evangelicals was matched by the fact that core Christian Right activists within the state GOP had not been on the Bush bandwagon from the beginning; during the early stages of the 2000 Republican presidential race, Minnesota's Republican party had favored Alan Keyes, not then-Governor Bush, as its preferred nominee (Gilbert and Peterson 2003, 181). The president's multiple visits to Minnesota during the 2002 U.S. Senate race helped to shore up his support, yet work remained to be done to mobilize Republican voters fully for the Bush reelection effort.

As in many other states, congregations became a focal point for recruitment and mobilization efforts for the Bush–Cheney ticket in Minnesota. Protestant and Catholic churches were targeted with both national and state party resources. One visible aspect of this effort was the Catholic Outreach Tour, sponsored by the Republican National Committee, which visited Minnesota in early July. This tour emphasized Catholic social teachings on abortion and traditional marriage, urging Minnesota Catholics to vote Republican on the basis of these two issues. As U.S. Representative Mark Kennedy told one gathering, "Republicans support [Catholic teachings on abortion and marriage,] and the Democrats oppose them" (Diaz and McKinney 2004). Although the Archdiocese of St. Paul and Minneapolis distanced itself from the tour directly, follow-up efforts in many parishes through the summer and fall reinforced the primacy of abortion and same-sex marriage as key issues bringing Catholics and Republicans together.

A continuing problem for Republican organizers was the presence of multiple religious voices on the issues Republicans most wished to use in mobilizing Minnesota Christians to their side. For example, when a state constitutional amendment to ban same-sex marriage was discussed at a Minnesota House committee public hearing in March 2004, clergy spoke both for and against the amendment (which the full legislature ultimately failed to approve) (Brunswick 2004a). Rallies in favor of the amendment were matched, in size and media coverage, by rallies opposed to it, and religious activists were present and public in their faith-politics links for both events (Brunswick 2004b).

Similarly, one of the largest preelection rallies in Minnesota occurred in early October, when a national movement to highlight poverty as a moral issue came to St. Paul (Hopfensperger 2004). Led by evangelical social activists Jim Wallis and Tony Campolo, the rally and its explicitly religious message served again to frame moral issues in a context that suggested that Republicans were not the only people who spoke and thought about political issues from a faith-based perspective.

The candidates themselves worked to put religious language and concepts into their numerous campaign visits. Again, the Republican desire to express the only religiously oriented message was blunted not only by Democratic counters but by media coverage that presented both sides as making such appeals. For example, Vice President Dick Cheney told a Minneapolis rally in mid-July, "I just want to see Christian men back in the White House for four more years" (Lopez and Walsh 2004). When asked one month later by a Minnesota voter if he was a Christian, John Kerry replied, "Yes, I am a Christian, but that should not be what decides whether somebody votes for me. . . . Some people try to use values to drive a great big wedge between Americans. But most of those values they are talking about are narrow values, calculated to divide" (Schmickle and Von Sternberg 2004).

Republican efforts to rally religious Minnesotans also were stifled by actions that hurt more than helped the cause. One well-publicized incident from a central Minnesota county involved an organizer who sought to build a chapter of Teen Age Republicans with the following message: "This group will be a grassroots movement to learn about how America got started, the difference between Republicans and Democrats, why the nation is split, why God is detested by our opponents and will be a force for the Republican Party in Renville County, not to be ignored" (Grow 2004). Republican and DFL party officials decried the statement, and a local newspaper publisher summed up the prevailing view: "Out here, we park our politics at the [church] door" (Grow 2004).

Despite these potential setbacks, the Republican campaign effort for Bush–Cheney did build positive momentum heading into the campaign's final two months. Polling results from late August through mid-October ranged from a two-point Bush lead to a ten-point Kerry advantage, with the majority of polls showing Kerry with a five- to seven-point lead—right at the edge of most polls' error margins (Von Sternberg 2004a, 2004b). A *Star-Tribune* poll conducted October 9–11 found Kerry with a 48 percent to 43 percent edge (with 2 percent for Ralph Nader and 7 percent undecided); more significantly for the Bush campaign, this same poll found that more than 50 percent of respondents believed the United States was on the wrong track, and fewer than 50 percent expressed approval of the president's job performance (Von Sternberg 2004b). This basic level of pessimism appeared in nearly every poll during the final weeks of the campaign—an obstacle that ultimately the Bush campaign could not overcome.

The October 9–11 *Star-Tribune* poll also revealed interesting trends across religious categories. Among Catholics, Kerry led by only 47 percent to 42 percent—well within the margin of error and probably reflecting the heavy Republican emphasis on reaching out to Catholic voters (Von Sternberg 2004b); Minnesota was one of several states in which full-page advertisements targeted at Catholic voters ran in the *Star-Tribune* shortly before Election Day. Among voters with no religious preference, Kerry led by 75 percent to 14 percent—an advantage that widened slightly by Election Day. Although poll data for evangelicals are difficult to evaluate (the *Star-Tribune* poll defines evangelicals differently than exit polls), Bush clearly held a substantial lead in this category, as expected.

Final efforts to mobilize supporters reflected the importance of Minnesota to the overall Electoral College picture, as well as the closeness of the race. Without a same-sex marriage ban on the ballot, Christian Right groups did not have the same mobilizing tools as their counterparts in Ohio and other states (Haga 2004a); nonetheless, all observers agree that their support of Bush–Cheney was considerable. The state Republican party put 55,000 volunteers into get-out-the-vote efforts, with teams in every precinct and more than 1 million contacts made in the final four days; the DFL countered with 20,000 volunteers, 750,000 phone calls, and nearly 100,000 e-mails per day in the final week (Schmickle and Gordon 2004).

The Republican campaign specifically included churches as targets of mobilization in the final days. The MFC sent voter guides to 3,300 churches across the state; the guides did not specifically endorse any candidate, but their emphasis on the familiar array of moral issues made clear which side was preferred (Schmickle and Gordon 2004). Many churches also encouraged voting without expressing any clear preference. One megachurch in the Twin Cities suburbs scheduled several prayer times on the Sunday before Election Day, urging members to consider voting as "a method of Christian stewardship" (Schmickle and Gordon 2004).

2004 Presidential Election Results and Analysis

Ultimately, despite the considerable efforts of Republican activists to support the Bush campaign, John Kerry and John Edwards benefited from strong DFL support and their own hard work to win the state's ten electoral votes. The Kerry–Edwards ticket received 1.45 million votes (51.1 percent) for a 98,000-vote margin over Bush–Cheney (47.6 percent). The final margin was greater than in 2000, suggesting again that a presidential Democratic majority continues to exist in Minnesota.

Exit poll data reveal several key factors contributing to Kerry's victory, as well as leading indicators of President Bush's electoral support. Table 7.2 presents a selected sample of exit poll results, echoing the preceding analysis. The sharp split between the Bush and Kerry camps is evident in the vote choices of Iraq war supporters (87 percent to 13 percent for Bush) and opponents (86 percent to 12 percent for Kerry). Similarly large differences emerge over candidate characteristics (strong leadership as the key quality produces a 66-point Bush edge) and issue salience (economy-first voters gave Kerry a 69-point advantage). Most demographic factors cluster toward the middle of table 7.2, although advanced education and youth favor Kerry more strongly. The exit poll data show an almost even partisan split among 2004 voters—38 percent Democrat, 35 percent Republican; hence, Kerry's advantage among moderate Minnesotans (45 percent of the sample, 57 percent to 42 percent for Kerry) helps to explain his victory margin.

Table 7.2 also reveals the salience of religious factors in the campaign. Echoing the 2000 results nationally and in Minnesota, church attendance continued to distinguish Bush/Republican voters (regular church attenders) from Kerry/Democratic voters (non–church attenders); the gap is especially pronounced among this latter category, which voted overwhelmingly (79 percent to 19 percent) for Kerry. The Catholic vote—which, as we have seen, was pulled in different directions by religious interests during the campaign—turned out to be split evenly between the candidates. The white conservative Protestant vote, not surprisingly, was overwhelmingly Republican.

Finally, the much-discussed issue phrase "moral values" also distinguishes Bush and Kerry voters. Almost one-quarter of Minnesota voters cited moral values as their most important issue, and such voters broke 77 percent to 21 percent for Bush. The moral values segment of the electorate was larger in Minnesota than nationwide, although its support for the president was marginally lower than it was nationwide. Although speculating with precision about what voters who chose moral values as the most important issue were thinking about is difficult, two arguments appear plausible. First, none of the other possible choices in the exit poll's most important

Table 7.2 Selected Indicators of Minnesota Presidential Preference, 2004

Category/characteristic	Exit Poll Results			
	% of Exit Sample	Bush	Kerry	Margin
	%			
Disapproved of Iraq war decision	51	12	86	Kerry +74
Economy/jobs most important issue	18	15	84	Kerry +69
Non–church attender	14	19	79	Kerry +60
Postgraduate education	17	35	64	Kerry +29
Age 18–29	20	41	57	Kerry +16
Political moderate	45	42	57	Kerry +15
Female	52	46	52	Kerry +6
Catholic	28	49	50	Kerry +1
Income over $100,000	21	53	46	Bush +7
Suburban	41	54	45	Bush +9
Weekly church attender	38	62	37	Bush +25
U.S. safer from terrorism now	52	77	22	Bush +55
Moral values most important issue	24	77	21	Bush +56
Strong leader most imp. quality	19	83	17	Bush +66
Approved of Iraq war decision	46	87	13	Bush +74
White conservative Protestant	19	91	9	Bush +82

Notes: Ralph Nader and other third-party candidates excluded; thus, totals do not round to 100.
Source: 2004 National Election Pool exit poll for Minnesota.

issue question (taxes, education, Iraq, terrorism, economy/jobs, health care) focused on the personal qualities of the candidates); hence, the less specific term "moral values" stands out as the one response that captures the deep affinity many citizens hold toward President Bush as a leader, especially since the September 11 attacks. Second, as discussed above, in Minnesota articulation of key national issues as "moral" or values-based is not confined solely to the Republican and/or Christian Right base; there can be no doubt that for many Minnesota voters, opposition to the Iraq war and to President Bush's broader agenda also was best captured by "moral values," as opposed to the more specific alternative issue choices presented.

Moving beyond the broad picture suggested by exit poll results, a regression analysis of individual-level vote choice reveals the most salient factors explaining presidential voting. Table 7.3 presents a full regression model of presidential vote choice in Minnesota, including supporters of Ralph Nader and other minor-party candidates as an intermediate choice between Kerry and Bush. In this model, positive coefficients

152   GILBERT

Table 7.3   Regression Analysis of 2004 Minnesota Presidential Vote
(OLS estimates)

Independent variable	Coefficient	Std. error
Catholic	0.025	(0.025)
Church attendance	−0.018	(0.012)
Secular	0.007	(0.038)
Moral values most important issue	0.319	(0.033)[a]
Party identification	0.259	(0.020)[a]
Political ideology	0.011	(0.021)
Bush job approval	0.473	(0.015)[a]
Terrorism most important issue	0.307	(0.036)[a]
Iraq most important issue	0.028	(0.031)
Female	−0.022	(0.023)
First-time voter	0.048	(0.044)
Education	−0.022	(0.012)[b]
Union household	0.037	(0.024)[c]
Married	−0.044	(0.027)[c]
Nonwhite	−0.074	(0.043)[c]
Age	0.002	(0.009)
Income	0.004	(0.008)
Suburban resident	0.067	(0.063)
Constant	1.812	(0.136)[a]

[a]Significant at .01 level.
[b]Significant at .05 level.
[c]Significant at .10 level.
Source: 2004 National Election Pool exit poll for Minnesota.

indicate greater support for the Republican candidate, and all variables have been recoded to run from low to high (for example, church attendance is coded from "never" through "more than weekly") or Democratic/liberal through Republican/conservative (Bush's job approval, for example, is recoded so that disapproval is on the bottom of the scale and approval is on top). Variables also are grouped into three categories for easier comprehension: religious factors, political measures, and demographic characteristics. The model predicts a healthy 80 percent of the variance in presidential vote choice.

One striking result in the table 7.3 model is how little salience attaches to demographic factors. Well-educated voters, voters living in union households, and nonwhite voters (who represent only 7 percent of the Minnesota electorate) were predictably more inclined to vote for Kerry. Married voters also were more likely to support Kerry, after the regression model parses out factors correlated with marriage; the exit poll showed married voters supporting Bush by 52 percent to 47 percent, but church attendance and support for moral values capture this effect more strongly in the model than the "married" variable. Other possible demographic predictors—such as gender, age, suburban residence, and income—are not significant in the full model.

Table 7.3 also reminds observers of U.S. politics that religious influences on voter choices do not always emerge from summary and proxy measures such as church attendance. By itself, church attendance does not predict presidential voting in the table 7.3 model; in fact, more frequent church attendance leads to greater Democratic voting after other factors are incorporated—the opposite of what straightforward exit poll results show. Of course, the reason for this result is that going to church represents the beginning of an ongoing, complex process of influence, rather than determining a specific political outcome in and of itself. Moreover, the results are not affected by what kind of church one attends regularly. In Minnesota, Lutherans (most of whom are not conservative, politically or theologically) and Catholics exist in roughly equal numbers, and many Minnesota churchgoers therefore are likely to attend congregations that are engaged in social justice movements and preach a very different theological perspective on local, state, and national issues from what would be heard in an evangelical setting (Gilbert and Peterson 2003, 170).

The political gap resulting from church attendance also is reflected in the insignificance of the "Catholic" variable in the table 7.3 regression model. Catholics did split 50 percent to 49 percent for Kerry, with regular Mass-attending Catholics supporting Bush by 54 percent to 44 percent and less frequent Mass attenders favoring Kerry by 55 percent to 44 percent. Church attendance clearly matters here, but its salience in effect cancels out the distinct influence of Catholic adherence. Being secular (no church attendance) also has no independent effect on vote choice—demonstrating from the reverse angle that not going to church means that other factors determine a secular person's vote, not simply the fact that seculars do not attend.

These table 7.3 results point squarely to the critical importance of issues and political variables in determining the 2004 vote choices of Minnesotans. Party identification, as always, is a strong predictor, and presidential job approval also clearly delineates Bush and Kerry supporters. Two issues also stand out: moral values and terrorism. Both of these issues—when cited as most important by voters—tend to predict Bush voting: 77 percent to 21 percent for moral values, 87 percent to 13 percent for terrorism. The president benefited from specific voter approval of his handling of terrorism, as well as from voter perceptions that he embodies particular values and a vision for the nation. At the same time, these positions certainly repel Democratic voters, whose dislike for Bush and/or his policies are reflected in the job approval variable.

Beyond the Presidential Vote:
More Good News for the DFL

Although the Minnesota DFL accomplished its primary goal of holding the state for John Kerry, the party made other significant gains in November 2004. The Republican state House majority was dramatically reduced; a thirteen-seat gain by the DFL lowered the gap to sixty-eight to sixty-six in favor of the GOP—still a majority but not nearly enough to assert the same level of political influence as in the 2003 and 2004 legislative sessions. Most DFL gains came in Twin Cities suburban districts, several of which have shifted back and forth in the past decade between the two major parties. The DFL mobilization of voters in favor of the Kerry–Edwards ticket appears to have had the corollary effect of increasing the DFL vote share in these competitive districts—enough to tip the balance in several cases.

This DFL advantage did not extend to other races, however. No shifts occurred in the state's congressional delegation, which remained at four Republicans and four Democrats. The most competitive race came in the Sixth District, where incumbent Mark Kennedy held off challenger Patty Wetterling by 54 percent to 46 percent—much closer than anticipated. Wetterling is well known in Minnesota and nationwide for her advocacy efforts on behalf of missing children and their families, and Kennedy ran a series of attack advertisements to fend off Wetterling's reputation and independent support from liberal groups such as MoveOn.org. Kennedy is the de facto Republican choice to run for Minnesota's open U.S. Senate seat in 2006 (now held by retiring Democrat Mark Dayton); hence, the fallout among voters from his close race and negative appeals will be a critical factor to watch in the next election cycle.

Assessing the Minnesota Christian Right: 2004 and Beyond

We can safely say that the Christian Right remains a potent influence in Minnesota politics, especially within state party circles and in the interest group universe, but its ability to deliver elections statewide remains circumscribed. There can be no question that Christian Right support has been critical in helping Republicans gain effective parity with the Minnesota DFL. Moreover, as has happened elsewhere, President Bush has mobilized more activists into Republican politics—as well as countermobilizing new voices into Democratic and liberal activism. Significantly, in Minnesota some of this Democratic and liberal activism has religious ties, and as long as religious voices are found on both sides of hot-button issues such as Iraq, the war on terror, abortion, and same-sex marriage, the ability of the Christian Right to monopolize religious rhetoric in the public square will be limited.

The ability to determine electoral outcomes is just one way to evaluate effectiveness and influence, however. What stands out in considering the Christian Right in Minnesota is its high degree of integration within the Republican party. The presence of Christian Right leaders and allies in key party positions, in addition to leaders and allies serving in office, indicates considerable operational control over the party's platform and priorities. The critical issues facing Christian Right groups today are either growing in visibility and salience (e.g., same-sex marriage and related issues of sexual orientation in public and private settings) or kept alive by incremental steps while waiting for national conditions to change (e.g., abortion politics in the period prior to changes in the composition of the U.S. Supreme Court that might alter the status quo). Framing the war on terror and the Iraq conflict in theological terms only adds to the Christian Right's prominence, although specific state policy initiatives related to security issues are more limited in scope.

Thus, the future of the Christian Right as an electoral force in Minnesota remains uncertain, and this mixed assessment is largely a product of the Christian Right's success in becoming a key player within the state GOP. Minnesota state politics is markedly more polarized and antagonistic than it was twenty or even ten years ago, and the ascendance of more conservative, Christian Right–influenced Republican legislators and officeholders has contributed greatly to this state of affairs (Brunswick 2004c; Duchschere 2005; Haga 2004b). The ill will generated by the Kerry–Bush 2004 battle and failures to compromise in three successive state budget cycles point to the continued partisan conflict that marked both the 2002 and 2004 election cycles, as well as the continued efforts of Christian Right activists to extend their influence within the Republican party and expand their influence over state government, which today sits tantalizingly close to a Republican majority in all branches. Such a triumph—hardly foreseeable twenty years ago, in the early days of Christian Right activism, but now possible in a state with even numbers of Republicans and Democrats—would open the door for Christian Right groups to remake the state's laws and reorient state spending to satisfy their long-sought policy goals.

Notes

1. I use the terms DFL and Democrat/Democratic interchangeably in this chapter.

2. Mondale was selected by the DFL to replace Paul Wellstone, who was killed in a plane crash twelve days before the election.

References

Allen, Martha Sawyer. 2004. "Bush Is One of Them, but Is He Their Guy?" *Minneapolis Star Tribune*, 24 April, 7B.

Brunswick, Mark. 2004a. "State Marriage Bill Gets First OK." *Minneapolis Star Tribune*, 10 March, 1A.

———. 2004b. "Counter-rally at Capitol." *Minneapolis Star Tribune*, 26 March, 1B.

———. 2004c. "Kiffmeyer Takes Flak, Pushes on." *Minneapolis Star Tribune*, 25 September, 1A.

Diaz, Kevin, and Matt McKinney. 2004. "GOP Seeking Catholic Inroads; Some Criticize Religious Outreach as Polarizing." *Minneapolis Star Tribune*, 3 July, 1A.

Duchschere, Kevin. 2005. "Senator, Mother, Rising Star." *Minneapolis Star Tribune*, 1 January, 1B.

Elazar, Daniel J., Virginia Gray, and Wyman Spano. 1999. *Minnesota Politics and Government*. Lincoln: University of Nebraska Press.

Gilbert, Christopher P., and David A. M. Peterson. 1995. "Minnesota: Christians and Quistians in the GOP." In *God at the Grassroots: The Christian Right in the 1994 Elections*, ed. Mark J. Rozell and Clyde Wilcox. Lanham, Md.: Rowman & Littlefield, 169–89.

———. 2000. "Minnesota 1998: Christian Conservatives and the Body Politic." In *Prayers in the Precincts: The Christian Right in the 1998 Elections*, ed. John C. Green, Mark J. Rozell and Clyde Wilcox. Washington, D.C.: Georgetown University Press, 207–25.

———. 2003. "Strong Bark, Weak Bite: The Strengths and Liabilities of the Christian Right in Minnesota Politics." In *The Christian Right in American Politics: Marching to the Millennium*, ed. John C. Green, Mark J. Rozell, and Clyde Wilcox. Washington, DC: Georgetown University Press, 167–86.

Grow, Doug. 2004. "Political Calling Put Religion into the Mix." *Minneapolis Star Tribune*, 19 September, 2B.

Haga, Chuck. 2004a. "Gay Marriage: Election May Hinge upon Divisive Issue." *Minneapolis Star Tribune*, 27 October, 1A.

———. 2004b. "Midwest Likely to Be in Limelight Once Again." *Minneapolis Star Tribune*, 5 November, 18A.

Hopfensperger, Jean. 2004. "Antipoverty March Will End with Capitol Rally." *Minneapolis Star Tribune*, 18 September, 4B.

Lopez, Patricia, and James Walsh. 2004. "Cheney Defends Pre-emption Policy; Vice President Addresses 1,000 in Minneapolis." *Minneapolis Star Tribune*, 18 July, 20A.

Pomper, Gerald M. 2005. "The Presidential Election: The Ills of American Politics after 9/11." In *The Elections of 2004*, ed. Michael Nelson. Washington, D.C.: Congressional Quarterly Press, 42–68.

Schmickle, Sharon, and Greg Gordon. 2004. "Two Days to Go for Broke." *Minneapolis Star Tribune*, 31 October, 1A.

Schmickle, Sharon, and Bob Von Sternberg. 2004. "State Fair Stumping." *Minneapolis Star Tribune*, 27 August, 1A.

Von Sternberg, Bob. 2004a. "Bush Inches up on Kerry, but Democratic Candidate Leads by 9 Percentage Points." *Minneapolis Star Tribune*, 15 September, 1A.

———. 2004b. "State up for Grabs, Poll Finds, Kerry's Lead Is No Lock." *Minneapolis Star Tribune*, 13 October, 1A.

CHAPTER EIGHT

Florida

So Close and Yet So Far

KENNETH D. WALD, RICHARD K. SCHER,

MATTHEW DESANTIS, AND SUSAN ORR

> "He was a great lawyer, Dan'l Webster, but we know who's the
> King of Lawyers, as the Good Book tells us, and it seemed as if,
> for the first time, Dan'l Webster had met his match."
> STEPHEN VINCENT BENET "The Devil
> and Daniel Webster" (1936)

LIKE HIS NAMESAKE IN THE CLASSIC SHORT STORY, FLORIDA'S DAN-
iel Webster appears to be on the losing side of a pitched battle with the
King of Lawyers. For the contemporary Daniel Webster, a Republican
who chairs the Florida Senate Judiciary Committee, Satan wears the guise
of the state's 1885 constitution and the black-robed judiciary that enforces
it. Webster's particular *bete noire*, Section 3 of Article 1, prohibits using
state revenue "directly or indirectly in aid of any church, sect, or religious
denomination or in aid of any sectarian institution." Fearing that such language might prevent churches and other religiously affiliated institutions
from receiving state funds to implement Florida's new prekindergarten
program, Webster is mulling an initiative campaign to remove the offending language from the Constitution (Date 2004).

Although Webster's animus against judges was occasioned by a mere
possibility of action, the social movement he champions, the Christian
Right, has long borne a grudge against state judicial authority. Time and
again, the Florida movement has capitalized on its political power to enact
policy goals via statute. More often than not, the victory has then been
snatched away by judges who find the laws unconstitutional. It happened
with a statue requiring parental notification of abortions by minor children, a state voucher program to fund private education, and now, Webster
anticipates, with the legislature's plan to authorize religious instruction by

state-funded private providers of preschool programs. Efforts to restrict judicial discretion by constitutional revision have failed to stop the trend, as have new procedures that increase the governor's power in the appointment of judges. Webster's initiative campaign represents only the latest front in an ongoing battle.

The desperation that has pushed Webster to consider a citizen's initiative against the Florida constitution makes for an interesting puzzle. Political scientists often are fascinated by the success of groups that appear to lack the kinds of resources that normally are considered essential for policy victories—money, organization, influential friends and allies, public support. The Christian Right in Florida—and, arguably, the United States in general—presents the inversion of the puzzle: How does a group that seems to have all the resources needed to influence policy repeatedly fall short of its goals?

Over the past quarter-century, Florida's Christian Right "has evolved gradually from an outsider social movement to a conventional interest group to a durable faction within a major party" (Wald and Scher 2003). It boasts several legislators as major supporters—Webster among them—and has enjoyed the limited patronage of the state's veteran Republican governor. On occasion, its members have occupied formal leadership roles in the state legislature and headed important state agencies. Many candidates for statewide and national office would not have been elected without its support. As a significant component of the party that dominates all organs of state government, it should be riding high. Yet despite its centrality to the levers of power and a mass base that, when energized, can play a crucial role in elections, the Florida Christian Right has been continually frustrated by structural barriers that limit its effectiveness. Although the movement has won on some issues, the overall record contains far more defeats than victories.

This chapter focuses on arenas where the Christian Right made news in Florida's 2004 campaign. The election of a Republican to fill the vacant U.S. Senate seat, together with the clear-cut victory of President George W. Bush in the presidential contest, shows how the Christian Right has remained an important player in state electoral politics. Yet just months after that triumphal election, the movement was decisively defeated in the Terri Schiavo case. Despite the Christian Right's determined efforts to maintain artificial life support for the severely brain-damaged woman— against the express wishes of her husband and legal guardian—the feeding tube was removed and Mrs. Schiavo eventually died. The Schiavo case illustrates graphically why the Florida Christian Right has so much difficulty turning its programmatic vision into binding public policy.

Inducing Attrition: The Context of the 2004 Election

The transformation of Florida from a one-party Democratic system to a dominant Republican system was largely complete when the parties began to gear up for the 2004 elections. Republicans held the governorship—Jeb Bush having twice defeated strong, well-financed, and well-organized Democratic contenders—and the two other state executive positions filled by election, attorney general and agriculture commissioner. The GOP boasted a two-to-one margin in the Florida House and occupied twenty-five of forty Senate seats. Although the Democrats appeared to have won the popular vote in the 2000 presidential election, the state's twenty-five electoral votes were cast for the Republican candidate—as they had been in five of the six previous presidential elections. Republicans also outnumbered Democrats by more than two to one in the state's delegation to the U.S. House of Representative. Nobody foresaw a radical shift in GOP dominance in 2004, not least because partisan redistricting had rendered the status quo in concrete: In November 2004, more than one-third of U.S. House seats, more than half the state Senate seats, and nearly two-thirds of the seats in the State House went uncontested.

Only two contests remained that were considered to be competitive: the presidency and the open seat in the U.S. Senate. After the fiasco of 2000, when Florida's electoral canvass ultimately was decided by the U.S. Supreme Court in *Bush v. Gore*, the race for the presidency in Florida was the subject of intense national speculation. Believing—with some justification—that they won the popular vote in 2000 but were denied victory by ballot error and fraud, the Democrats had pledged a major effort to capture the state for their party's presidential nominee in 2004.[1]

A close presidential race never developed in 2004. Democratic hopes had been deflated two years earlier when the party proved unable to mount a serious challenge to the two Republicans who were considered the architects of Bush's 2000 victory. In 2002 the president's younger brother, Jeb, won an easy reelection contest over Democrat Bill McBride. Katherine Harris, who had been both the state's chief election officer and the chair of the Bush presidential campaign in 2000, waltzed to an easy victory in her race for Congress, filling one of the safest Republican seats in Florida. Unable to capitalize on lingering resentment just two years after the 2000 contest and with a perceived northern liberal as their 2004 nominee, the Democrats were unlikely to carry the state.

The Republicans' 2004 presidential strategy in Florida was relatively simple. As it did elsewhere, the party put considerable effort into boosting Republican turnout in rural areas and among evangelical Protestants. Republican efforts to turn large churches into virtual precincts received some unfavorable national publicity in the summer when the Bush–Cheney campaign was discovered to have requested congregational directories and mailing lists from "friendly" denominations. Beyond increasing turnout, the Florida presidential strategy was intimately tied to the Senatorial contest. The national party was committed to finding a strong Senate candidate who would assist the GOP presidential campaign and avoiding weak candidates who might pull down the top of the ticket.

In contrast to the presidential race, many observers expected a serious contest for the open U.S. Senate seat. Unlike almost every other sphere of state politics, where Republicans were ascendant, the two parties had maintained something like parity in contests for the state's two U.S. Senate seats. The popular former Democratic governor, Bob Graham, had occupied one of the seats since 1987, and fellow Democrat Bill Nelson, a well-regarded congressman from the Space Coast, had won the other seat in 2000. Graham's decision to forego the prospect of another Senate term in favor of a campaign for the presidency created an open seat that Republicans coveted. Democrats needed to hold the seat to have any chance of regaining a majority in the U.S. Senate.

Without Graham on the ballot, nearly every Republican officeholder with a statewide reputation or aspirations was rumored to be considering a senatorial bid. Enter the White House. President Bush's chief political adviser, Karl Rove, was widely reported to have gotten very involved in both recruiting and discouraging potential candidates. Rove apparently settled on a member of Bush's cabinet—Housing Secretary Mel Martinez of Orlando. Martinez, who had been mulling a gubernatorial bid in 2006, was regarded both as a unifying figure and as a candidate who could energize south Florida's large Cuban community and make inroads among non-Cuban Hispanics—a Democratically inclined constituency concentrated in south and central Florida. Beyond boosting Martinez by channeling contributions and holding fundraisers, the GOP was said to have actively undermined campaigns by other challengers whose weaknesses might affect the Florida presidential vote. Katherine Harris—still considered a lightning rod who would stimulate intense Democratic countermobilization—apparently was promised support for a future statewide run if she stayed out of the 2004 Senate race. Other top GOP figures, such as State Treasurer Tom Gallagher and Attorney General Charlie Crist, also were induced to remain on the sidelines. Although the August primary ballot carried eight names, the number of serious GOP aspirants had been whittled down to just two: Martinez and former congressman Bill McCollum, the loser in the 2000 Senate race (Jacoby 2004).

Even with the active involvement of the White House, Christian conservatives were a significant factor in the campaign. The Christian Right is too large for Republicans to ignore but too controversial among main-stream voters for the party to embrace in statewide electoral contests. As a "necessary annoyance" (in the words of a GOP activist we interviewed in 2002), this constituency can veto unacceptable nominees but is not strong enough to determine the party's standard-bearer. That reality became apparent in the runup to the primary when the movement blocked the progress of a popular congressman but proved unable to catapult either of its favorites to the nomination against a determined party leadership working in tandem with the While House.

U.S. Representative Mark Foley of West Palm Beach, who dropped out well before the primary, illustrates the plight of GOP moderates who run afoul of the Christian Right. On the surface, Foley should have been an attractive candidate who could raise significant funding. A native of Newton, Massachusetts, who ran a family restaurant before entering politics, Foley was a respected member of the U.S. House of Representatives and a former state legislator. Foley had done exceptionally well in historically Democratic areas with what passed for a moderate voting record among GOP leaders in Florida. He ranked last among Florida Republicans on the Christian Coalition voting index; he voted with prochoice groups on almost three-fourths of roll calls between 1995 and 2001.[2] Although these qualities would have boded well for him in a general election, they prevented him from attracting the conservative support deemed essential for a successful primary election. Although Foley had been attempting to position himself as a social conservative by aggressively championing morality issues such as Internet pornography, he was outflanked from the right by other candidates. Furthermore, persistent rumors about Foley's sexuality, magnified by the publicity of a Senate race, undermined his campaign. Despite a vain request for privacy, Foley could not still the rumors or quell the threats that he would be "outed" by various publications during the race. Despite amassing nearly $3 million in campaign funds, Foley withdrew his candidacy.

At the other end of the ideological spectrum, two long-time Christian Right stalwarts also competed for the nomination but carried too much baggage to help the GOP's statewide campaign. State Representative Johnnie Byrd and the aforementioned State Senator Daniel Webster both announced their candidacies for the Senate seat. Byrd, who as speaker of the Florida House had pushed through legislation favored by the Christian Right, believed his voting record would gain him support from socially conservative voters (Salinero 2003; Ruth 2003). Although Byrd received the endorsement of the National Right to Life Committee, he was hurt by his behavior as House leader. During his tenure the GOP-controlled House was at constant loggerheads with the somewhat more moderate GOP-controlled

Senate—a conflict many observers attributed to Byrd's abrasive and uncompromising leadership style. Many observers believed that he was incapable of unifying the party, let alone forging a statewide majority among Independents and Democrats (Byrd 2004; Melone 2003). Before Byrd dropped out, Webster competed with Byrd for the support of the evangelical community (Bousquet 2004a). During his service as leader of the GOP House in the 1990s, Webster had allowed the organizer of the Florida Christian Coalition to work out of the speaker's office. Although Webster could claim seniority over Byrd and a better reputation as a leader who reached out to multiple factions, Webster had an organizational disadvantage by virtue of twenty years of uncontested races for his legislative seat. Unable to make headway against better-financed candidates, Webster withdrew before the primary. Byrd attracted an embarrassing 6 percent of the primary vote—finishing fourth behind a businessman with no political experience.

The Republican Primary Campaign

Just as Foley illustrated how a moderate would be unable to win the GOP primary, the fate of the two social conservatives showed that many Republican elites believed that extreme social conservatives could not carry a general election. That circumstance left the election as a two-candidate race with contestants from the business wing of the Republican Party. Both had distinguished records of public service, and both were widely considered electable.

Bill McCollum, a longtime member of Congress from the Orlando suburb of Longwood, was a pillar of the state GOP. With substantial name recognition gained during his leadership of the impeachment campaign against President Bill Clinton, McCollum had won the Republican nomination for the Senate just four years earlier—but lost handily to his fellow U.S. Representative, Democrat Bill Nelson. Despite the defeat, McCollum sometimes was regarded as the favorite for the nomination in 2004. Apparently the White House felt differently. McCollum's most formidable competitor, Mel Martinez, had carved out a successful career in Orange County (Orlando) politics, attracting considerable support from Democrats and Independents as well as Republicans. Although neither housing nor urban development were priorities during the president's first term, Martinez carried no significant baggage from his service in the Cabinet. He resigned the position and returned to Florida to campaign full-time for the Senate nomination.

The primary campaign illustrated two important patterns. First, as in advertising commercial products, the greatest spending reflects the need to differentiate brands that have no innate differences. (Examples include beer and toilet paper.) Second, both front-running candidates—believing they could carry mainstream Republicans in November—aimed their messages during the primary campaign at the Christian Right. With impeccable establishment credentials, each candidate could afford to run right in the primary and then to the center in the general election.

Primary voters usually are the most enthusiastic and ideologically extreme members of a party. In a race without party cues to guide voting decisions, the truest of the true believers may exercise influence out of all proportion to their numbers. Although evangelical Protestants, the base constituency of the Christian Right, constitute a minority of GOP primary voters (usually estimated at 20–30 percent), their large presence often makes them the major target of candidates. That was especially likely in a crowded, winner-take-all primary without a runoff. Accordingly, despite the different shades of Republicanism represented by the candidates, all tilted their campaign messages toward social conservatives.

Looking closely at past records, McCollum would have been the clear favorite to win Christian Right support. With his extremely strong denunciations of President Clinton during the impeachment hearings, McCollum had earned a reputation as something of a moralist. That impression was reinforced by a congressional record that matched the Christian Coalition voting scores of nationally known social conservatives and fellow Florida Republicans such as Joe Scarborough (now a conservative talk show host on MSNBC) and Charles Canady, who put the issue of "partial birth abortion" on the national agenda. That record was sufficient to earn McCollum the endorsement of Pat Neal, former chair of the Florida Christian Coalition.

Martinez, on the other hand, was a blank slate. In his only previous race for public office—a contest for the chairmanship of the Orange County Commission—he had lost the endorsement of local Christian conservatives to a primary rival (Griffin 1998). Once in office, he gained a reputation as a tax-cutter and fiscal conservative, a moderate Republican who reached out to Democrats to build coalitions. Martinez tangled on at least one occasion with the leader of the influential local group United Christians, which he condemned as "a political organization that utilizes faith for their own political ends" (Maxwell 1998).

Considering this background, one out-of-state reporter was not far off the mark when she framed the 2004 campaign as a contest between "conservative Bill McCollum" and "the more moderate Mel Martinez," a Florida version of the ongoing national "battle between social-movement conservatives and country-club Republicans" for control of the GOP (Milligan 2004). By the end of the campaign in August, that characterization was in tatters—the victim of the vicious campaign style for which Karl Rove was known.

Both candidates began their campaigns by building bridges to the Christian Right. McCollum set out early to establish his bona fides with Christian conservatives, speaking often in evangelical Protestant churches around Florida. Martinez trumpeted a direct tie to Ken Connor, long-time president of Florida Right to Life and, for a time, president of the Family Research Council, the influential national Christian Right organization. Although some observers interpreted Connor's endorsement of Martinez as a signal that most Christian Right organizations would weigh in on the latter's behalf, there was another explanation. Martinez and Connor were close personal friends from college days and had once been partners in a law firm. In his own ill-fated campaign for the Republican gubernatorial nomination ten years earlier, Connor had induced Martinez to stand as his running mate.

Both McCollum and Martinez faced specific challenges as they competed for the support of Christian conservatives (March 2004a). Martinez had three major issues to overcome. First, he was a Hispanic Catholic in a party dominated by non-Hispanic Protestants who were not always friendly to his religious faith and had a choice among three evangelical Protestants on the ballot. Although Florida's Cuban community has a reputation for conservatism, that orientation usually has not extended to the kinds of social policy questions that most engage evangelical Protestants. Second, as a trial lawyer who had been president of the state's Academy of Trial Lawyers, Martinez represented what had become a demonized profession among conservatives generally and Christian conservatives in particular. Finally, Martinez' record exhibited little emphasis on the core issues that animated the Christian Right. None of these factors made him a "natural" choice for evangelicals.

McCollum faced his own challenges. As a sitting member of Congress who had to take positions on controversial issues, McCollum did not always endear himself to the social conservatives in GOP ranks. Like GOP stalwarts such as Nancy Reagan, Orrin Hatch, and Trent Lott, McCollum endorsed government funding for embryonic stem cell research using embryos that were to be discarded by fertility clinics. Despite the blessing of a state Christian Coalition leader, this position lost him the support of the National Right to Life Committee, which had endorsed his 2000 senatorial bid (Bousquet 2004b). Moreover, McCollum geared his campaign around the war on terror—an issue that was not likely to galvanize social conservatives in a Republican primary (Jones 2004).

Under the leadership of John Dowless, the highly effective former organizer of the Florida Christian Coalition, the Martinez campaign sought to allay concerns about his commitment to social conservatism by meeting with high-profile clergymen throughout the state (Bousquet 2004a). Martinez campaign ads always emphasized his support for restrictive abortion laws. Martinez also pushed for Christian Right support by investing heavily in advertising and appearing on Christian radio talk shows in several important media markets. By constantly playing up his ties to President Bush—whom Christian Right voters considered one of their own—Martinez sought to improve his credibility among socially conservative voters. He emphasized his support for the Defense of Marriage Act and urged supporters to press Senator Graham to vote for the proposal. No doubt because of McCollum's moderate position on stem cell research, Martinez allied himself closely with President Bush's unalterable opposition to any federal funding for research using embryos beyond those that had already been created for experimental purposes. In a radio ad, Martinez neatly tied his escape from Cuba as a teenager with his opposition to gay marriage. Living in a society with same-sex marriage, he said, would be just like living under "a totalitarian dictator who had no respect for the traditional values of family and faith" (Dahir 2004).

The campaign turned ugly as Martinez sought to differentiate himself from McCollum. Like many other conservatives who were the target of a Karl Rove campaign, the socially conservative McCollum found himself portrayed as a first cousin of Teddy Kennedy. The congressman's support for bipartisan hate crime legislation, including penalties for attacks based on sexual orientation, along with his alleged employment of two homosexuals on his staff occasioned the absurd charge that McCollum was the "darling of homosexual extremists" (Patton 2004). Martinez' television ads also alleged that his opponent was "antifamily" for supporting stem cell research (Jacoby 2004). Having supported omnibus appropriations bills that funded the National Endowment for the Arts, McCollum was accused by the Martinez campaign of having voted for "anti-Christian and offensive pornographic art" (Bousquet 2004a). Just a week before the primary, Martinez sponsored a conference call in which leaders of several socially conservative organizations, such as the Traditional Values Coalition, told reporters that McCollum had lied by misrepresenting his voting record (Bousquet and Kumar 2004).

These tactics by the Martinez campaign drew rebukes from many sources. Governor Bush urged Martinez to stop the attacks on McCollum. Citing the negative campaign, the liberal *St. Petersburg Times* withdrew its editorial support for Martinez and instead endorsed McCollum just a day before the election. Florida's respected former Republican senator, Connie Mack, also wrote Martinez to condemn his use of what Mack called "political hate speech." The efforts to galvanize the most socially conservative members of the Republican party by transforming Martinez "from sunny moderate to snarling right-winger" (Jacoby 2004) brought endorsements from groups of social conservatives such as the American Family Association, National Right to Life, the Traditional Values Coalition, and the Florida Family Focus. The attacks may have cost Martinez some support from the GOP's admittedly small and dwindling moderate wing.

There was a remarkable irony in Martinez' charges that McCollum had enlisted in the homosexual lobby by employing two gay staffers. It turned out that two critical members of the Martinez campaign team—his chief strategist and finance director—were gay. This fact came to light when the *Washington Blade*, a gay newspaper, reported on meetings with John Dowless in a gay bar (Dahir 2004). Yet the charges never seemed to hurt Martinez, both because they were not widely reported during the campaign and because the unstinting support of Christian Right organizations apparently immunized him from any negative fallout.

Ultimately, Martinez won the primary with a healthy fourteen-point margin and 45 percent of the total vote. Most commentators attributed the victory to Martinez' intense television campaigns linking him with President Bush, his compelling "rags-to-riches" personal story, and voter perceptions that he was the "official" candidate sponsored by the national Republican party (Troxler 2004; March 2004b). The power of the Christian Right clearly influenced the final vote difference between two very similar candidates. McCollum's inability to appeal to the Christian Right, evident in the string of endorsements for Martinez from the movement's leaders, hurt him on primary day.

Just days after winning the primary by framing himself as a staunch conservative who would not back down from his positions, Martinez began his movement to the center by denying claims that he was an extremist, emphasizing his ability to work with Republicans, Democrats, and Independents alike (Bousquet and Kumar 2004). During the general election, there was significantly less mention of socially conservative issues, with the exception of parental consent to abortion and stem cell research. The only major effort to mobilize social conservatives involved repeated trips to Florida by Ralph Reed, the former organizer of the national Christian Coalition, who touted both Martinez and President Bush to rallies organized in large part by Christian churches. Having persuaded the Christian Right of his affinity during the primary campaign, Martinez had no further need to emphasize his social conservatism. Instead, he focused on the war on terror—an issue that allowed Martinez to tie himself to the president even more closely and to attack his Democratic opponent, Betty Castor, for being soft on terror. On Election Day, Martinez edged out Castor by a mere 1 percent of the vote—running nearly 300,000 votes behind President Bush while Castor ran even with the Democratic presidential ticket in Florida.

This pattern conforms to previous studies about the Christian Right as an electoral force in Florida. The movement has played a large role in primaries, when many less-intense partisans were uninvolved, but receded in importance as the visibility of the race increased. The efforts by Martinez to remake himself as a social conservative bear testimony to the continued importance of Christian Right sympathizers in the Florida Republican party. In addition, the preference of Christian Right elites for Martinez over Byrd and Webster—two candidates who had long carried water for the movement in the legislature—documents the growth of pragmatism in the social movement. Faced with a choice between a true believer who was unlikely to win and a latter-day fellow traveler with a good shot at victory, the movement opted for the more electable candidate.

Defeat from the Jaws of Victory: The Terri Schiavo Case

The results of the November 2004 election demonstrate the capacity of the Florida Christian Right to play an important role in selecting government officials. The Terri Schiavo case, by contrast, suggests the limits of electoral strategy.

In 1990 twenty-seven-year-old Terri Schiavo suffered a heart attack, apparently brought on by a potassium imbalance of undetermined origin.[3] The heart attack shut off blood to her brain for several minutes, putting her into what her doctors called a "persistent vegetative state." After several years and repeated confirmation of the diagnosis of permanent and severe brain damage by numerous respected neurologists, Mrs. Schiavo's husband, Michael, decided to remove her from life support. Although Mrs. Schiavo could breathe without the assistance of machines, she had lost her swallow reflex and had to be fed and hydrated by tubes. Reporting that Mrs. Schiavo had made clear her antipathy to being kept alive by machines, Michael Schiavo petitioned the courts in 1998 for permission to end her life by discontinuing the delivery of sustenance. The trial court "found by clear and convincing evidence that Theresa Schiavo was in a persistent vegetative state and that Theresa would elect to cease life-prolonging procedures if she were competent to make her own decision" (*Bush v. Schiavo* 2004, 3). According to brain scans, the lack of oxygen had prompted severe deterioration of her cerebral cortex—an irreversible condition. Mrs. Schiavo's parents, Bob and Mary Schindler, who had stopped speaking to their son-in-law in 1993, never accepted the medical diagnosis and insisted that their daughter could improve with therapy and eventually might even recover full cognitive function thanks to medical miracles.[4]

Over the next several years, the Florida courts heard a series of appeals brought by the Schindlers. Although the cases demonstrated impressive creativity, the medical witnesses called by Michael Schiavo's attorneys and those employed by the court all agreed that there was no chance Mrs. Schiavo would regain cognitive function. This finding did not deter the Schindler family, which employed a broad range of tactics in an effort to take control of their married daughter's medical treatment. Finally, on October 15, 2003, when a state circuit court once again decided in favor of Michael Schiavo's authority to remove sustenance from his wife, the case appeared to reach its sad end.

Showing considerable political prowess, however, the Schindlers managed to attract political support to their daughter's case. Arguing that Mrs. Schiavo would be murdered by her husband's decision, they enlisted the help of Governor Jeb Bush, social conservatives, and the Roman Catholic hierarchy in Florida. At the last minute, during a special session called late in 2003, they persuaded the Florida legislature to pass what became known as "Terri's Law"—legislation that expressly forbade removal of her feeding tube, under penalty of law. The law was passed not in the dead of night but amidst the full glare of publicity and with incredible efforts at mass mobilization. Indeed, the law's advocates so overloaded the legislature with telephone calls, faxes, and e-mails that the communication system collapsed under the strain (Melone 2004). Although the law was of dubious constitutionality, its passage had the effect of staying any action until the Florida Supreme Court ruled on Michael Schiavo's appeal against it. Just six days after Terri Schiavo's feeding tube was first removed, it was reinserted on orders of Governor Bush.

In September 2004 Michael Schiavo's appeal against Terri's law was upheld by unanimous decision of the Florida Supreme Court. Although a state district court had previously ruled against Terri's Law on several grounds, the state's highest court zeroed in on what it considered two egregious violations of the basic doctrine of separation of powers. The legislation in question gave the governor authority to overrule a final decision reached by a competent court after full and careful consideration of all evidence. Apart from authorizing the executive branch to tread on territory reserved for the judiciary, the court concluded, the law also amounted to an unconstitutional delegation of legislative power to the executive. Despite further attempts at delays through appeals to higher courts, a state judge then ruled that the feeding tube be removed on March 18, 2005.

Rather than end the battle, the impending deadline only stimulated it further. Emboldened by their gains in 2004, Republicans in the Florida

House brought forward another bill that they thought was crafted more generally than the legislation struck down by the Florida Supreme Court in 2004. Under this new bill, anybody in a persistent vegetative state who had not expressly indicated beforehand a desire to end sustenance would continue to receive food and water. The law was made retroactive so that it would apply to Mrs. Schiavo. House Republicans also attempted to out-flank the Florida state court system by moving the case to federal courts, where new issues could be raised. The case was taken up by the U.S. Congress—with the active encouragement of the newly elected senator from Florida, Mel Martinez.

Although the Florida Christian Right was not alone in this effort and probably was less important than the governor and many out-of-state organizations, it was extremely active in the attempt to circumvent state court rulings. The original Terri's Law was sponsored by Daniel Webster in the Florida Senate and pushed actively by House Speaker Johnnie Byrd. To handle the state's legal appeals, Governor Bush turned to Ken Connor—Mel Martinez' long-time friend and former national head of the Family Research Council.

Although we would not gainsay the motivations that drove these efforts, we also cannot overlook the political calculations that may have reinforced them. Terri's Law, which was passed late in 2003, often was portrayed as an integral part of Republican campaign strategy in 2004. The goal was to stimulate higher turnout among evangelicals—who, supporters argued, had not been particularly energized in the 2000 election. As Ken Connor himself acknowledged, "the Legislature and the governor acting in a decisive way . . . will galvanize the base of the Republican Party because most of that base is pro-life" (Wallsten 2003). A leader of the protests outside Terri Schiavo's hospice, Operation Rescue's Randall Terry, similarly noted that "This pro-life, pro-family governor could not afford to not intervene in some way," lest he undermine the Republican effort to attract evangelicals to the GOP (Goodnough 2003). Some Republicans believed that Johnnie Byrd's energetic championing of the Schiavo case in 2003 was an effort to improve his standing before the GOP Senatorial primary less than a year later. One such critic, Republican Tom Lee of Tampa, denounced the 2003 legislation as an effort "to use this woman's life as a political football to appeal to the Christian conservatives in this state" (Wallsten 2003). Even some of the legislators who toed the party line by voting for the legislation came to regret doing so (Melone 2004). Ironically, considering that the law supposedly was passed to aid the GOP in 2004, a December 2003 poll revealed that two-thirds of Floridians opposed the law and three-fourths believed that spouses should have the right to make such decisions (Associated Press 2003).

Tom Lee was not a marginal force in the state Senate; he was a widely respected legislator who was slated to become the Senate president in 2005—which did not bode well for efforts to restore some form of Terri's Law after the Florida Supreme Court struck it down late in 2004. Lee was one of six Senate Republicans who had voted against the law in 2003. In mid-March 2005, during the regular legislative session, the Florida Senate refused to go along with a second incarnation of Terri's Law, voting twenty-one to sixteen (with three abstentions) against a weaker version than the House measure. With that action, the case left Florida to enter the national political arena.

The only remaining mystery in the Schiavo affair involved the behavior of Governor Jeb Bush, who assumed direct, hands-on leadership of the effort to maintain Mrs. Schiavo on artificial life support. Apart from pressing the legislature to pass the original Terri's Law and its failed successor, Bush repeatedly encouraged state agencies to fight the judiciary at every turn. He recruited a prolife physician to observe Mrs. Schiavo directly, later reporting that she showed signs of "minimal consciousness" that had been undetected by armies of medical experts in previous comprehensive examinations. Indeed, the *Miami Herald* reported on the basis of at least three sources that Bush had ordered state officials to seize Mrs. Schiavo, under a dubious legal pretext, and was dissuaded only when local law enforcement authorities in Tampa warned that they would resist state agents with force if necessary (Miller 2005). Although the governor's office denied the account, the *Herald* stood by the story. Only then did Bush regretfully give up his efforts and grudgingly accept the authority of the judiciary.

Throughout Job Bush's governorship, Florida has often been one of the laboratories where political themes and public policies subsequently introduced by his brother's presidential administration have received trial runs. Might the governor's aggressive campaigning for the Schindler family have been another instance of the younger brother serving the goals of the national administration by handing it an issue that would build support among Christian conservatives? Other cynics have imagined that the Schiavo case was the governor's effort to build electoral support in anticipation of a senatorial campaign in 2006 or a presidential campaign in 2008.[5] Although such considerations can never be ruled out entirely, they seem to be unlikely explanations for the governor's behavior.

In 1996 Jeb Bush joined the Catholic church. Like other converts who often embrace their new religious identity more ardently than those born to the faith, Bush may simply have been personally moved by the appeals of the Schindler family and Catholic doctrine regarding the immorality of euthanasia.[6] Whatever the source, a governor who generally had held the

Christian Right at arm's length became the most visible statewide symbol of its efforts. Ironically, Jeb Bush's unwillingness to breach the law by seizing Mrs. Schiavo generated a blistering denunciation by the fervent demonstrators who maintained a vigil outside the hospice where she spent her last days.

Why the Christian Right Failed in the Schiavo Case

As a social movement, Christian conservatives did not enter the realm of politics for symbolic gratification or merely material benefits. As appealing as those incentives have been, the movement has always focused on a broader aim: nothing less than the transformation of public policy in the state of Florida. That goal is the appropriate standard, then, by which to judge the movement's success.

On its face, the Schiavo case was an issue for which the stars were nicely aligned for a Christian Right victory. The issue itself was not overtly partisan, which meant that people who might have opposed social conservatives were not necessarily hostile. The governor, who previously had tried to keep the movement on a tight rein, was an active force on behalf of efforts to keep the feeding tube in place. The facts of the case also built some support for the Schindler family's opposition to the termination of sustenance. First, Terri Schiavo had left no written instructions that clearly conveyed her wishes about how she was to be treated in such a situation. Few twenty-seven-year olds in good health think to do that. Thus, the issue became a matter of Michael Schiavo's word and the testimony of Terri's friends against the assurances of her biological family; the fact that Michael Schiavo had fathered two children with another woman after his wife had suffered brain damage did not help his case. Second, the videotape that the family smuggled out of Mrs. Schiavo's hospice appeared to show Terri Schiavo as a conscious and reactive person. As is often the case when sober words conflict with vivid imagery, medical testimony that patients in a persistent vegetative state often appear as if they are functioning was less powerful than the pictures displayed on television. Finally, although the issue was framed as a right-to-die case, Terri Schiavo was not going to be disconnected from a respirator or denied medical attention; she was to be refused food and water. The prospect of starvation, even for a comatose person who was to be heavily sedated, struck a nerve with many observers. All told, the Schiavo case should have been an issue on which the Christian Right could prevail.

Previous studies have noted how social facts—particularly the diversity that characterizes a large state such as Florida—have limited the Christian Right's electoral reach and policy influence (Wald and Scher 2003;

Wald, Tartaglione, and Scher 2000). On occasion, movement activists have squandered their advantages by overreaching and offending erstwhile allies. The Christian Right's failure in the Schiavo case is not a matter of electoral impotence or offensive behavior; it can be attributed principally to a pair of structural barriers that often have impeded the movement: the differences between Republicans in the Florida House and Senate and the role of the judiciary.

Wald and Scher (2003) discuss the differences between the two chambers of the Florida legislature. Much as the U.S. House and Senate tend to differ in tone and temperament, so do the equivalent chambers of the Florida legislature. Whereas the House tends to be regimented procedurally and peopled by individuals who tend to the extremes, the Senate grants individual members considerable procedural leeway and seems to soften the ideological hard edges of its members. Whereas the House often has been likened to a partisan battlefield, Senate veterans still talk about the prevalence of civility in the upper chamber. According to some legislators who have moved from the House to the Senate, there is greater pressure in the upper house to consider the statewide implications of legislation than in the House, which is apportioned into much smaller and more homogeneous districts. In the perspective of the Florida Christian Coalition's executive director, senators "think their ideal of public policy is superior to everybody else's," and "nobody can reason with them" (Follick 2005). A well-placed informant told us that Governor Bush had mused about changing the Senate's name so that its unruly members would stop thinking of themselves as U.S. Senators with a statewide mission!

These differences were apparent when the first Terri's Law was passed in 2003. Both the Senate president and his chief deputy had personal knowledge of the conditions associated with persistent vegetative states. After dealing with his parents' deaths, the former had actually written the Florida law establishing the right of guardians to remove feeding tubes, and his deputy had only recently authorized discontinuation of artificial sustenance for his elderly mother, who soon died at the age of 89 (Melone 2004). Although they had bowed to the groundswell and voted reluctantly for Terri's Law in 2003, they were determined not to retreat from their principles again. Many of the dissident Republicans cited personal experience or broad concerns about political philosophy. Noting that the Senate bill to replace Terri's Law would mandate continued feeding when family members differed over treatment, one GOP senator succinctly declared, "I don't want my sister overriding my wife" (Follick and Dunkelberger 2005). Others cited their beliefs that government should not be making decisions that are best left to family members—a staple of GOP platforms for decades.

Given these sentiments, we hardly should be surprised that the GOP-dominated Florida Senate twice refused to go along with attempts to circumvent the judge's ruling in 2005. In a body that still follows party discipline, nine of the Senate's twenty-six Republicans voted with all but one Democrat against repassage of a kind of Terri's Law during the 2005 session.[7] The contours of the vote suggest something of the internal tensions dividing the Republican majority. All four female Senate Republicans joined the opposition to legislative intervention. Although there were Republicans with similar traits who supported the Webster bill, the dissenters also stood out from their GOP colleagues by virtue of northern birth, membership in nonevangelical religious denominations (e.g., Catholic, Presbyterian, Jewish), and business/law backgrounds.

In addition to role differences between representatives and senators, the campaign to maintain Terri Schiavo on life support was undercut by the judiciary. Many allies of the Schindler family railed against the state judiciary for what they considered its willingness to disregard the law and Mrs. Schiavo's best interests. From the harsh rhetoric directed against him as biased, neglectful, vindictive, and incompetent, one might imagine Judge George Greer as a perfect liberal target for conservative opponents.

In fact, but for his rulings in the Schiavo case Judge Greer might have been mistaken for a supporter of the Christian Right. According to a newspaper profile (Levesque 2005), the judge was a conservative Republican and a churchgoing Southern Baptist who abhorred judicial activism. As Greer saw it, his decisions were simply a matter of following the law. The Florida constitution, unlike its federal counterpart, has strong and explicit provisions regarding the right to privacy, specifying that individuals are to be free from unwarranted governmental intrusions in their personal affairs. In the 1990 case known as *In Re Guardianship of Browning*, the Florida Supreme Court asserted that the "state may not override the clearly expressed wishes of a patient to be disconnected from a feeding tube" and indicated that "oral declarations" to next-of-kin are sufficient to establish the wishes of the patient (Dorf 2003). The trial courts that heard the cases filed by the Schindler family repeatedly accepted the judgment offered by court-appointed physicians that Mrs. Schiavo was in a "persistent vegetative state" and affirmed her husband's authority to act as her guardian in making medical decisions. Judge Greer's findings were motivated not by his personal predilections but by his philosophy of judicial interpretation—a belief that judges should interpret the law as written. Ironically, Greer was precisely the kind of judge social conservatives often hold out as an exemplar—someone who did not read his personal convictions into the law but attempted to interpret the law as it was written.

Nor was Greer an anomaly. During the long course of legal proceedings in the Schiavo case, the Schindler family repeatedly and unsuccessfully appealed Greer's decision to the federal Court of Appeals in Atlanta. Despite the passage of federal legislation encouraging the federal courts to consider the appeal, the appeals court continued to reject the case. In an unusual written opinion, one of the court's most conservative members—a Republican appointee—condemned the federal legislation for overreaching the separation of powers. "When the fervor of political passions moves the executive and legislative branches to act in ways inimical to basic constitutional principles," wrote Judge Stanley F. Birch Jr., "it is the duty of the judiciary to intervene" (Goodnough and Yardley 2005). Like Greer, Judge Birch set aside his decidedly conservative personal convictions because he understood his role as a guardian of the Constitution. His principled commitment to the judicial role contributed to stopping legislation championed by the Christian Right. Much the same probably can be said of the three Republican appointees to the Florida Supreme Court who joined with their four Democratic brethren to strike down Terri's Law in a unanimous decision. Such structural barriers continue to hamper implementation of public policies by a movement that has achieved considerable electoral success.

In Stephen Benet's classic short story quoted at the beginning of the chapter, the fictional Daniel Webster bests the King of Lawyers—none other than Satan himself, masquerading as a member of the bar. In Florida, the modern-day Daniel Webster, the most visible Christian Right official in the state, repeatedly has been bested both by his colleagues in the state Senate and by various judges. The contemporary Webster's plight underlines what would-be revolutionaries often have discovered after gaining access to the levers of government: The U.S. political system has a genius for resisting radical changes—even those proposed by people and movements who style themselves conservatives.

Notes

1. The official 2000 canvass indicated that the Bush–Cheney ticket received 537 more votes than the Democratic nominees, but scholars have provided persuasive evidence that poor ballot design in Palm Beach County cost the Gore-Lieberman ticket many more votes than that (see Wand et al. 2001).

2. The voting scores were obtained from successive biennial editions of the *Almanac of American Politics*.

3. The facts of the case recounted here are derived from the 2004 decision of the Florida Supreme Court (*Bush v. Schiavo*, SC04-925).

4. The postmortem examination showed that the trial courts had been right and the Schindlers had been wrong. The autopsy confirmed that Mrs. Schiavo had suffered massive brain damage that was permanent and irreversible by treatment or therapy. Having lost her vision, she could not have been looking at people, as she seemed to be in the widely broadcast videotapes (see Brown and Murray 2005).

5. Despite Jeb Bush's personal popularity, he carries some family baggage that may hinder a presidential run in 2008. His daughter's treatment for drug addiction and his wife's continued residence in Miami during his gubernatorial terms both raised issues that may concern Christian conservatives.

6. In spite of the opposition of both the pope and American Catholic bishops to the death penalty, however, Governor Bush has signed more than thirty death warrants for convicts sentenced to execution (see data in http://www.fadp. org/jebwarrants.html).

7. Two Republican senators who had not voted in the first roll call supported legislative intervention on the revote. The measure still fell short, on an 18–21 roll call vote (with one abstention).

References

Associated Press. 2003. "Poll: Most Florida Voters Oppose 'Terri's Law.'" CNN. com, 7 December.

Bousquet, Steve. 2004a. "Republicans Court the Faithful." *St. Petersburg Times*, 21 June.

———. 2004b. "Endorsement Stirs up Stem Cell Controversy." *St. Petersburg Times*, 20 July.

Bousquet, Steve, and A. Kumar. 2004. "Attacks Intensifying in Senate Contests." *St. Petersburg Times*, 25 August.

Brown, David, and Shailagh Murray. 2005. "Schiavo Autopsy Released." *Washington Post*, 16 June, A1.

Bush v. Schiavo. 2004. Supreme Court of Florida, SC04-925, decided 23 September. Available at www.findlaw.com.

Byrd, Ted. 2004. "Byrd Builds on Evangelical Conservative Bedrock." *Tampa Tribune*, 11 August.

Dahir, Mubarak. 2004. "Anti-Gay Senate Candidate Has Two Gay Advisers." *Washington Blade*, 16 July.

Date, S. V. 2004. "Voters May be Asked to Remove Florida's Church-State Ban." *Palm Beach Post*, 16 October.

Dorf, Michael E. 2003. "How the Florida Legislature and Governor Have Usurped the Judicial Role in the Schiavo 'Right to Die' Case." Writ: Findlaw's Legal Commentary, 29 October, available at www.writ.news.findlaw.com/dorf/20031029. html.

Follick, Joe. 2005. "Senators Torn over Schiavo Decision." *Gainesville Sun*, 17 March.

Follick, Joe, and Lloyd Dunkelberger. 2005. "Attempts to Keep Feeding Tube Stall." *Gainesville Sun*, 18 March.

Goodnough, Abby. 2003. "Victory in Florida Feeding Case Emboldens the Religious Right." *New York Times*, 24 October.

Goodnough, Abby, and William Yardley. 2005. "Congress Rebuked for Schiavo Efforts." *New York Times*, 31 March.

Griffin, Michael. 1998. "Religious Right Might be Left Out." *Orlando Sentinel*, 18 October, G-3.

Jacoby, Mary. 2004. "Karl Rove's Florida Frankenstein." Salon.com, 8 October. Available at www.salon.com/news/feature/2004/10/08/florida_senate_race/index_np.html (accessed February 6, 2006).

Jones, Allison North. 2004. "In Second Bid, McCollum Wears Antiterrorism Badge." *Tampa Tribune*, 9 August.

Levesque, William R. 2005. "Quiet Judge Persists in Schiavo Maelstrom." *St. Petersburg Times*, 6 March.

March, William. 2004a. "Christian Right Vote Key for GOP Rivals." *Tampa Tribune*, 11 July.

———. 2004b. "GOP Bigwigs Back Martinez in 'Wide Open' Senate Race." *Tampa Tribune*, 13 July.

Maxwell, Scott. 1998. "Fliers Rile Faith Groups." *Orlando Sentinel*, 2 October.

Melone, Mary Jo. 2003. "If Byrd Flew North, Would the Mischief Go with Him?" *St. Petersburg Times*, 28 October.

———. 2004. "The Swarm that Moved a Legislature Buzzes Still." *St. Petersburg Times*, 20 February.

Miller, Carol Marbin. 2005. "Police 'Showdown' over Schiavo Averted." *Miami Herald*, 26 March.

Milligan, Susan. 2004. "Senate Surprise: Democrats Pulling Ahead in Close Races." *Boston Globe*, 11 April.

Patton, Charlie. 2004. "Swipes Begin to Sting for McCollum and Martinez." *Florida Times-Union*, 31 August.

Ruth, Daniel. 2003. "The Schiavo Case: So Much for Legislating with Dignity." *Tampa Tribune*, 26 October.

Salinero, Mike. 2003. "Faith-Based Initiative Clears Committee." *Tampa Tribune*, 19 March.

Troxler, Howard. 2004. "GOP Primary Escalates into Ugly, In-Party Squabbling." *St. Petersburg Times*, 29 August.

Wald, Kenneth D., and Richard K. Scher. 2003. "'A Necessary Annoyance?': The Christian Right and the Development of Republican Party Politics in Florida." In *The Christian Right in American Politics: Marching to the Millennium*, ed. John Green, Mark J. Rozell, and Clyde. Wilcox. Washington, D.C.: Georgetown University Press, 79–100.

Wald, Kenneth D., Maureen Tartaglione, and Richard K. Scher. 2000. "Answered Prayers and Mixed Blessings: The Christian Right in Florida." In *Prayers in the Precincts: The Christian Right in the 1998 Elections*, ed. John C. Green, Mark J. Rozell, and Clyde Wilcox. Washington, D.C.: Georgetown University Press, 115–44.

Wallsten, Peter. 2003. "Decision Could Aid GOP at the Polls." *Miami Herald*, 22 October.

Wand, Kenneth W. Shotts, Jasjeet S. Sekhon, Walter R. Mebane Jr., Michael C. Herron, and Henry E. Brady. 2001. "The Butterfly Did It: The Aberrant Vote for Buchanan in Palm Beach County, Florida." *American Political Science Review* 95:793–810.

CHAPTER NINE

Colorado

An Uphill Climb

CARIN LARSON

WHEN COLORADO'S U.S. SENATOR BEN NIGHTHORSE CAMPBELL (R) announced that he would not seek another term in 2004, two wings of the Republican party rallied behind two different candidates to replace him. On paper, the two candidates had many similarities of great importance to the Christian Right. Both were prolife conservative Catholics who supported the Federal Marriage Amendment, which defined marriage as a union between a man and a woman. Yet Christian conservatives in Colorado were enthusiastic about one and fearful of the other. Republican Congressman Bob Schaeffer easily attracted local evangelical groups with his record in the U.S. House supporting such issues. In contrast, the only association conservative Christians had with Pete Coors was his family's beer company.

In many ways, the race between Schaeffer and Coors embodies the tension within the Republican party ever since the Christian Right originated. Sometimes these factions work together successfully, as in President Bush's 2004 reelection bid in Colorado. On other occasions, such as in the Colorado Senate race, bitter infighting occurs. Coors won the primary, and Christian conservatives showed little enthusiasm for his general election campaign, which he lost to the Democrat Ken Salazar. After the election, there was some speculation that this infighting might have cost the Republican Party not only the Senate seat but control of the state legislature as well. A careful look at the election results suggests that there is some truth to that claim, although other factors probably were involved. In any event, the 2004 election in Colorado is a warning to Republican and Christian Right activists alike.

I begin this chapter by reviewing the political history of Colorado and the unique social landscape that makes cooperation between moderate and conservative Republicans particularly difficult. I then move to a discussion of the Christian Right and the perception of the city of Colorado Springs as home to the fundamentalist wing of the Republican party. After examining the more prominent Christian Right organizations in the state, I turn my attention to the 2004 Senate race, which provides a window into the influence of evangelical voters in Colorado politics. The challenges faced by the Christian Right in Colorado have implications for the success of the movement nationally, as well as for the future makeup of the Republican party.

Colorado's Political Landscape

The disappointing results of the 2004 election for Colorado Republicans are not simply a reflection of their relationship with the Christian Right at a single point in time. The divide between moderates and conservatives within the Republican party reflects, in part, a geographical division in the state. Although there are fundamental ideological differences between moderates and conservatives, there are other factors in Colorado's landscape that make cooperation between the two groups even more difficult.

Colorado Springs, which is located in the central region of the state, is widely recognized as a hotbed of social conservatism. The city is home to more than 100 Christian ministries, and many of its residents belong to one of the 162 evangelical Protestant churches within the city limits.[1] The list of ministries includes Focus on the Family—headed by James Dobson, who has come to be a significant figure in the national Christian Right movement. Focus on the Family has a $122 million budget and more than 1,300 employees; it broadcasts Dobson's radio program on 3,500 stations across the United States (Farrell and Mulkern 2005). Focus on the Family is regarded as a magnet for other Christian groups, providing a haven for cooperation among several different ministries.

The headquarters of the National Association of Evangelicals also is in Colorado Springs, although most of its political work takes place at the federal level out of its office in Washington, D.C. Several Christian college ministries are headquartered in the city—such as Campus Crusade and Navigators, which conduct outreach on secular campuses. Finally, mission organizations such as Compassion International and the International Bible Society make their homes in Colorado Springs as well. Both direct their attention to needs and mission-based issues abroad.

Why have so many Christian organizations made their way to Colorado, and to Colorado Springs specifically? The migration seems to have begun in the 1980s when Focus on the Family, the largest ministry functioning out of the area, moved its offices from California to Colorado. Perhaps the migration has something to do with the beautiful landscape, which for many Christians is spiritually inspirational.

Given the makeup of the city, the fact that Republicans win by large margins in the districts in and around Colorado Springs is unsurprising. Republican state representatives in this area are known to win with 75 percent of the vote.

Just sixty miles north, however, is a different story. According to Sharon Johnson of the Focus on the Family state affiliate, the Rocky Mountain Family Council (RMFC), "Pro-life Republicans in Denver County could get in one phone booth" (interview with author, 14 March 2005). The Denver metropolitan area is a hub of economic activity. It has a large telecommunications industry and a large blue-collar population. In general, the relatively few Republicans here value fiscal restraint and states' rights and care less about the social issues that are of primary concern in Colorado Springs. Most Denver residents are social liberals; they are exposed to greater religious and cultural diversity because Denver has a larger minority population than Colorado Springs. Republican candidates are likely to lose big in Denver.

Enter a Christian Right composed mostly of evangelicals from the Colorado Springs community, who must learn to work with Republicans from the Denver metro area—the state capital and home to the Colorado GOP headquarters. Although Colorado also includes distinct regions such as the Eastern Plains; the western slope, which is full of ski resorts; and southern Colorado, the Denver–Colorado Springs corridor is where the majority of the state's population resides. Consequently, there is a cultural barrier that makes penetrating the state capital in Denver difficult for cultural conservatives. Christian conservatives are somewhat isolated, which might explain in part why their influence is limited. Moreover, the demographics of Colorado Springs are such that Republican candidates and conservative interest groups are rarely seriously challenged and therefore are not forced to develop skills of compromise and strategic bargaining apart from their work in Denver.

Looking beyond the Republicans' intraparty squabbling, we find a teeter-totter political identity within the state as a whole. Jim Chapman, executive director of the Rocky Mountain Family Council, calls Colorado a "Prozac state" because of its history of seemingly temperamental political shifts and the diversity within its borders (interview with author, 20 April 2005). The same state that is home to more than 100 Christian ministries is home to the nation's fourth-largest gay and lesbian population. Many social liberals reside in Boulder—a university town that hosts Naropa University, which is built on the Buddhist tradition. Ethnically the state is very diverse, with an increasing Hispanic community and a large Native American population. Most residents are transplants who have moved to Colorado for its mountainous landscape and mild climate. "They come to recreate and procreate," says Chapman. Consequently, unlike its neighbors Utah or Kansas, Colorado is not a "red" state. In 2004 commentators classified it as purple.

During the 1970s Colorado leaned left. Democratic strongholds such as Denver and Boulder received an influx of migrants from California, who came to Colorado to find open space to settle and preserve. As a result, Democrats consistently were elected to the governor's seat, and the party controlled a large percentage of the seats in the state legislature. In recent years, however, Democrats have not fared as well. The 1990s brought several new industries to the state, along with the ballooning numbers of Christian ministries headquartered in Colorado Springs. The last time the state voted for a Democratic presidential candidate was in 1992, when it supported Bill Clinton. The state was one of three that flipped from "blue" to "red" in 1996, supporting Republican candidate Bob Dole over the Democratic incumbent. In 1998 Bill Owens became the first Republican governor the state had seen in a few decades.

In the 2000 presidential race, Colorado was placed comfortably in the Republican column; indeed, the conservative parts of the state beat out the more liberal parts on Election Day. Denver voted 62 percent to 31 percent for Al Gore over George W. Bush and Boulder County supported Gore over Bush by 50 percent to 36 percent; by contrast, Colorado Springs's El Paso County voted for Bush over Gore by 64 percent to 31 percent, and nearby Douglas County supported Bush over Gore by 65 percent to 31 percent.[2] Although the state has leaned Republican in recent years, in 2004 the state was considered a "swing" state. The state's economy was faltering and had a larger Hispanic population than in years past, and the election was up for grabs.

Moreover, even though registered Republicans outnumber Democrats by 180,000, a large percentage of Republicans are classic libertarians. Accentuating the moderate–conservative divide in the Republican Party, the libertarian crowd takes particular issue with Christian Right policy that restricts individual rights, such as a ban on gay marriage or restrictions on abortion. According to Robert Zwier, "Colorado is home to a rugged individualism and an antigovernment ethos not particularly rooted in religious perspectives" (Zwier 2003, 192). Christian Right groups are aware of the libertarian strain in Colorado, and some appear to take that factor into consideration. According to Chapman, many Christian Right policies could be interpreted as intolerant or bigoted if evangelicals do not present them effectively. "Social conservatives have to be shrewd," he said. Chapman's comment suggests a political sophistication on the part of the Christian Right in Colorado to get along and work strategically amid grave diversity. In other instances, however, infighting between conservatives and moderates causes great rifts within the party. Christian conservatives actually campaigned against two moderate Republican candidates during the general election, specifically over the issue of school vouchers. The Parents Alliance for Choice in Education (PACE) of Colorado sent flyers to voters criticizing the Republican candidates; the ad stated that in opposing school vouchers, the candidates "[refused] to put children first." One target of these efforts was state Rep. Ramey Johnson (R), who ended up losing her seat to the Democratic challenger (a candidate who also opposed school vouchers) by forty-one votes. PACE does not claim responsibility for Johnson's loss, saying that Johnson herself jeopardized her seat when she voted against a school choice bill in the previous session of the state legislature (Bartels 2004). From a political strategy standpoint, however, PACE appears to have put its immediate commitment to school vouchers before a long-term look at the benefits of a Republican-controlled state legislature that might be more supportive of its agenda. Nor did PACE, which comprises mostly Christian conservatives, produce a third-party candidate who might have backed its policy preference. In this instance, then, Christian conservatives appeared to be so adamant about their support of the school choice initiative that they wanted to punish members of their own party, with no regard to the danger it posed to their own agenda down the road. After her loss, Johnson said that the Republican party in Colorado is participating in a "circular firing squad" (Bartels 2004). Indeed, the party suffered many casualties in 2004. Ultimately it lost control of both houses in the state legislature, in addition to Campbell's seat in the U.S. Senate.

In this case, we see little in terms of political bargaining and compromise and instead find amateurish behavior, politically speaking. Taken together, there is a diverse set of approaches among the Christian Right, and the absence of a united front could partly explain their losses in the 2004 election.

The Colorado Christian Right

Many observers assume that with so many Christian ministries in one location, the Christian Right of Colorado is an influential political player in the state. This perception is reinforced by media accounts that depict Colorado Springs as entirely evangelical Christian. According to *Harper's* magazine, for example, Colorado Springs is "home to the greatest concentration of fundamentalist Christian activist groups in American History" (Sharlet 2005, 41). In a study of Christian Right influence in state Republican parties in 2000, Conger and Green (2002) find the Christian Right in Colorado to be very influential.[3] According to their results, Christian Right activism in Colorado resembles movement activism in Virginia and Alabama. Because this research was based solely on perceptions of strength by political elites, the findings are debatable. A GOP official might say Christian groups are largely influential in the state because he or she perceives them as a threat. In 2004 the Christian Right targeted moderate candidates and arguably contributed to their loss—causing harm to the Republican Party. There is some anecdotal evidence to suggest the Christian Right in Colorado is an influential political player. There also is an equal amount of anecdotal evidence to suggest the opposite.

The Christian Right is hardly preaching to the choir in its advocacy efforts. There is great diversity within Colorado; many residents and groups oppose the movement's socially conservative agenda. Another limitation on the Christian Right is that there appears to be little coordination between politically active conservative groups. This lack of coordination prevents them from producing a united front in negotiating with the Republican party.

Furthermore, the nature of Christian organizations in the state explains the lack of political force one might expect. Many of the organizations in Colorado Springs are not politically oriented in any way; they are mission-based organizations that are committed to preaching the gospel, apart from any political messages. Examples include organizations such as Campus Crusade for Christ or Compassion International. Campus Crusade's outreach is specific to college campuses nationwide; it provides fellowship circles for Christian students on secular campuses. Compassion International seeks to provide financial and spiritual support to poor children overseas by linking them with a sponsor in the United States. Although the employees within these organizations are mostly conservative Christians and thus potential Christian Right members, they are not necessarily active in the movement. Organizational membership in these cases is not the same as being part of the Christian Right.

In addition, Christian Right groups in the state that are politically motivated focus primarily on races and issues on the national agenda. For example, although Focus on the Family emerged as a major player in the 2004 election season, it was minimally involved in its home state of Colorado. Focus on the Family was one of the primary sponsors (along with the

Family Research Council) of ivotevalues.org—a voter registration drive that conducted outreach primarily in evangelical churches. The packet of materials given to church liaisons recruited by Focus on the Family included a ten-step churchwide voter registration strategy, outlining how church members can form committees to register fellow congregants. The ivotevalues.org campaign also included special outreach to pastors on how to preach on Sundays leading up to the election. Focus on the Family and the Family Research Council distributed sermon outlines to all their state affiliates in the weeks leading up to the November election. Because Focus on the Family has its headquarters in Colorado, one would imagine that it would take a special interest in Colorado politics. Yet that is true in only a handful of cases; moreover, most of its local involvement is dictated by issues facing the state legislature. Focus on the Family had little involvement in the 2004 election in Colorado—especially after Schaeffer, whom Dobson (as a private citizen) endorsed, lost the primary to Pete Coors.

Thus, even though there is a large constituency of Christian conservatives in the state, Christian Right state affiliates must rally the troops at the time of an election. Two state Christian Right groups are most prominent: Focus on the Family's Rocky Mountain Family Council and the Christian Coalition of Colorado (CCCO). Concerned Women for America, another prominent Christian Right group nationally, does not have a state director in place currently but has been active in Colorado politics in the past.

The RMFC is the state affiliate to Focus on the Family and the Family Research Council. The RMFC is an educational and advocacy group that seeks to inform citizens on issues concerning the traditional family, abortion, marriage, and education and then hopes they will vote accordingly. Begun in 1991, the group has an annual budget of $300,000 and employs three staff members. As an affiliate of Focus on the Family, the group sometimes is the recipient of criticism leveled at Dobson's actions on the national scale. For example, the RMFC hosted a lobbying day at the state legislature in March 2005 and was greeted by protestors dressed in SpongeBob SquarePants costumes. The protestors were responding to claims Dobson had made a few months before the event that an educational video to be shown in schools starring SpongeBob was endorsing homosexuality. The RMFC's link with its parent organization is difficult to ignore in Colorado because Focus on the Family has a national reputation. Drivers in Colorado are likely to see bumper stickers that say, "Focus on Your Own Damn Family"—a reflection of the frustration many residents have with Focus on the Family's agenda to define the traditional family structure.

For the most part, the RMFC functions independently from Focus on the Family headquarters and spends its time at the state legislature.

The RMFC offices are located right outside of Denver, with easy access to the state legislature—and thus at a greater distance from Focus on the Family headquarters in Colorado Springs. In 2003 the RMFC distributed 2,500 informational packets to pastors and churches across the state urging them to reject Amendment 33, which would have allowed video gaming at five Front Range racetracks. Other recent legislative successes for the group include a joint resolution passed by the state legislature that states its support for the Federal Marriage Amendment that would define marriage as between a man and a woman. Also in 2004, the legislature passed a bill that would require schools to notify parents and allow students to be excused when human sexuality is discussed in the classroom. As a 501(c)3 organization, the RMFC cannot endorse specific candidates, but it does participate in get-out-the-vote drives at churches and evangelical groups in the state. The RMFC makes little effort to coordinate its efforts with the Republican Party. "We try to remain distinct from the GOP," said Sharon Johnson, the group's legislative director.

The CCCO—the state affiliate of the national organization—is the other Christian conservative player in Colorado politics. Although the national organization is largely defunct, the organization in Colorado remains active, albeit with a loose infrastructure. The CCCO has no official office space and no full-time employees. Instead, it consists largely of the efforts of a few energetic individuals. For example, CCCO president Chuck Gosnell has been a vocal advocate of the traditional family structure and prolife policy. He was particularly outspoken over a custody battle between a lesbian and a former lesbian in 2004. A Colorado judge ruled that the women would share custody but that the former lesbian, who had converted to Christianity, could not expose the daughter to anything considered to be "homophobic" as part of her religious upbringing. Gosnell was quoted in media reports as saying that the judge's ruling ultimately recognized gay divorce (which necessarily implies gay marriage) and that the CCCO would work to impeach the judge. Nothing ever came of the impeachment efforts, however, and the judge's decision was upheld by a Colorado Court of Appeals.

Even with no full-time staff, the CCCO claims to maintain a network of 30,000 supporters, with varying degrees of involvement. Most CCCO members are in El Paso and Douglas counties, which includes Colorado Springs. In 2004 the organization sent out 400,000 voter guides, according to its own records. The CCCO is less concerned about remaining distinct from the GOP than is the RMFC; the CCCO has worked to send delegates to the Republican Party's state convention who would be friendly to the Christian Right agenda. Part of the CCCO's agenda is to try to control the party from the inside out. The group's efforts to maneuver within the party might be a cause of the great division I note at the beginning of this chapter. According to Scott Russell, political director of the Colorado Republican Party, "There is a sense among Republicans that a conservative wing of the Republican Party is trying to kick out anybody who is not a social conservative" (interview with author, 6 April 2005). Thus, one can assume that the CCCO is not being received warmly by moderate Republicans who feel threatened by its presence.

In sum, Christian Right activity in the 2004 election was largely a result of these two organizations. Because there was little coordination between the two, ascertaining their overall impact is difficult. Although the two groups agree on policy positions, the RMFC makes a concerted effort to shape legislation at the state level apart from party politics. Meanwhile, the CCCO works with the Republican party and takes a more active role in elections. As I discuss below, the RMFC and the CCCO used very different tactics with regard to their involvement in the U.S. Senate race.

This situation is a far cry from previous Christian Right activity in Colorado, which assembled a much broader and more powerful coalition. In 1992, for example, Christian conservative groups wrote and mobilized supporters of Amendment 2, which sought to repeal local bans on discrimination on the basis of sexual orientation in Denver, Boulder, and Aspen. Christian groups perceived these local ordinances as part of the "homosexual agenda," granting special rights to gays and lesbians. Christian activists within the state banded together to form a new group, Colorado for Family Values (CFV), that was created specifically to pass Amendment 2. Individuals from national organizations such as the Traditional Values Coalition, Focus on the Family, the Eagle Forum, and Concerned Women for America sat on the group's board and advised leaders about political strategy. Amendment 2 was written by Christian activists, and enough Colorado residents signed petitions to put it on the 1992 ballot. Colorado allows for ballot initiatives to be placed there by the citizens without approval from the legislature. By a 53 percent to 47 percent margin, Colorado voters passed Amendment 2.

Although the amendment never went into effect—it was challenged all the way to the U.S. Supreme Court, where in May 1996 it was overturned on the basis of the Fourteenth Amendment to the U.S. Constitution— the 1992 coalition stands in stark contrast to the Christian Right groups in 2004. Colorado for Family Values no longer exists, and the RMFC and CCCO are separate entities that experience great challenges to their agenda in such a diverse state. There clearly is a population of conservative Christians that have the potential to be energized, but the Christian Right lacks a significant infrastructure to do so. Moreover, most residents of Colorado—Christian conservatives and their counterparts alike—have a deep love for the outdoors. Chapman suspects that orientation makes Christian Right recruitment efforts even more difficult. He believes Coloradans simply do not desire to be politically active even when they believe an issue is important. "A rally for marriage with thousands in attendance is just not going to happen in Colorado," said Chapman.

Although Colorado did not have a ban on gay marriage ballot initiative in 2004, Focus on the Family, the national organization that was heavily involved in the bans of same-sex marriage in 2004, has said Colorado is on the list for the 2006 election. The group is likely to seek to create an infrastructure comparable to that for Amendment 2. The *potential* for the mobilization of Christian conservatives probably is what leads to the perception of the movement's strength and influence. Little appears to have changed since Zwier's assessment of Colorado in 2003: "The Christian Right has a seat at the Republican table but has not yet been able to set the table's agenda" (Zwier 2003, 192).

The Christian Right and the 2004 Colorado Senate Race

The Republican Senate primary between Pete Coors and Bob Schaeffer and the subsequent general election race between Coors and Democrat Ken Salazar provide a unique opportunity to assess the Christian Right's influence in the 2004 election. If Christian conservatives are vital to the Republican party's success, a close race such as this is likely to illuminate that fact. According to Sharon Johnson of the RMFC, Coors's win over Schaeffer in the primary made rallying Christian conservatives in the general election even more difficult for the Republican party. Although the candidates held similar positions on policy, they were not equal in the eyes of the Christian Right. The primary drew a line in the sand between the Christian Right and the Republican party that would affect elections across the state in 2004—and perhaps in years to come. Competition between moderates and conservatives reflects the battle within Republican politics in general. According to columnist E. J. Dionne (2004), Coors represented the market values of the Republican Party; he is a businessman who shows women in bikinis in a beer commercial to sell the product. On the other hand, Schaeffer represented family values that would trump economic prosperity if it had to. Dionne asserts, "The Coors-Schaffer primary went to the heart of the core contradiction in American conservatism"—in this case pitting family values against economics.

Whether one agrees with the foregoing classification of the two candidates and their values or not, Christian Right groups clearly saw them in this light. Indeed, Schaeffer was a social conservative. He served three terms in the U.S. House of Representatives, after previously serving as a state senator in Colorado. During his time in office, Schaeffer became a friend of Christian Right groups. Speaking as a private citizen, James Dobson endorsed Schaeffer for the U.S. Senate. So did Gary Bauer, Phyllis Schlafly, and Michael Farris—all Christian Right leaders at the national level. Schaeffer was consistent in his policy positions on restricting abortion and gay rights—positions that were favorable to the Christian Right's agenda.

Coors agreed with Schaeffer on many, if not all, issues of importance to the Christian Right. He repeatedly emphasized his prolife position and his opposition to gay marriage. However, policies enacted at Coors Beer Company seemed to conflict with Coors's platform. "The Christian community wants you to walk the talk," said Johnson. "They are not going to separate Coors from Coors Beer Company, nor should they." The CCCO—which was more politically aggressive than the RMFC, at least in the context of the campaign—is credited with discovering during the primary that the company's health plan covered abortions for employees (Florio 2004c). Coors changed the policy shortly thereafter. Perhaps even more damaging, the company was one of the first in the nation to grant benefits to same-sex couples. Pete Coors himself happened to be the company representative who began an outreach to the gay community in San Francisco in the 1970s. His campaign's handling of the homosexuality issue never fully satisfied Christian conservatives.

One debate with Salazar on the NBC's *Meet the Press* (October 10, 2005) was particularly damaging. When Coors was asked about his company's position on homosexuality, he described the policies as good business, separate from politics. Media outlets gave the issue a great deal of attention. Coors was quoted in the *Rocky Mountain News* defending the company's policies by saying, "The employees in that (gay) community are hardworking, good and loyal. We felt we had the ability to extend benefits to them" (Florio 2004a). A few months later, the newspaper reported that "Pete Coors' company will be among the sponsors of the Black & Blue 2004 Festival in Montreal, a weeklong gay benefit that attracts up to 80,000 people to events such as the Leather Rail, Raunch Fetish Night and a male nude revue. . . . Coors Light is one of two free beers that will be served at the official launch cocktail party" (Florio 2004b).

Coors's response to these questions did not satisfy social conservatives, to say the least. During the primary, Schaeffer pointed out the inconsistencies in Coors's positions relative to his company's. Christian Right groups helped Schaeffer do this. In a memo to the Colorado Friends of the Campaign for Working Families, Gary Bauer endorsed Schaeffer, saying the following after the U.S. Senate did not vote to bring the marriage amendment up for debate: "Maybe it's not fair to judge Pete Coors by the actions of his company and company he keeps. But after yesterday's Senate vote against the marriage amendment, I'm not willing to take any chances. Are you?" Meanwhile, Schaeffer's supporters within the state painted Coors as someone who would promote a "radical homosexual agenda." One mailing that was paid for and distributed by the CCCO pictured a drag queen showing off his naked buttocks and holding a six-pack of Coors Light. The group also sent a flier to more than 100,000 residents that criticized Coors for running "one of the most gay-friendly companies in the nation" (Couch 2004a).

The Colorado Republican Party's backing of Coors is a mystery at first glance. According to Scott Russell, the Colorado GOP's political director, Schaeffer had the majority of support from Colorado party activists and won the state convention with more than 60 percent of the vote from delegates. Seeds of doubt came after party leaders looked at Salazar's fundraising. Russell said, "It is my perception that while Bob Schaeffer's conservative political philosophy is in line with the vast majority of Republicans in Colorado, most did not think that he had any chance against Salazar, and a race that Coors lost by 100k, would have been lost by twice that much if Schaeffer was running." Schaeffer and Coors were in a dead heat throughout most of the primary. Coors loaned $1.45 million of his own money to the campaign—not a trivial amount but not much given his net worth of more than $10 million (Couch 2004b).

Ultimately, by most activists' accounts the party's decision to back Coors was a strategic decision. Party leaders assumed that Coors would enjoy free advertising in the form of a beer can; in hindsight, this advertising helped Salazar more than Coors. Initially Colorado Governor Bill Owens said he would support Schaeffer; after reported conversations with Republican elites in Washington, D.C., however, Owens came out in favor of Coors—on the day he was supposed to appear side-by-side with Schaeffer. Many perceived Owens' flip-flopping as evidence of his aspirations for a position in Washington. The move harmed his standing with conservative circles, according to RMFC staff members. Coors also was endorsed by retiring Senator Ben Nighthorse-Campbell, a moderate Republican who had switched parties (from Democrat to Republican) while in office. Coors won the primary handily—a surprise to most analysts—but not by winning over Christian conservative groups. He received 66 percent of the vote in Denver County but only 56 percent of the vote from El Paso County, where Colorado Springs is located. He received 61 percent statewide.

The Republican Rift and the General Election

Following the primary, the Christian Right was hesitant, to say the least, about supporting Coors. "He would have voted correctly, we just couldn't get excited about him," said Peter Brandt, director of public policy at Focus on the Family (interview with author, 30 December 2004). Brandt noted the lack of enthusiasm he observed across evangelical groups in Colorado: "He did not do a good job of exciting our folks." At one point Coors made what has been described as a "pilgrimage" to ask Dobson for his support. Although the details of that meeting are unknown, Coors apparently did not win Dobson over. Although Dobson was featured in National Republican Senatorial Committee advertisements for Republicans in tight Senate races such as Tom Coburn's in Oklahoma and John Thune's in South Dakota, he did little for Coors.

Other Christian groups appeared open to granting Coors their support if he was willing to reach out to them. After the *Meet the Press* debate with Salazar, the CCCO invited Coors to speak before its members to clarify his position on gay marriage and policy favoring homosexuals. Coors declined the invitation. Although a few CCCO leaders nonetheless campaigned for Coors as individuals, the organization had a hard time mobilizing its members.

The RMFC reacted similarly. According to Sharon Johnson, it was easy for Schaeffer's supporters to feel abandoned by the Republican party. Personally, Johnson was offended by the Coors beer commercials that featured twins in bikinis and a variety of sexual innuendos. What bothered conservatives was not so much the alcoholic beverage he was selling as how he tried to sell it. Chapman also noted the beer commercials and had a difficult time ignoring them when he found himself in the voting booth. Ultimately, however, Johnson said she had no trouble voting for Coors: "I think he would have been far better for evangelical values and for appointing judges." Johnson did not think all evangelicals would agree with her, however: "There were a lot of evangelicals who didn't think through the long-term benefits."

Another issue that dissuaded evangelicals—and other voters—from supporting Coors was his support for lowering the drinking age to eighteen. Although Coors defended his position by using a philosophical argument in favor of states' rights, that position nonetheless resonated with citizens' fears already in place over Coors's company and its economic incentives. For example, Johnson said that she knew a local firefighter who voted for Bush for president but voted for Salazar for Senate simply because he had seen eighteen-year-old victims of drunk driving.

Even with Bob Schaeffer repeatedly saying after the primary that not voting for Pete Coors was a vote for Ken Salazar, the Christian Right in Colorado appeared to take little action to mobilize evangelicals for the Republican nominee. Conservatives across the state appeared to be so disenchanted with the party that they campaigned against the Republican candidate in several cases (e.g., state Rep. Johnson). Sometimes moderate

Republicans could not support a conservative candidate. In the Third Congressional District, a conservative won the party's five-way nomination but then could not garner enough support from moderate Republicans to win the general election.

Anecdotally at least, antagonism between Republicans and the Christian Right appears to have contributed to a Democratic victory in the Senate race. If evangelicals sat out the Senate race or voted for Salazar, one can fairly say that the lack of mobilization by the Christian Right cost Coors and the Republican party the seat. Yet there were factors apart from Coors's inability to enthuse Christian conservatives that went wrong. Coors was not a strong campaigner. He was criticized for being too philosophical in his talks before large crowds. He never mastered the art of the stump speech. During a nationally televised debate he said North Dakota when he meant to say North Korea. Hence, Coors simply may have been a poor candidate, and that is why he lost the seat.

The Democrats easily capitalized on Coors's weakness. Colorado Democrats in 2004 were especially effective in making the most of Coors's wanting to lower the drinking age to eighteen. One 527 group, Citizens for a Strong Senate, ran a particularly damaging television ad in the weeks leading up to the election; the ad showed a series of mangled cars as the announcer said, "As far as Pete Coors is concerned, it doesn't matter if it's bad for kids, as long as it's really good for business."

Money also played a huge role in the Colorado Senate race. Together the two candidates spent $16 million, making the race the most expensive in Colorado history. Salazar outspent Coors by $1 million. Republicans also were hit hard by 527 groups that supported Salazar, including the Alliance of Colorado Families, the Coalition for a Better Colorado, the Alliance for a Better Colorado, and Forward Colorado. If the Republican party chose Coors on the basis of his financial capabilities, those hopes went unrealized.

Another factor that one should not ignore is Salazar's campaign, which was particularly effective. First, Salazar had name recognition. As the attorney general of Colorado, he was the only Democrat to win statewide office in Colorado since 1994. He is a fifth-generation Coloradan with deep roots in the San Luis Valley. He has been a farmer, a small business owner, and a natural resources lawyer over the course of his career. Portraying him as a native son of Colorado in campaign ads required little effort; commercials showed him driving around the state in a pickup truck, wearing a cowboy hat. He was portrayed as a man of the people, in contrast to Coors the beer tycoon. As a Catholic and Hispanic, Salazar also had unique appeal to a large segment of the Colorado population. Since 1990 the state's Hispanic population has grown by 70 percent; in 2004 it accounted for 17 percent of Colorado's overall population. According to exit polls, 79 percent of

Hispanics voted for Salazar, and 82 percent of Hispanic Catholics voted for him. Slightly fewer—73 percent—voted for John Kerry for president. With the increasing number of Hispanics in the state, we should not be surprised that Democrats sensed the tide turning in 2004. They spent $7 million on state legislature races—twice the amount Republicans spent. Overall, Democrats gained seven seats in the state House and one in the state Senate.

The Religious Vote in 2004

Despite anecdotal claims that Pete Coors lost because he was unable to rally Christian conservatives, there appears to be a demographic and perhaps financial explanation for why Democrats might have had the edge. With Hispanics emerging as a solid bloc, Democrats running for statewide office now had a base to which they could appeal. Moreover, there apparently were many more Democratic 527s active in the state than similar Republican groups. To reexamine the suggestion that the absence of Christian conservatives cost Coors the race, I examine the National Election Pool exit polls data from the 2004 election to see if evangelicals voted for Coors and compare their behavior against other religious traditions. I use the percentage of votes for President Bush as a baseline. Because Bush apparently had greater appeal in the state—he beat john Kerry by 5 points—I suggest that this figure represents the potential constituency that Coors could have tapped into for the Senate race.

As table 9.1 illustrates, evangelicals voted overwhelmingly for Coors— more than any other religious tradition—despite the lack of mobilization efforts on the part of Christian Right groups; however, not as many evangelicals voted for Coors as they did for Bush.[4] Seventy-eight percent of evangelical Protestant voters supported Coors in the general election, whereas 85 percent of evangelicals voted for Bush. This gap raises the possibility that there were more evangelical Protestant voters available to Coors—or whoever the Republican candidate for Senate was—who simply were not tapped in 2004. If Coors had had greater appeal to these Christian conservatives and received 85 percent of the evangelical Protestant vote, would he have beaten Salazar? In other words, could Schaeffer—a Christian Right candidate with a greater chance of receiving 85 percent of the evangelical Protestant vote—have beaten Salazar? Keeping all other votes constant, I manipulate the data to examine the outcome of the Senate race with Coors receiving 85 percent of the evangelical vote. Interestingly enough, if most of the additional evangelical voters given to Coors in this hypothetical scenario were subtracted from the Salazar column, the result indeed would have been within a fraction of a point of Coors coming out

Table 9.1   Coors and Bush Vote by Religious
Tradition, Colorado (%)

Religion	Coors	Bush
Evangelical Protestant	78	85
Mainline Protestant	44	50
Hispanic Protestant	37	47
Black Protestant	14	14
Catholic	54	59
Hispanic Catholic	21	25
Mormon	75	82
Other Christian	53	70
Jewish	27	24
Other faiths	36	36
Unaffiliated	23	25

Source: National Election Pool exit polls, conducted by Edison Media Research/Mitofsky International 2004.
$N = 2,585$.

on top, assuming no percentage of error. Of course, Coors did not accomplish this vote percentage among evangelicals. Schaeffer, however, with
the enthusiasm from the Christian Right community, could have received
85 percent of the evangelical vote. Thus, there is a slight chance that the
Republicans could have saved the seat if they had nominated Schaeffer.

To examine this possibility further, I restrict my analysis to Bush voters and take particular notice of the vote pattern for evangelicals who did
not vote for Coors. I examine whether there were enough evangelicals who
voted for Salazar that a Schaeffer candidacy could have stolen.

As table 9.2 shows, 8 percent of evangelical Bush voters voted for Salazar, and only a few refrained from voting altogether. There is barely a large
enough pool for Schaeffer to have dipped into to retrieve evangelical votes
from Salazar, but it is possible. This outcome would have required Schaeffer
to stop all Republican "defectors" in their tracks, leaving Salazar with no
support among evangelical Bush supporters. Yet the percentage of Republican "defectors" is even larger outside the evangelical category. Collectively,
13 percent of nonevangelicals who voted for Bush did not vote for Coors;
11 percent of Catholic Bush voters and 15 of mainline Protestant Bush voters
chose Salazar. These numbers suggest that Salazar had at least some appeal
among Republican-leaning voters, and it is difficult to imagine that this
would not be true for the evangelical population as well.

The results suggest that there is a *slight* possibility that Schaeffer could
have beaten Salazar—and that the evangelical vote made the difference
in the Senate race. That hypothetical scenario, however, rests on several

Table 9.2   Bush Voters and Senate Vote by Religious Tradition, Colorado (%)

Religious Tradition	*Coors*	*Salazar*	*Did not vote*	*Other*
Evangelical Bush voters	89	8	2	1
Mainline Protestant Bush voters	83	15	—	1
Catholic Bush voters	87	11	1	1
All other nonevangelical Bush voters	84	13	1	2

Source: National Election Pool exit polls, conducted by Edison Media Research/Mitofsky International 2004.
$N = 2,585$.

assumptions that make the finding inconclusive at best. First, libertarians who supported Coors might not have supported Schaeffer. Schaeffer may have had too many ties to the Christian Right for some voters to find him attractive. So although he may have had a larger percentage of the evangelical vote than Coors, he probably would have lost votes from libertarians or perhaps other religious minorities that would have feared his association with the Christian Right. Second, the alternate outcome also depends on the assumption that virtually all evangelicals who voted for Bush and did not vote for Coors chose instead to vote for Salazar. To have beaten Salazar, Schaeffer would have needed to pull voters away from Salazar rather than simply appealing to nonvoters.

The data do not conclusively demonstrate that Schaeffer could have saved the Republican seat. According to the exit polls, 56 percent of Independents voted for Salazar, compared to 40 percent for Coors. Ten percent of Republicans voted for Salazar, and 4 percent of Democrats voted for Coors. Clearly Salazar had an edge, especially among Independents, that contributed to his victory, apart from the infighting in the Republican party. The data do suggest that there was room for improvement among evangelicals and that their votes mattered in the race. The data suggest that Schaeffer might have been a more competitive candidate. There is at least some possibility that Christian conservatives shot themselves in the foot by not supporting Coors. At the very least, their support for Coors could have made the race incredibly close.

Conclusion

The Christian Right faced an uphill climb in the 2004 election. Although there is a large constituency of evangelical Protestants in Colorado

Springs, the state organizations have not yet fully integrated them into the Christian Right movement or the Republican Party. Moreover, evangelical groups do not have a united front. RMFC staff members say they disagree with the CCCO's tactics during elections (possibly referring to the ad placed by the CCCO depicting Coors as a drag queen). Moreover, after 2004 moderate Republicans will be even less inclined to welcome Christian conservatives into the party after being threatened by them in several state House races. Rhetorically, at least, many moderates are still blaming evangelicals for Coors's loss as well. For their part, conservatives blame moderates for not putting Schaeffer on the ballot in the first place. The Bush campaign seemed to successfully bridge the division, or at least avoided igniting the fault lines.

Nonetheless, Republican success in the future is likely to hinge on the ability of conservatives and moderates to get along. Key to these efforts will be candidates that can address the agendas of both camps. Schaeffer appeared to be a candidate who could appeal to conservatives without ostracizing moderates, although his affiliation with Christian Right figures could have harmed him in that respect. He won over delegates at the state convention and did nothing to tarnish his relationship with Christian conservatives over the course of the campaign. He lacked name recognition and a war chest, however. In contrast, the Republican party may have been too presumptuous in its choice of Coors as a candidate. Party leaders assumed that name recognition would matter more than securing appeal to evangelicals in the state.

The future of the Christian Right in Colorado is unclear. If Christian groups work to secure a marriage amendment on the ballot in 2006, it will be interesting to see how Republican candidates fare that time around. With the help of Focus on the Family and other national organizations, perhaps the state will see something like the mobilization among religious groups that occurred for Amendment 2 in 1992. Colorado does appear to be a few elections away, however, from turning into a "blue" state. Democrats are correct in putting their hope in the large influx of Hispanics. In light of that fact, conservative and moderate Republicans will have to work together and appeal to independents to succeed at the voting booth.

The case of Colorado suggests that the national Christian Right movement must continue to compromise and get along with the moderate wing of the Republican party. Conservative Christians must broaden their outreach to incorporate minority groups because the Hispanic population may determine election outcomes across the country in years to come. Finally, Christian Right organizations themselves must learn to work together if they wish to have the most influence possible. In many swing states, Christian Right success at the ballot box is an uphill climb.

Notes

1. North American Religion Atlas, http://www.religionatlas.org (accessed April 15, 2005).

2. This point was made in the 2004 *Almanac of American Politics* (Barone and Cohen 2004).

3. Conger and Green (2002) replicate a study first done by Persinos (1994). Persinos put Colorado's Christian Right in the least influential grouping, along with the Christian Right in states such as North and South Dakota, Wisconsin, and New York.

4. "Evangelical" characterizes respondents who classified themselves as Protestant when asked their religious affiliation and then also answered positively to the question, "Would you describe yourself as a born-again or evangelical Christian?" The National Election Pool exit polls were conducted by Edison Media Research/Mitofsky International 2004; $N = 2,585$. The data were appropriately weighted.

References

Barone, Michael, and Richard E. Cohen. 2004. *The Almanac of American Politics.* Washington, D.C.: National Journal Group.

Bartels, Lynn. 2004. "GOP Assailed for Defeat: Jeffco Republican: Party 'Prostituted' Itself on Vouchers." *Rocky Mountain News,* 16 November; available at http://rockymountainnews.com/drmn/election/article/0,1299,DRMN_36_3331828,00.html (accessed March 30, 2005).

Brandt, Peter. 2004. Interview with author, 30 December.

Conger, Kimberly H., and John C. Green. 2002. "Spreading Out and Digging In: Christian Conservatives and State Republican Parties." *Campaigns & Elections* 23 (1): 58–65.

Couch, Mark P. 2004a. "Coors' Stance on Gays Attacked; A Mailing by the Christian Coalition Rips the GOP Senate Candidate for Gay-Friendly Policies at Coors Brewing Co." *Denver Post,* 1 August, C3.

———. 2004b. "Coors, Salazar Clash on Economy, Security; Senate Hopefuls Also Get Personal during Second Debate." *Denver Post,* 17 September, B4.

Dionne, E. J. 2004. "GOP Values—and Those Twins." *Washington Post,* 13 August, A25.

Farrell, John Aloysius, and Anne C. Mulkern. 2005. "Dobson Seen as Driven, Divisive—as Respect Rises, Worries Surface; The Evangelical Leader's Resounding Plunge into Politics Has Stirred Both Democrats and the GOP." *Denver Post,* 27 April, A1.

Florio, Gwen. 2004a. "Business Background Guide; Coors' Path to Politics." *Rocky Mountain News,* 13 July; available at www.insidedenver.com/drmn/election/article/0,1299,DRMN_36_3034875,00.htm (accessed April 25, 2005).

———. 2004b. "In Mailing, Coors Says He Shares Company's Values." *Rocky Mountain News*, 5 October; available at www.rockymountainnews.com/drmn/election/article/0,1299,DRMN_36_3230721,00.html (accessed April 24, 2005).

———. 2004c. "Salazar to Coors: Reveal Coverage on Abortions." *Rocky Mountain News*, 19 October, 8A.

Persinos, John F. 1994. "Has the Christian Right Taken Over the Republican Party?" *Campaigns and Elections* 15, no. 9:21–24.

Sharlet, Jeff. 2005. "Inside America's Most Powerful Megachurch." *Harper's Magazine* (May), 41–54.

Zwier, Robert. 2003. "The Christian Right and the Cultural Divide in Colorado." In *The Christian Right in American Politics: Marching to the Millennium*, ed. John Green, Mark J. Rozell, and Clyde Wilcox. Washington, D.C.: Georgetown University Press, 187–207.

CHAPTER TEN

Oklahoma

A Battle of Good versus Evil

SHAD B. SATTERTHWAITE

THE 2004 ELECTIONS WERE TOUTED AS THE MOST IMPORTANT IN years. Analysts predicting large voter turnouts were not disappointed when polls closed on November 2. Oklahoma was no exception. With a heated race for the U.S. Senate and a ballot loaded with salient referenda issues, voters in the Sooner State had ample reason to go to the voting booths. Churchgoing voters were reminded from the pulpit to make their voices heard. For many, casting a vote was more than a civic duty—it was a moral imperative.

Campaigning in Tulsa in August 2004, Republican U.S. Senate candidate Tom Coburn said, "This is a battle for the culture of America, and I would describe it as a battle of good versus evil (Martindale 2004)." With moral issues such as the lottery, gaming, and gay marriage on the Oklahoma ballot, many voters probably agreed. Area churches and other organizations waging a values campaign led a charge to defeat several ballot measures. Despite the rhetoric and hard campaigning, however, not all conservative positions dominated when the polls had closed and the dust finally settled.

For decades most statewide and congressional offices were held by Democrats, who also controlled both houses in the legislature. This situation has reversed in the past decade; the majority of these offices now are held by Republicans. Oklahoma clearly has seen a shift in its electorate. Results from a poll conducted by the University of Oklahoma are indicative of these changes. Respondents were asked if they considered themselves Republican or Democrat. Overall, 43 percent considered themselves Republican and 41 percent identified as Democrats. The results are interesting in comparison with actual registration statistics, which show that 51 percent of registered voters are Democratic and only 38 percent are Republican (Casteel 2000).

Oklahoma's experience is similar to that of several other southern states. Voters in the Sooner State support conservative issues and the politicians who espouse them. A 2003 poll found that 73 percent of Oklahomans would support placing a monument displaying the Ten Commandments in Oklahoma's Supreme Court building (Ellis 2003). In a 2000 poll that asked Oklahomans to name the person they admire most (Grelen 2000), Jesus of Nazareth was the clear choice (29 percent), followed by Abraham Lincoln (9 percent). A vast majority (83 percent) believe partial-birth abortions should be banned (Zizzo 2001), and Oklahoma has a law that requires schools to begin each day with a moment of silence.

Background of the Christian Right in Oklahoma Politics

Oklahoma politics have a long history of being tied to conservative causes, and religion has played an active role in influencing policy outcomes (Morgan and Meier 1980; Bednar and Hertzke 1995; Satterthwaite 2005). Conger and Green (2002) found that Oklahoma was one of five states where Christian conservatives maintained the perception of a strong influence in state Republican parties relative to their original 1994 study as well as their 2000 analysis. Oklahoma is home to several large Christian ministries, including Oral Roberts University and the Rhema Church and Bible Training Center. These ministries often encourage members of their congregations to vote, especially on moral issues. Richard Roberts, president of Oral Roberts University, referred to the 2004 election as "perhaps one of the most crucial elections in history" and urged students to register to vote in Oklahoma or vote by absentee ballot in their home states (Sherman 2004).

Nancy Bednar and Allen Hertzke (1995) note the impact of the Christian Coalition in Oklahoma. In particular, they point to the effectiveness of the signature voter guides distributed by the group during election campaigns. Before the voter guides were distributed, candidates throughout the state received a survey asking for their stance on several issues selected by the Christian Coalition. Results were tabulated, and the voter guides were printed and distributed in districts throughout the state.

The activities of the Oklahoma Christian Coalition have not been without controversy, however. After the 1998 elections, Democratic State Senator Dave Herbert sued the organization for libel, claiming that the voter guide was wrong on every issue attributed to him—including a charge that he favored decriminalization of sodomy and bestiality. Herbert took the case to the Oklahoma Supreme Court after it was dismissed by a district court judge. The state's Supreme Court agreed with the lower court's ruling that the statements in the voter guide were "protected political speech (Talley 1999)."

After losing in a very close election in 2000, another state senator filed a similar suit against the Oklahoma Christian Coalition. The Christian Coalition mistook a vote cast by Democratic Senator Ed Long of Enid and attributed it to Democratic Senator Lewis Long of Glenpool in one of the voter guides it distributed during the 2000 campaign. Christian Coalition Executive Director Ken Wood wrote a letter apologizing for the error, but Senator Lewis Long continued with the libel suit, taking it to the Oklahoma Court of Civil Appeals after a district court failed to find actual malice. Although the courts ultimately rejected Long's defamation claim, it did spur legislation. Both houses of the Oklahoma legislature approved a measure that would subject a candidate who knowingly lies about another candidate's voting record to a $50,000 fine. The legislature considered language to apply the bill to interest groups as well, but supporters couldn't muster enough votes. The bill was vetoed by Governor Frank Keating, who argued that the "bill inappropriately limits the 1st Amendment right of freedom of speech" (Ervin 2000).

Despite a recent increase in political activity, the Oklahoma Christian Coalition is not the biggest religious player in Oklahoma politics. That distinction probably applies to the Baptists. In his book *Inside U.S.A.*, journalist John Gunther (1947) listed five groups that "all have something to do with running Oklahoma": the Baptist church, oil interests, old folks, the education lobby, and "county rings." The Baptist General Convention has actively opposed several state ballot questions. In 1982 the Convention contributed more than $80,000 to oppose pari-mutuel betting. The Baptists also opposed a 1984 ballot question that would have authorized liquor sales by the drink. The lead spokesman against the issue was the editor of the *Baptist Messenger*, and Baptist clergy actively opposed it from the pulpit. Baptist support also was a key element in defeating a 1994 lottery question. These actions prompted a columnist to write, "Churches, when they wield their influence, still pack a powerful wallop in affairs of state. Religious groups formed an almost solid phalanx against the lottery and were instrumental in getting out the vote" ("Lottery Lessons" 1994).

Other churches have been active in Oklahoma politics as well. The Oklahoma Conference of United Methodists and the State Association of Free Will Baptists also contributed to the 1982 campaign against pari-mutuel betting, for example. In fact, moral political issues in Oklahoma have been one area in which a variety of religions have found common ground. Bednar and Hertzke (1995) point out how well received Roman Catholic Senator Don Nickles and Mormon Representative Ernest Istook were at a large Pentecostal church in Oklahoma City during the 1994 campaign. Prior to the defeat of a proposed constitutional amendment that would have legalized casino gambling in 1998, Oklahoma's Roman Catholic governor, Frank Keating, met with religious leaders from various churches across the state and said, "When February 10 [the election date] is over and we defeat this . . . let us all join in an ecumenical war to advance moral and spiritual growth" (Greiner 1997).

If moral issues have been a force in bringing various churches together, the 2004 election in Oklahoma was no exception. Galvanized by several issues, many church leaders joined together for a common cause. Baptist General Convention of Oklahoma spokesman Ray Sanders noted that people of faith were taking a great interest in the election because of the ballot questions relating to gambling, the lottery, and same-sex marriage. Sanders said that he "could not remember any other time when election issues have had such a unifying effect on faith communities, bringing together Baptists, Churches of Christ, Assemblies of God, Methodists, Catholics, Mormons, and nondenominational churches to oppose the expansion of gambling and other issues" (Sherman 2004).

The 2004 U.S. Senate Campaign and the Role of the Christian Right

Observers from both parties had their eyes on Oklahoma's race for the U.S. Senate in 2004. An open seat with strong candidates from each party meant that the election was going to be a swing race that could change the U.S. Senate's party balance.

The Primaries

In fall 2003 Oklahoma's senior senator, Don Nickles, announced that he would be retiring from the U.S. Senate after serving four terms. The announcement set off a chain of events in both political parties to fill the newly open seat. On the Democratic side, U.S. Representative Brad Carson, from Oklahoma's second district, quickly emerged as the clear frontrunner. Carson, a sixth-generation Oklahoman, Rhodes scholar, and former White House fellow, had been reelected in 2002 with 74 percent of the vote. Early polls indicated that he had the most statewide name recognition of any declared candidate in either party and maintained a lead in any head-to-head match up.

Things weren't so simple for the Republicans. After Nickles' announcement, Oklahoma City mayor Kirk Humphreys stepped down from office to devote time to his campaign for the Senate. Humphreys had picked up some key endorsements, including Nickles; Oklahoma's other U.S. senator, Jim Inhofe; and U.S. Representative Tom Cole. Humphreys also was able to get a lead in fundraising, bringing in more than $1.2 million through the first quarter of the year. At the outset, Humphreys' primary challenge came from Bob Anthony. Anthony had been the first Republican in sixty years elected to the statewide office of the Oklahoma Corporation Commission. A known vote getter, Anthony was reelected with ease in three subsequent elections. Prior to his entrance into politics, Anthony served as president of his family's retail store chain, C. R. Anthony Company. He had personal wealth that he could invest in his campaign for the U.S. Senate.

The dynamics of the race changed when Tom Coburn entered the race in March 2004. Coburn was a Muskogee physician and former three-term (1995–2001) U.S. Representative from Oklahoma's second congressional district. A Southern Baptist, the politically conservative Coburn talked openly about his religion and even cast issues such as the national debt in moral terms. As a member of Congress he introduced several conservative bills involving issues such as abortion and prayer. Coburn vowed to introduce similar legislation as a U.S. senator. Coburn's entrance into the race caught the state's Republican establishment off guard. Most had already openly endorsed Humphreys and even helped to secure financial backing for him. Coburn had wide name recognition in the eastern part of the state and a hardcore group of supporters that he could count on during the campaign.

Humphreys began to feel the effects of Coburn's candidacy almost immediately. Asked about the impact of Coburn's candidacy on his ability to raise money, Humphreys replied, "I think in Washington, it's had the effect of parking a lot of money on the sidelines. In the state, there is some effect like that but not that great. Most of the in-state donors, a lot of them got on board with us before he got in the race" (Casteel 2004a). The Club for Growth—a political action committee (PAC) dedicated to limited government and lower taxes—contributed heavily to the Coburn campaign. Before the primary election in July, Humphreys spent nearly $2 million on the campaign, including nearly $1 million of his own money.

Three weeks before the primary, Coburn ran three radio spots. One pointed to his qualities as a physician, another emphasized his fulfillment of his campaign pledge to serve only three terms in Congress, and the third highlighted his Christian background and values. Two of the ads were critical of Humphreys's television commercials, which featured endorsements by retiring Senator Nickles, Senator Inhofe, and former Congressman J. C. Watts. The announcer in Coburn's radio ads referred to Humphreys's commercials, "where a whole bunch of Oklahoma politicians try to tell us who they think should be Oklahoma's next senator," and said that "a few other people would like to weigh in." The radio ad then had testimonials from Coburn supporters (Casteel 2004b).

Five days before the primary, a group of real estate organizations sponsored a forum and invited all Senate candidates of both parties to participate. Questions quickly turned to moral issues. People in attendance asked the candidates about their stances on same-sex marriage, prayer in school, the term "under God" in the Pledge of Allegiance, and the hanging of the Ten Commandments in public areas. All of the candidates spoke in opposition to gay marriage and in support of the others. Coburn said, "Our founders knew the only way we could be successful is if we were a moral society." Humphreys noted that he had the Ten Commandments on the wall of his office when he was the mayor of Oklahoma City. Although the forum had little impact on the outcome of the election, it illustrates the degree to which voters were concerned about moral issues (Greiner 2004).

Ultimately, Coburn won the primary with 61 percent of the vote. Despite the efforts of his campaign and all of the endorsements, Humphreys captured only 25 percent of the vote; Anthony received 12 percent. Humphreys also was hurt by relentless attacks coming from the Anthony campaign. Some observers characterized Anthony's attacks as a "murder-suicide strategy." Although the attack ads didn't help Anthony, they certainly hurt Humphreys, who pledged—along with Coburn—to only run a positive campaign.

The General Election

Brad Carson had a slight lead in the polls in early August, but Tom Coburn's campaign—coming off a resounding victory in the primary election—began to pick up momentum, and his polling numbers surpassed Carson's. After a series of unfortunate comments from Coburn, Carson went back on top in post–Labor Day polls. Among the comments were Coburn's description of the election as one of "good versus evil." Although Coburn claimed he didn't intend to say that Brad Carson was evil, the Carson campaign capitalized on the remark and tried to portray Coburn as an extremist. Coburn also referred to state legislators as a bunch of "crapheads in Oklahoma City." The state Democratic Party purchased billboard space with those remarks along major freeways around Oklahoma City, where Coburn needed support. Coburn also questioned whether all members of the Cherokee Nation were Indians. To make matters worse, a story broke about a former patient of Coburn who claimed he had sterilized her without permission.

Throughout the rest of September and into early October, polls showed a very tight race, with many polls giving the edge to Carson. The race gained national attention, and Coburn and Carson were thrown into the media spotlight. They were invited to appear with Tim Russert on NBC News' "Meet the Press," and C-SPAN carried nationally one of their debates in Oklahoma. Both of the national parties regarded the campaign as winnable and devoted a lot of resources to their candidate.

Religion and values took center stage throughout the campaign. Two days after Coburn initially used the term, National Republican Senatorial Committee Director Patrick Davis cast the race as one of "good versus evil." An infuriated Carson released the following statement: "We are Americans, Oklahomans, God's children, and it is disgusting to refer to this race as one of 'good versus evil.' As a Christian and a family man, I'm deeply offended by being referred to as 'evil.' I have been called a lot of things in my political life; no one has ever referred to me as 'evil'" (Casteel 2004c).

The Christian Coalition put out one-page voter guides that featured presidential candidates George W. Bush and John Kerry on the left half and Coburn and Carson on the right half. Under the candidates were a list of issues and their positions. Issues included passage of a federal marriage protection amendment, public financing of abortions, federal funding for faith-based charities, and federal gun registration and licensing, among others. The guide noted that both senatorial candidates supported passage of a federal marriage protection amendment and that Coburn supported the others. It noted that Carson either opposed the other issues or did not respond to the survey.

Throughout the campaign, Carson and Coburn defended their stances on abortion. Carson stated during the October 20 debate, "As a Baptist, I believe abortion is wrong in every instance. I believe as a matter of public policy it is moral only in the case of rape, incest, and for the life of the mother." Coburn criticized Carson for being too lenient on the issue. Coburn had performed two abortions as a physician—in each case to save the mother's life. "It's not a choice of whether or not you take a life," Coburn stated. "It's a choice of whether you save a life. In all other instances I am not for abortion" (Bellamy 2004). Some analysts also were critical of Coburn's position. During the Coburn–Carson debate on "Meet the Press," Tim Russert pressed Coburn on some of his earlier remarks regarding the issue. Russert asked Coburn whether he would apply the death penalty to doctors who perform abortions. Coburn responded, "If somebody intentionally takes life at any stage throughout the country, except to save a life, and that's innocent life, I think we have to use the law that's on the books to respond to that."

The candidates differed on other issues as well. Carson supported increased federal funding for education. Coburn wanted to reduce federal spending and claimed that education was a state and local matter. Coburn argued that, as a physician, he was better qualified to deal with health care issues. Carson, on the other hand, accused Coburn of "being out of touch with average Oklahomans," many of whom didn't have insurance and could not qualify for Medicaid. Both supported reimportation of lower-priced prescription drugs from Canada. Carson vowed to protect the current Social Security system, whereas Coburn favored allowing Americans to set up their own accounts. Both candidates said they would protect military installations in Oklahoma from being closed (Krehbiel 2004).

Both Senate candidates received numerous endorsements. Carson was careful not to appear tied to the national Democratic party—a mistake other Oklahoma Democrats had made in the past. He often cast himself as a member of the "Oklahoma Party" and played down his support for John Kerry. Coburn attracted several endorsements and visitors, including Elizabeth Dole and the president's father, George H. W. Bush. Among others who came to Oklahoma to campaign for Coburn was James Dobson, founder of Focus on the Family. Dobson stumped across Oklahoma, urging supporters to fast and pray on the weekend before the November 2 election. Dobson argued that a vote for Carson would equal a vote for U.S. Senators Tom Daschle, Ted Kennedy, and Patrick Leahy. Singling out Leahy, Dobson said, "Patrick Leahy is a 'God's people' hater. I don't know if he hates God, but he hates God's people" (Snyder 2004a).

Indeed, Dobson's analysis resonated with many Oklahomans. The race was not simply Coburn versus Carson; it was portrayed as a race that could turn control of the U.S. Senate over to the Democrats. The state's largest newspaper, the *Daily Oklahoman*, endorsed Coburn largely on that basis. The paper argued that Carson could do a credible job representing Oklahoma, but the thought of turning the Senate over to Carson's party was too much of a risk. "Lest you think it makes little difference," the editorial noted, "here are some of the folks who could chair important committees if the Democrats regained control: Robert Byrd (Appropriations), Joe Biden (Foreign Relations), Ted Kennedy (Labor) and Pat Leahy (Judiciary)" (*Daily Oklahoman* 2004).

The tone of the race became very negative, and voters were inundated with ads and direct mail. One such ad was sponsored by Americans United to Preserve Marriage, a group headed by Gary Bauer. The ad featured a picture of the *Washington Blade* newspaper. The voiceover says, "This is the *Washington Blade*. It's a gay newspaper, and it covers gay political plans. September 5th last year it reported, quote, Politicians like Brad Carson might well support our right to marry. But the *Blade* explains gays should stay quiet about it now, or the truth might hurt Carson in Oklahoma. If gay activists seem sure Brad Carson will eventually come out for gay marriage, can you be sure he won't?" The ad closes showing a picture of Carson and the words, "A Risk to Your Values."

The ad prompted Oklahoma's Democratic governor, Brad Henry, to issue a statement saying that Carson did indeed represent Oklahoma values and that Carson's support for traditional marriage was well known and documented (Casteel 2004d).

Negative ads also were run against Coburn. One featured a malpractice case brought against him involving the sterilization of a young woman. The case was dismissed, but the woman came forth during the campaign to tell her story. Ads claimed she was sterilized without her consent. In addition to television ads, direct mail flyers featuring the woman and her case were distributed throughout Oklahoma.

Toward the end of the campaign both candidates vowed to be more positive and pull the negative ads, but the damage already had been done. Letters to the editors of newspapers around the state voiced the same theme: The negativity had gotten out of hand.

When the polls closed, Coburn won with 52 percent of the vote; Brad Carson garnered 41 percent, and Sheila Bilyeu, an independent candidate who claimed that the government implanted a receiver in her head in the 1970s and sent messages to annoy her, captured 6 percent of the vote. According to exit polls, Coburn received support from 55 percent of voters who attended religious services regularly and 65 percent of voters who claimed to be prolife. Carson received 36 percent and 25 percent, respectively, from those groups (*SurveyUSA* 2004).

During his victory speech Coburn said, "I will not be ashamed of my faith; I will stand for my faith, and that will influence my ability to work in the U.S. Senate." For his part, Carson urged his followers to support Coburn and said his prayers were with him (Myers and Martindale 2004).

2004 State Ballot Questions and the Role of the Christian Right

Direct democracy is a familiar feature of Oklahoma government. Oklahomans have voted on an average of seven ballot measures a year for the past two decades. During the 2004 election Oklahomans faced nine such questions. Four of these questions dealt with moral issues on which religious organizations took a stance. State Question 705 and its companion, State Question 706, created a lottery and trust fund; State Question 711 placed a ban on gay marriage in the state; State Question 712 allowed gaming machines in tribal casinos and three licensed racetracks; and State Question 713 imposed an increased tax on tobacco products.

Although other moral issues appeared on Oklahoma ballots in the past, they faced strong opposition from the religious community and were defeated. Despite the opposition, many supporters were able to repackage the measures and get them back on the ballot at a later date, at which point the voters approved them. In all cases, these questions were pitched as tools for economic growth. The following are examples.

In 1974 a state question that would have authorized betting on horse races was defeated. The issue came back and was placed on the ballot in the fall of 1982. The collapse of the Penn Square Bank that year signaled an end to the oil boom Oklahoma enjoyed in the 1970s. Oklahoma's horse industry touted pari-mutuel betting as a means to bring in new jobs and benefit the state's economy to the tune of more than $500 million per year; some advocates claimed that it could turn into a billion-dollar industry (Greiner 1982). Voters apparently agreed and voted overwhelmingly to approve the measure.

In 1984 citizens voted in support of liquor by the drink despite opposition from area churches. Supporters argued that Oklahoma's liquor practices were out of step with the rest of the nation and that this situation put the state at a disadvantage in trying to attract tourism and promote conventions. Previous attempts to pass liquor by the drink where rejected by voters in 1972 and 1976.

Two ballot measures placed on the ballot in the 1990s were defeated despite economic arguments. The horse racing industry and religious groups—former foes—teamed up to defeat a state question that would have established a state-sponsored lottery in Oklahoma in 1994. Churches and horse groups joined forces again in 1998 to defeat a measure that would have legalized casino gambling in the state.

State Questions 705 and 706

During the 2002 gubernatorial campaign, Democratic candidate Brad Henry made the lottery a major part of his platform. He argued that unless someone came up with a better plan or a tax increase, a lottery would be the best way to fund education. After his inauguration, Henry introduced the measure to the Oklahoma state legislature. The legislature passed a resolution to place the issue on the ballot for voters' approval. Opponents were successful in delaying the special election for nearly two years; it finally was placed on the ballot for November 2004. State Question 705 proposed the creation of a lottery, and State Question 706 created a lottery trust fund.

State Question 712

Interestingly, the horse racing industry was one of the biggest proponents of State Question 712—a measure that would allow gaming machines in tribally owned casinos throughout the state as well as in three licensed racetracks. Horsemen and racetrack owners were struggling in Oklahoma and looked to New Mexico as a model. The New Mexico legislature passed a law in 1997 that allowed limited slot machines at racetracks. These machines soon became, in the words of a race commissioner, "the life-blood for [the] tracks," which would have gone under otherwise (Thornton 2004a).

Churches in Oklahoma rallied to defeat the lottery and gaming proposals. The Oklahoma Baptist General Convention led the charge. Sunday, October 3, 2004, was declared "dollar day"; congregants were asked to contribute an extra dollar to be earmarked for the campaign against the lottery and gambling. Some congregations took a second offering; some put all of the day's contributions toward the cause. Pastors decried the ballot measures from the pulpit. One referred to the election as "a battle for the soul of our state" (AP 2004). Before the campaign was over, the Convention had contributed more than $200,000 to Oklahomans for Good Government, an organization that campaigned against the lottery and gambling measures.

Oklahomans for Good Government ran an ad called the "gambling mouse" that was accompanied by a website, www.gamblingmouse.com. The ad featured a computer-generated mouse that was enticed by a gambling promoter to take the bait. Despite warnings, the mouse went ahead and the trap sprung. The commercial ended with a plea to vote "NO" on State Questions 705, 706, and 712. The commercial also could be viewed online. The companion website had links to articles and organizations opposed to gambling, as well as a game that underscored the antigambling theme.

In addition to making contributions to the Oklahomans for Good Government organizations, churches did a great deal within their own organizations. The Oklahoma Conference of the United Methodist Church featured a website that presented the perils of gambling. The Baptist General Convention printed and distributed flyers containing summaries of the state questions and biblical references to each. The flyers had the following caption: "How a Christian votes is not determined by public opinion polls, partisan politics or promises of financial gain. The issue for a Christian is: *what does the Bible say and what would Jesus have me do?*" The bottom of the flyers read, "PRAY and VOTE, November 2."

Despite these efforts, opponents of the two ballot questions knew they were going to be outspent. The race was cast as a "David versus Goliath" fight. Forrest Claunch, head of Oklahomans for Good Government, said, "We expect to be outspent. Clearly, gamblers have an affinity for giving money to these campaigns" (Snyder 2004b). To combat the big money spent by supporters of the lottery and gaming issues, churches were counting on a neighbor-to-neighbor outreach campaign. Describing the operation, Baptist General Convention of Oklahoma spokesman Ray Sanders said, "It will be very strong from the pulpit. It will be very grassroots, how moms and pops across Oklahoma feel about keeping Oklahoma grand" (Talley 2004).

State Question 711

Legislators also approved State Question 711, which defined marriage to be between one man and one woman and provided that same-sex marriages in other states would not be valid in Oklahoma. After the measure was referred by legislators, opponents filed a lawsuit asking that it be removed from the ballot. The suit was backed by the American Civil Liberties Union (ACLU). Legal briefs were submitted by two legislators and the state's attorney general. The Oklahoma Supreme Court refused to block the measure, and it was placed on the November ballot.

Unlike the lottery or gambling measures, State Question 711 never was an economic issue. From the outset, polls indicated that it would be approved overwhelmingly by the voters. Opponents of the ban on gay marriage ran a small grassroots campaign, but it was largely ineffective. Two groups formed in support of the measure: Oklahomans for the Protection of Marriage and the Protecting Oklahoma Families Fund. Together both groups raised about $16,000. Church leaders expressed their views from the pulpit, but they did not engage in a concerted advertising effort to pass the measure.

State Question 713

Oklahoma last increased its sales tax on tobacco products in 1987. By 2004 Oklahoma's tax rate on tobacco ranked forty-second of the fifty states. Most of the states that had lower cigarette taxes were tobacco-producing states. Oklahoma also boasted a high per capita rate of smokers. Concerned lawmakers regarded an increase in the cigarette tax as a way to raise more money and discourage people, especially youth, from smoking. The legislature approved the inclusion of the measure on the November ballot.

Organizations with a stake in the outcome lined up to sell their position to Oklahoma voters. The tobacco industry contributed heavily to the campaign to defeat the tax increase, with most of the money coming from tobacco giants such as Philip Morris and RJ Reynolds. Supporters of the tax increase included health care organizations and insurance groups. Although churches did not play as active a roll, they did take a stance to support the tobacco tax. One editorial in the *Baptist Messenger* stated, "SQ 713 is worthy of our support because of its benefits to health concerns" (Yeats 2004a). A poll conducted by University of Oklahoma professor Michael Givel found wide support among Christians for the tobacco tax. Nearly 80 percent of respondents who identified themselves as Christians favored State Question 713 (Cooper 2004).

Religious groups spent the most resources opposing the lottery and gaming machine issues. They were just as emphatic about their support for the ballot measure banning gay marriage, although they did not feel a need to actively promote the issue through advertising. John Yeats, the editor of the *Baptist Messenger*, summarized the issues: "This we know for sure—if only the people who attend Oklahoma Baptist churches and other evangelical churches show up at the polls and cast their ballots in agreement with the morals expressed in the Bible, the gambling initiatives don't stand a chance of passage, and the marriage definition SQ 711 will pass by a huge majority. More evangelicals are registered to vote than at any time in our state's history. The next step is to go to the polls and vote our biblical convictions. Do not fall prey to the rhetoric and false promises. Refuse to allow a promised economic gain to outweigh convictions and wisdom" (Yeats 2004b).

Election Outcome

When the battle was over and the votes were counted, "good" did not completely triumph over "evil." Despite pleas from religious leaders and warnings that gambling in any form would eat away at the state's moral fiber, voters sided with their pocketbooks to create a state-sponsored lottery and permit gaming machines in tribal casinos and horse racing tracks. On the other hand, Republican candidate Tom Coburn was elected to the U.S. Senate; his campaign themes guaranteed a future voting record that would champion conservative causes. In addition, State Question 711, defining marriage as between one man and one woman, was overwhelmingly approved by a margin of three to one. Thus, the election yielded mixed results for the Christian Right.

President Bush, Tom Coburn, and the marriage definition amendment received the highest percentage of votes from evangelical Protestants. As Table 10.1 illustrates, the president performed better in all religious traditions than Coburn, despite Coburn's constant appeal to people of faith.

Table 10.1   2004 Oklahoma General Election Votes by Religious Category for Bush, Coburn, and the Marriage Definition Amendment (%)

Religious Category	For Bush	For Coburn	For Marriage Amendment
Evangelical Protestant	77.8	69.3	86.8
Mainline Protestant	62.1	52.5	62.0
Black Protestant	25.3	18.7	75.9
Catholic	65.7	62.4	66.7
Other Christian	62.6	46.2	76.8
Other Faiths	37.5	32.1	56.4
Unaffiliated	43.0	27.8	55.7
Total	**65.2**	**56.0**	**75.5**

Source: 2004 National Election Pool, Oklahoma.

Voters who claimed not to be affiliated with any particular religion also cast more votes for Bush than for Coburn. Clearly President Bush was very popular in Oklahoma. Coburn was not as successful as he would have liked to have been in riding on the president's coattails. Part of the explanation lies in the tone of the race itself. The campaign became extremely negative, and many voters were turned off by this climate. As a result, an unknown independent political candidate with no financial backing was able to garner more than 86,000 votes (6 percent) in the race for the U.S. Senate.

The ballot measure defining marriage enjoyed broad support across religious affiliations. Although churches spoke out in support of the measure, that this measure was going to pass by a large margin was a foregone conclusion. Unlike the campaign to defeat the lottery and gaming machines, little money was raised to campaign in support of SQ 711. For many voters, it was solely a moral issue. Whereas the lottery and gaming machine campaigns promised increased revenue and jobs for the state of Oklahoma, the amendment defining marriage offered little in the way of economic benefits.

The two issues churches fought the hardest to defeat, the lottery and gambling, both passed, with nearly 65 and 60 percent of the vote, respectively. Church groups were outspent and could not overcome a massive advertising campaign to get the measures passed. For example, the group Oklahomans for Education and Jobs spent more than $3 million to promote passage of SQ 712, which ended restrictions on gaming machines. This amount represents nearly ten times what opponents of the measure spent. Table 10.2 shows the percentage of the vote each state question received.

Table 10.2 2004 Oklahoma General Election Votes for State Ballot Questions (%)

Ballot Question	For Proposal
SQ 705, Creation of state lottery	64.7
SQ 706, Trust fund for state lottery	68.0
SQ 711, Marriage definition amendment	75.5
SQ 712, Gaming machines in tribal casinos	59.4
SQ 713, Cigarette tax increase	53.3

Source: Oklahoma State Election Board.

The tobacco tax increase passed by a narrower margin, with 53 percent of the vote. Groups with close ties to the tobacco industry contributed nearly $2 million to defeat the tobacco tax increase. Unlike area churches and other groups opposing the lottery and game machine issue, supporters of the tobacco tax contributed heavily to promote its passage. Hospitals and other health and medical groups nearly matched the spending of the tobacco industry.

The election turned out to be bittersweet for many Christian conservatives. After the election returns were in, former Republican legislator and vocal opponent of the lottery and gambling Forrest Claunch said, "The sun's going to rise tomorrow, and the Lord's still going to be the Lord, but that doesn't mean He's going to be pleased with what has happened today." Claunch expressed concern over future social problems such as divorce and bankruptcies that would result from gambling: "The churches will have to step up and minister to those people and help them with the lives that are damaged, and the state will just go on, crowing about the revenue they've got" (Thornton 2004b).

The gaming, lottery, and tobacco measures were regarded as a victory for Oklahoma's Democratic governor, Brad Henry, who endorsed them as a way to increase state revenues. Religious organizations apparently couldn't match the advertising punch or appeal of the state-sponsored lottery. Although Christian conservatives cheered Tom Coburn's victory in the U.S. Senate race, economic arguments obviously trumped moral appeals to reject the lottery and gaming machines.

References

Associated Press. 2004. "Baptists Organizing Campaign against State Questions." Associated Press state and local wire, 4 October.

Bednar, Nancy L. and Allen D. Hertzke. 1995. "Oklahoma: The Christian Right and Republican Realignment." In *God at the Grass Roots: The Christian Right in the 1994 Elections*, ed. Mark J. Rozell and Clyde Wilcox. Lanham, Md.: Rowman and Littlefield, 91–107.

Bellamy, Clayton. 2004. "Carson, Coburn Given Boxing Gloves but Hold Punches in Debate." Associated Press state and local wire, 20 October.

Casteel, Chris. 2000. "More Oklahomans Call Themselves Republicans—Poll, Voter Records Don't Match." *Daily Oklahoman*, 22 October.

———. 2004a. "Humphreys Looks for Jump in Race." *Daily Oklahoman*, 16 May.

———. 2004b. "Coburn Plans to Launch Radio Ads." *Daily Oklahoman*, 5 June.

———. 2004c. "Carson Objects to Use of 'Evil' Referring to Senate Race." *Daily Oklahoman*, 2 September.

———. 2004d. "Adwatch: U.S. Senate Race." *Daily Oklahoman*, 27 October.

Conger, Kimberly H., and John C. Green. 2002. "Spreading Out and Digging In: Christian Conservatives and State Republican Parties." *Campaigns and Elections* 23, no. 1 (February): 58–65.

Cooper, Scott. 2004. "Smokin' and Other State Questions." *Oklahoma Gazette*, 20 October.

Daily Oklahoman. 2004. "Carson or Coburn? In a close call, we recommend. . . ." *Daily Oklahoman*, 24 October.

Ellis, Randy. 2003. "Poll Shows Oklahomans Support Displaying Ten Commandments." *Daily Oklahoman*, 6 September.

Ervin, Chuck. 2000. "Group Admits Guide Mistake." *Tulsa World*, 18 November.

Greiner, John. 1982. "Consultant Sees Billions in Horse-Racing Industry." *Daily Oklahoman*, 5 November.

———. 1997. "Keating Asks Churches to Lead Defeat of Casino Proposal." *Daily Oklahoman*, 14 September.

———. 2004. "Senate Hopefuls Speak Out: Gay Marriage, School Prayer Addressed at Event." *Daily Oklahoman*, 23 July.

Grelen, Jay, C. 2000. "Poll Finds Wide Admiration for Jesus." *Daily Oklahoman*, 25 December.

Gunther, John. 1947. *Inside U.S.A.* New York: Harper & Brothers.

Krehbiel, Randy. 2004. "Finding an Area of Agreement." *Tulsa World*, 22 October.

"Lottery Lessons." 1994. *Daily Oklahoman*, 12 May.

Martindale, Rob. 2004. "Carson, Coburn Clash over 'Evil.'" *Tulsa World*, 31 August.

Morgan, David R., and Kenneth J. Meier. 1980. "Politics and Morality: The Effect of Religion on Referenda Voting." *Social Science Quarterly* 61:144–48.

Myers, Jim, and Rob Martindale. 2004. "U.S. Senate Race: Coburn Triumphs in Senate Contest." *Tulsa World*, 3 November.

Satterthwaite, Shad. 2005. "Faster Horses, Older Whiskey, and More Money: An Analysis of Religious Influence on Referenda Voting." *Journal for the Scientific Study of Religion* 44:105–12.

Sherman, Bill. 2004. "For Religious Voters, Elections Hold Critical Importance." *Tulsa World*, 10 October.

Snyder, Carmel Perez. 2004a. "Marriage, Family Advocate in State to Support Coburn." *Daily Oklahoman*, 23 October.

———. 2004b. "Henry to Talk Lottery as Group Vows Defeat." *Daily Oklahoman*, 8 August.

SurveyUSA. 2004. "Carson Losing Ground in Fight against Coburn for U.S. Senate." Poll conducted for KJRH-TV Tulsa and KFOR-TV Oklahoma City, October 28–30.

Talley, Tim. 1999. "Senator Takes Libel Appeal to High Court." *Daily Oklahoman*, 10 June.

———. 2004. "Campaigns Gear Up for Lottery Vote." Associated Press, 23 August.

Thornton, Tony 2004a. "Slots Credited with Track Turnaround." *Daily Oklahoman*, 10 October.

———. 2004b. "SQ 712: Ballot Item Makes for Strange Bedfellows." *Daily Oklahoman*, 4 November.

Yeats, John. 2004a. "Tell the Truth, Trust the People." *Baptist Messenger*, 28 October.

———. 2004b. "Gamblingmouse.com." *Baptist Messenger*, 21 October.

Zizzo, David. 2001. "Abortion Poll Finds Mixed State Support—Most Surveyed Back Some Allowances." *Daily Oklahoman*, 21 January.

CHAPTER ELEVEN

California Ménage à Trois:

The Christian Right, the Republican Party, and Arnold Schwarzenegger

J. CHRISTOPHER SOPER AND JOEL S. FETZER

> Whatever starts in California unfortunately has a tendency to spread.
>
> JIMMY CARTER

> There is science, logic, reason; there is thought verified by experience. And then there is California.
>
> EDWARD ABBEY

ACCORDING TO THE QUOTATIONS THAT BEGIN THIS CHAPTER, CALIfornia is either a trendsetter for the rest of the nation or so idiosyncratic it could never be a harbinger of things to come. Christian Right activists in the state certainly hope the latter is true. The 2004 election in California demonstrated again the limitations that beset a movement whose goals are not shared by a majority of the state's electorate. Most notably, Proposition 71—an initiative to provide public funding for embryonic stem cell research—passed comfortably in the November election, although the Christian Right was united in its opposition to that initiative. Just as important, the gubernatorial recall election of 2003 highlighted how the Christian Right's association with the state Republican party is problematic at best. In that special election, California voters ousted Democratic Governor Gray Davis from the state's highest office and replaced him with Republican Arnold Schwarzenegger.

The 2003 recall election could help to resurrect a Republican Party that recently seemed consigned to political irrelevance, but Schwarzenegger's liberal views on social issues, as well as some of his own lifestyle choices in the past, stray dramatically from those of most conservative Christians, to say the least. Both of these elections underscored how muted the Christian Right voice is in California politics. Although the Christian Right is not politically powerless in state politics, by itself the movement cannot shape public policy, nor is it a controlling faction in the state's GOP. In both cases, it must reach beyond its natural constituency of white, evangelical Protestants to have an impact on politics. At the same time, the movement's leaders are wrestling with the advantages and disadvantages of pursuing a pragmatic or ideological approach to politics.

The Religious and Political Culture of California

The primary obstacle to Christian Right political mobilization in California is demographic: There are too few conservative Christians in the state. The Christian Right generally derives its principal strength from white, evangelical Protestants (Green 2000). The 2004 National Annenberg Election Survey reported that 17 percent of registered voters in California were evangelical or born-again white Protestants. By contrast, more than half or close to half of registered voters in Tennessee (51 percent), Kentucky (50 percent), Mississippi (46 percent), Arkansas (49 percent), and Georgia (41 percent), to name a few states, were white, evangelical Protestants. Even ostensibly "blue" states such as Washington (26 percent) and Oregon (27 percent) had larger percentages of white evangelicals than California. Of the thirty-four states for which the survey had data, only six states (Connecticut, Maryland, Massachusetts, New Jersey, New York, Utah) had a lower percentage of white evangelicals registered to vote than did California (National Annenberg Election Survey 2004; California Opinion Index 2005).

Although California is more liberal than many states, evangelical Protestants in California are no less conservative than their religious counterparts in Tennessee, Mississippi, or Georgia. Polls over the past decade have consistently shown that white evangelicals in California have more conservative attitudes on a wide range of social issues than any other subgroup in the state. According to a 2004 poll (Field Poll 2004), 79 percent of evangelical Christians in California opposed same-sex marriages, nearly two-thirds (63 percent) favored amending the Constitution to define marriage as a union between a man and a woman, and a plurality (49 percent to 42 percent) favored laws that would make obtaining an abortion more difficult.

From the standpoint of the Christian Right, the "problem" is not that evangelical Protestants have adopted the state's liberal values but that overall the state is liberal or moderate on the social issues that matter most to the Christian Right. A 1997 poll indicated that 62 percent of Californians supported first-trimester abortions, and a majority favored publicly funded abortions for indigent women (Field Poll 1997). The percentage of Californians who wanted no changes in the state's abortion laws or who wanted to make obtaining an abortion easier remained virtually unchanged between 1991 (72 percent) and 2004 (71 percent). Only 22 percent of registered voters in California favored laws that would make obtaining an abortion more difficult (Field Poll 2004). This high percentage of support for legalized abortion in California is even more telling given that the state's abortion policies are among the most liberal in the nation (Russo 1995). Californians are more evenly divided on the rights of gays and lesbians, but the state is moderate to liberal on this issue as well. A 1997 poll indicated that 45 percent of the state's population believes that homosexual relations are always or almost always wrong; a nearly identical percentage (47 percent) feels that homosexual relations are not at all wrong or only sometimes wrong (California Opinion Index 1997). A majority (56 percent) disapproves of allowing two people of the same sex to marry and benefit from regular marriage laws, although most Californians (67 percent) approve of granting legal recognition of family rights to domestic partners, allowing child custody rights for homosexuals (69 percent), and permitting gays and lesbians to serve in the military (58 percent). A 2004 poll indicated that a majority of registered voters (54 percent) opposed amending the U.S. Constitution to define marriage as a union between a man and a woman (Field Poll 2004).

Part of the reason for the state's policy liberalism is that a sizable percentage of the state's registered voters (15 percent) report that they have no religious preference (National Annenberg Election Survey 2004), and the policy views of these voters is consistently liberal. Seventy-five percent of these secular voters approved same-sex marriages, 80 percent opposed amending the U.S. Constitution to define marriage as between a man and a woman, and 58 percent believed that California should make obtaining an abortion easier (Field Poll 2004).

The political ideology of the state's population acts as a final impediment to Christian Right political mobilization: Self-identified political conservatives and liberals are almost evenly matched in the state. In the six statewide elections from 1994 to 2004, the percentage of voters identifying themselves as conservatives fluctuated from a low of 28 percent in 2004 to a high of 34 percent in 2000. The percentage of self-described liberals in those elections reached a high of 37 percent in 2000 and a low of 26 percent in 2004 (Los Angeles Times Poll 2000; California Opinion Index 2005). The state may not be as liberal as the media often assume, but it also is not as conservative as it would need to be for the Christian Right to be a dominant electoral force. The conservative social views of white, evangelical Christians are nearly evenly matched in their political impact by the liberal positions of secular voters. The winning formula for elections in California has been and still is to be found in the ideological center or slightly left of center—which is not where the Christian Right and the Republican Party have positioned themselves for much of the past two decades.

Despite these cultural and religious barriers, the California Christian Right at times has had a political impact in the state, primarily because the state's political institutions provide an ideal context for social movement mobilization. Few states have been as affected by progressive political reforms as California. California was one of the first states to adopt political primary elections; initiative, referendum, and recall votes; and nonpartisan city elections, as well as outlawing pre-primary endorsements by political parties (Mayhew 1986; Gerston and Christenson 1995; Hyink and Provost 1998; Field 2005). Because political parties are structurally weak, they are open to takeover by groups that are willing and able to commit time and resources to party activism. Candidates for elective office need the support of activist groups in the electorate that can mobilize voters for political primary elections. Finally, interest groups and their supporters dominate referendum and initiative campaigns. These progressive innovations have enabled well-organized social movements to have some political impact—which is precisely what the Christian Right has done over the past two decades.

Christian Right Mobilization in Republican Party Politics

As in other states, the impetus for Christian Right activism in California was growing dissatisfaction among conservative Christians with the state's liberal social policies on abortion, gay rights, and religion in public schools. From a resource perspective, conservative Christians proved to be ideal for political activism; group leaders recruited members through sympathetic evangelical and fundamentalist churches (Gilbert 1993). Several groups emerged to challenge the state's liberal social policy, including the California Republican Assembly, the California ProLife Council, the Traditional Values Coalition, and the Christian Coalition. Notably absent in California were the Moral Majority and Concerned Women for America, which have been politically significant in other states (Soper and Fetzer 2003).

Once mobilized, the Christian Right set its sights on the state Republican Party, where control has vacillated between moderates and conservatives for the past fifty years. In the 1950s moderates controlled the party, but the migration of many midwesterners and southerners into the state in the 1940s and 1950s changed the state's political culture and fueled a conservative backlash in the state GOP (Elazar 1972). The party became far more conservative on law and order, taxation, labor, and race. The transformation of the Republican Party eventually led to Ronald Reagan's two terms as California's governor. At the time, the fervor and organizational strength of the right wing in California, particularly in Orange County, were unmatched elsewhere in the country (Schuparra 1998; McGirr 2001).

As governor, however, Reagan was more libertarian than social conservative. In 1967, for example, he signed the Beilenson bill, which enacted the nation's most liberal abortion law (Cannon 1998). The same was largely true for Republican governors George Deukmejian (1982–1990) and Pete Wilson (1990–1998), for both of whom crime was a cornerstone social issue. The election of the prochoice Wilson in 1990 solidified the movement of the state GOP in a socially moderate direction.

As the Christian Right began to gain a foothold in the party in the early 1990s, however, antagonism grew between moderates and conservatives in the party. The annual party conventions in the 1990s became public feuds between Christian Right activists and the prochoice governor. During his eight-year tenure as governor, Wilson urged the party to adopt a modified prochoice position, distanced himself from the state party leadership, and had an increasingly antagonistic relationship with Christian conservatives in the party. In response, some delegates to the party's 1991 convention tarred and feathered the governor in effigy (Peterson 1991).

Because the state GOP was relatively weak, it was open to the tactics of grassroots organizing and get-out-the-vote drives utilized by Christian conservatives; by 1993 such activists controlled thirty-eight of the fifty-eight county GOP Central Committees and were a significant influence in the state Republican party (Nollinger 1993; Persinos 1994). A study of conservative Christian influence in state Republican parties (Conger and Green 2002) concluded that Christian conservatives had lost some ground in California but were still moderately influential in the state GOP.

The Christian Right voice often has been represented in the state party platform. The 2004 platform, for example, described the GOP as the "Party of Life," supported "reversal of *Roe v. Wade*," and affirmed the party's support "for the protection of innocent human life at every stage, from the pre-born to the elderly." The platform also opposed "granting to homosexuals special privileges, including marriage, domestic partnership benefits, and child custody or adoption" (www.cagop.org/about/platform).

Intraparty battles between social-issue moderates and social-issue conservatives for control of the state party chair have become commonplace, however. In 2001 conservatives retained control of the state party chair position despite a well-financed challenge from the party's moderate wing and support from the Bush White House for the socially moderate candidate (Barabak 2001; Wildermuth 2001). By contrast, in 2003, for the first time in more than a decade, the party elected a social-issue moderate, Duf Sundheim, as GOP chair.

The very forces that made the party susceptible to a takeover by the Christian Right have limited what the movement has been able to accomplish within the state GOP. Because the state party is weak, it has had few of the resources candidates need and none of the sanctions they fear. For example, California's parties do not control the nomination process, and they have not historically contributed a very large percentage of the money needed for political campaigns. Nor has control of the party meant that the Christian Right has enjoyed the power to shape the issues debated within a given election. No state in the union has more candidate-centered elections than California; more often than not the Christian Right has found itself responding to a set of issues defined for it by candidates or the media. Governor Wilson, for example, consistently used divisive wedge issues for his political purposes. The most notorious examples occurred in 1994, when he linked his reelection bid to support for Proposition 187—a referendum that called for cutting off undocumented immigrants' access to most public services—and in 1996, when he and the GOP supported Proposition 209, an anti–affirmative action measure. Wilson easily won reelection in 1994, and Christian Right organizations endorsed both propositions. Yet immigration and affirmative action were not issues that were central to the movement's political self-understanding.

Although the Christian Right periodically has controlled the state GOP, the movement's electoral impact has been less significant. As table 11.1 demonstrates, white evangelical Christians—the core of the Christian Right movement—are at best an important, but not controlling, faction among Republican voters. Evangelicals reached their high-water mark in the 1994 midterm election. In that contest evangelicals accounted for 17 percent of all voters in the state and 24 percent of all votes cast for Republican House candidates. A decade later, in the 2004 presidential election, the percentage of Christian Right voters in the state had fallen to 11 percent of all votes cast, although they still represented 24 percent of all Republican identifiers.

The Christian Right also has been involved in the electoral process in California. In 1990 Christian conservative candidates won 60 positions on San Diego County's school and hospital boards (Bruzzone 2003). Movement leaders also have recruited candidates and helped to nominate some of them in Republican primary elections throughout the 1990s. Although Christian conservatives were a minority of the state's electorate, they magnified

Table 11.1   Political Characteristics of White Christian Right Voters, California, 1994–2004

Characteristic	1994	2000	2004
% Conservative	61	68	
% Moderate	32	25	
% Republican	60	73	
Christian Right as percentage of electorate	17	10	11
Christian Right as percentage of GOP vote	24	22	24

Note: Data for 1994 and 2000 from Voter News Service exit poll; data for 2004 from National Election Pool exit poll. Christian Right voters were defined in 1994 and 2000 as those who considered themselves "part of the conservative Christian political movement, also known as the religious right." Equivalent voters in 2004 described themselves as "white," "conservative," and "Protestant" or "other Christian." Data for 2000 and 2004 weighted to achieve demographically representative sample.

their significance by voting predominantly in Republican primaries. As we note below, Christian Right voters represented about one-quarter of GOP votes over the past decade, which makes them an important constituency within the party. On the other hand, candidates even remotely identified with the Christian Right have historically done poorly in statewide races. The Christian Right often has gotten its favored candidates nominated in the primary but thereby has torpedoed the GOP's chances in the general election. The Christian Right casualties in previous races have included Robert "B-1 Bob" Dornan and Tom Bordonaro.

The most recent example was the 2002 GOP gubernatorial primary. That race pitted the socially moderate former Los Angeles mayor, Richard Riordan—the candidate favored by the Bush White House and most of the state's elected Republicans—against socially conservative political neophyte Bill Simon. Simon appealed to the right, particularly to Christian conservative voters; Riordan reached out to swing voters. Two months before the election, Simon trailed Riordan by 37 percentage points (*California Journal* 2002; Cannon 2002). Simon eventually won the Republican race by 18 percentage points—an unprecedented 55-point reversal in less than sixty days.

Christian conservatives were instrumental in Simon's victory. Turnout for the election was low (33 percent), and the swing voters to whom Riordan appealed did not turn out in large numbers, whereas conservative Christians did. The race also witnessed a concerted effort by then-Governor Gray Davis to aid Simon's campaign. No doubt aware of the positive fate for

Democratic candidates in statewide races when they run against socially conservative opponents, the Davis campaign decided to spend $10 million dollars on television commercials attacking Riordan's credibility during the Republican primary. Brilliant or diabolical, this effort helped to seal Riordan's fate. In the general election, Davis defeated Simon by 5 percentage points—proving again that candidates closely identified with the Christian Right do not win statewide races in California.

Although conservative Christians have maintained fealty to their political principles in state party battles, the Christian Right also has been willing at times to modify those ideals to help get socially moderate Republicans elected to office. In 1994 the movement supported dozens of "stealth" candidates who minimized their formal ties to the Christian Right (Soper 1995). The Christian Coalition especially took this path, consistently emphasizing a wide variety of issues in its voters' guides. The effect has been to make moderate Republican candidates seem acceptable to conservative Christians. The Christian Coalition all but endorsed socially moderate GOP candidates Michael Huffington, Matt Fong, Bill Jones, and even Pete Wilson in their bids for statewide office, and Christian conservatives have consistently voted for moderate Republican candidates.

The severe electoral decline of the state GOP in the past decade has further intensified the battles between social moderates and conservatives within the party. Between 1996 and 2004, the number of Republicans representing California's fifty-three congressional districts fell from twenty-five to twenty. The Republican caucus in the eighty-member State Assembly declined from forty-one to thirty-two, and Republicans lost three seats in the forty-member State Senate, dropping from seventeen to fourteen. Finally, the GOP has lost the past four presidential races in the state and the past four contests for the U.S. Senate.

The Christian Right has taken much of the blame for the party's electoral failures over the past decade (Cannon 1998, 2004). In particular, the party's conservative positions on abortion, gay rights, school vouchers, gun control, and the environment have alienated California's voters. It is difficult to imagine a candidate who opposes abortion rights and gun control or who favors school vouchers or very conservative restrictions on the rights of gays and lesbians winning a top-of-the-ticket race in California (Skelton 2000). Nonetheless, these views prevailed within the state GOP, in large part because of conservative Christians' role in the party. Over the past decade, an unhealthy relationship seemed to bind the Christian Right and the state Republican Party; neither partner benefited much from their mutual commitment, but neither could imagine abandoning their union.

Then came Arnold.

The 2003 Gubernatorial Recall Election

The seeds for the 2003 gubernatorial recall election were planted nearly 100 years ago, when California became one of eighteen states that would eventually adopt the recall process. The threshold to qualify a recall for the ballot is particularly low in California; the number of signatures required to force a statewide recall race is just 12 percent of the vote for the governor in the previous election. Governor Davis germinated the process in various ways. He had the genuine misfortune of being governor in the midst of a state energy crisis that included an increase in electricity prices by as much as 900 percent and rolling blackouts in some cities in the summer of 2001 (Block 2003). Davis ran a negative reelection campaign in 2002 that depressed voter turnout—which, in turn, reduced the number of signatures that would be needed for the recall to qualify for the ballot. Although Davis won reelection that year, shortly thereafter he shepherded the state into a $38 billion budget deficit. Never particularly popular with the voters—and even less so after his shenanigans in the 2002 race—Davis bore the brunt of his political missteps, and his opponents launched a recall campaign that quickly secured the necessary signatures to qualify for a special election to be held in October 2003. In addition to voting for or against the recall, voters would select a preferred candidate for governor if the recall passed.

Eventually, 135 serious and not-so-serious candidates of various political persuasions qualified as candidates for governor on the recall ballot. The candidates included adult film actress Mary Carey; child television star Gary Coleman; numerous "ordinary" citizens looking for their fifteen minutes of fame; and more mainstream political figures such as Green Party candidate Peter Camejo; independent candidate Arianna Huffington; Republicans Peter Ueberroth and Tom McClintock; and the Democratic Lieutenant Governor, Cruz Bustamante (Lesher 2003). The *coup de grace* was delivered when Arnold Schwarzenegger announced his candidacy for the governor's office on *The Tonight Show with Jay Leno*. For once, California seemed to be living up to its image as a political freak show.

Although Schwarzenegger had nothing to do with organizing the recall election, it quickly became apparent that he could be its biggest beneficiary. As a social-issue moderate, Schwarzenegger would have had great difficulty winning a Republican primary election. Christian conservative voters frequently had demonstrated that they could thwart the efforts of moderates to win a party primary. The recall election, however, allowed Schwarzenegger to skip the primary and appeal directly to California's general electorate, which is moderate to liberal on social issues. He also stood a very good chance of winning—something no Republican candidate had done for a significant statewide office in nearly a decade.

In addition to his obvious star power and the unprecedented media attention focused on his gubernatorial campaign, Schwarzenegger proved to be an adept candidate who far exceeded the low expectations his opponents and the media placed on him (Cannon 2003). Moreover, his positions on issues such as abortion, gay rights, immigration, and taxes closely mirrored those of the California electorate. Political pragmatism dictated that Republicans of all stripes support Schwarzenegger's candidacy, which is precisely what the state party apparatus did. Forty of the fifty-eight county chairs endorsed Schwarzenegger, as did the entire California Republican Party board.

Schwarzenegger's candidacy presented the Christian Right with a difficult dilemma. Although a victory by Schwarzenegger might provide the Christian Right with more access to the governor's office than they had enjoyed during Democratic administrations, Schwarzenegger represented the most liberal wing of the Republican Party. He was prochoice, pro–gay rights, and pro–gun control. He said that the Clinton impeachment made him "ashamed" to call himself a Republican. He had publicly admitted using steroids, and in a 1977 *Oui* magazine interview Schwarzenegger bragged about participating in orgies. Finally, during the latter stages of the campaign several women accused him of sexual harassment—a charge he almost implicitly acknowledged when he apologized for his past mistreatment of women (Marquez 2003). Schwarzenegger's fiscal conservatism makes him a Republican, not his views on social issues. Even more problematic for the Christian Right was that one of Schwarzenegger's Republican opponents, Tom McClintock, was closely identified with the Christian conservative movement. McClintock was prolife, and he opposed gay rights. In a 1997 article for the *Christian Science Monitor*, McClintock wrote, "Religion thus formed the foundation of American liberty: the 'self-evident' truth that the rights of all people are endowed not by the state, but by their creator" (Garza 2003).

In short, ideological purity dictated that Christian conservatives support McClintock—and some of the movement leaders did. The Traditional Values Coalition (TVC) aired a one-minute television spot showing Schwarzenegger's face morphing into that of Democratic Governor Gray Davis. The group's founder, the Reverend Lou Sheldon, pointed out that the message the group was sending was that "there is no difference between Arnold Schwarzenegger and Gray Davis" (Marinucci 2003). The national headquarters for the 1 million-member TVC are in California, where Sheldon has had a high profile on gay-rights issues for the past twenty years (Dunlap 1994).

Not all national Christian Right leaders opposed Schwarzenegger's candidacy, however. Pat Robertson all but endorsed Schwarzenegger on his television show, saying "I'm a body-builder. . . . So I think the weight lifters of the world need to unite" (Rich 2003). Perhaps trying to mend fences with Christian conservatives, Schwarzenegger said in a television interview with Sean Hannity of Fox News that he opposed partial-birth abortions and gay marriages. He also said that he supported prayer in school and parental notification laws (Haddock 2003). The state Christian Coalition and the California Republican Assembly were notably silent on the recall election.

Political pragmatism, rather than ideological purity, proved more compelling to Christian conservative voters in the recall election. Of the Christian Right voters in the 2003 election, 2 percent voted for Democrat Bustamante, 22 percent for the socially conservative McClintock, and an overwhelming 76 percent for the socially moderate-to-liberal Schwarzenegger. If one only includes religious-right members in a regression parallel to that in table 11.1, the only relevant variables with a statistically significant effect on one's odds of voting for Schwarzenegger instead of McClintock are Female ($b = -0.668$; $p < .05$) and Income ($b = 0.233$; $p < .05$). Perhaps Christian Right women were more committed to McClintock's prolife position on abortion or found Schwarzenegger's previous behavior toward women more troubling. Conversely, well-off evangelicals might have perceived Schwarzenegger's economic agenda as more advantageous to the rich than McClintock's.

The 2003 recall election results seemed to confirm that voters who identify with the Christian Right in California are so closely enmeshed with the Republican party that they will not abandon even the most liberal party candidates. The election also demonstrated that a social issue moderate in the GOP could win a statewide race with or without the support of the Christian Right. In contrast to so many of his previous Republican counterparts for statewide office, Schwarzenegger expanded his base beyond partisan Republican voters; he received 46 percent of the vote total from registered Independents and even 21 percent of the vote from registered Democrats. He also did particularly well among self-described moderates, who represented 31 percent of the vote total; this group voted for Schwarzenegger over Bustamante, his closest competitor, by a 53 percent to 28 percent margin.

Once in office, Schwarzenegger lived up to Christian conservatives' worst fears. He also discovered the limits of his "nonpartisan" appeal. Two days before President Bush's 2004 campaign visit to the state, Schwarzenegger distanced himself from the president's position on gay marriage by saying on the *Tonight Show* that he would be "fine" with same-sex marriages if California voters approved, and he proclaimed that he "had no use for a constitutional amendment" that would take the power away from states to define legal marriages (Salladay 2004). Schwarzenegger also signed into law several bills supported by gay rights groups and opposed by the Christian Right. One measure required health insurance companies to offer the same benefits to same-sex domestic partners that they offer married spouses. Another expanded the definition of gender in hate crimes and discrimination law to protect transgender individuals from harassment. In response, TVC chairman Lou Sheldon issued a press release stating, "Schwarzenegger has sided with the homosexual and drag queen lobby in muddying the biological realities of male and female" (Sheldon 2004). Not only did these bills raise the ire of the Christian Right, they also received virtually no support from Republican members of the State Assembly and Senate. Finally, after months of silence on the issue, Schwarzenegger endorsed Proposition 71, an initiative on the 2004 ballot that would provide $3 billion for embryonic stem cell research. Putting himself at odds with his party at both the state and national levels, Schwarzenegger said, "I am very much interested in stem cell research, and I support it 100 percent" (Matthews and Garvey 2004).

In signing these bills and endorsing Proposition 71, Schwarzenegger has shown himself to be politically astute. Polls in the state consistently show that California voters are weary of what they regard as excessive partisanship from both Democrats and Republicans; demonstrating political independence from his own party, therefore, reinforces a positive image voters have of Schwarzenegger as being "above" party politics. Because Schwarzenegger's moderate-to-liberal views on social issues correspond more closely to those of Californians than do the views of the Christian Right, periodically showing his independence from that movement also made good political sense for the new governor (Weintraub 2004). When Schwarzenegger has not been actively opposing key aspects of the Christian Right agenda, he has essentially ignored them. In 2004, for example, San Francisco mayor Gavin Newsome issued marriage licenses to same-sex couples—in direct violation of the voter-approved initiative Proposition 22, which stated that only marriages between a man and a woman are valid and recognized in the state of California. In response, Schwarzenegger called on Newsome to respect the law but did nothing to try to stop him. A year later, however, the governor faced a wrenching political dilemma when the Democratic-led legislature passed a bill legalizing gay marriages in the state. Having seen his public approval ratings plummet for much of the preceding year, particularly among Democrats and independents, Schwarzenegger had little choice but to placate his Republican, Christian conservative base and veto the bill (Skelton 2005).

Schwarzenegger's victory in the 2003 recall election initially buoyed the fortunes of the state Republican party. In 2003 the state GOP raised more money than its Democratic counterpart for the first time in five years. That same year also witnessed the most significant Republican gains in party registration in more than a decade (Cannon 2004). Although statisticians remind us that correlation is not causation, one can hardly fault Schwarzenegger's supporters for concluding that his political pragmatism and social issue liberalism were responsible for the party's relative success. The question was, and is, whether the new governor's popularity was short-lived and whether it would translate into Republican victories in the 2004 elections.

The 2004 Elections

Proposition 71 was the most significant issue for the Christian Right on the 2004 ballot. The measure was specifically designed to circumvent President Bush's stem cell policy, which had restricted research in the field; it proposed that the state would raise $3 billion over ten years to promote embryonic stem cell research in the state. Despite opposition from the Christian Right, the initiative passed by a comfortable 59 percent to 41 percent margin.

Ironically, initiatives historically have been one vehicle for Christian Right activism in state politics. To qualify for the ballot, an initiative must be signed by registered voters amounting to 5 percent of the total votes cast for governor in the most recent gubernatorial election. To qualify for the 2006 election, for example, an initiative would need to be signed by 373,816 registered voters. Initiatives play to the political strengths of the Christian Right movement—the enthusiasm and vitality of activists and the interconnection of movement participants through evangelical churches throughout the state (Allswang 2000). Although the political parties sometimes take a stand on a particular initiative, they provide few of the resources necessary to get an initiative on the ballot or to publicize it for an upcoming election. On sociocultural issues, ideological interest groups and wealthy individuals dominate the process. Between 1979 and 2000, for example, the Christian Right was instrumental in placing eight initiatives on the ballot—six dealing with gay and lesbian rights and two with the use of state educational vouchers for public or private schools, including religious schools. Initiatives, in short, have been an effective way for the Christian Right to get some of their key issues on the legislative agenda.

Getting an initiative onto the ballot is one thing, but getting a majority of the voters to support it is another. In the case of the Christian Right, with one exception the initiatives they have supported have not passed. The voucher initiatives, Proposition 174 in 1993 and Proposition 38 in 2000, proposed that the state would provide a voucher to all school-age children (kindergarten through twelfth grade) to help pay for tuition and fees at private schools, including private religious schools. The Christian Right provided vocal support for both initiatives. Yet the voters rejected the two voucher initiatives by identical 70 percent-to-30 percent margins. The Christian Right has not been much more successful on propositions dealing with gay and lesbian rights; Proposition 6 in 1978 was the first to deal with this issue. If passed, the proposition would have allowed schools to fire an employee for advocating or practicing homosexuality and would have prohibited them from hiring gays or lesbians. Lou Sheldon, founder of the TVC, was the chief architect of this proposition. Proposition 6 failed by a 58 percent-to-32 percent margin. Voters also soundly defeated two other propositions from the 1980s that would have declared AIDS an infectious disease and placed carriers of the disease on a special list.

Of course, what is good for the conservative Christian goose also is good for the socially liberal gander. The Christian Right is not the only social movement in the state that can mobilize effectively for an initiative campaign, nor is it alone in taking advantage of the initiative procedures to bypass political party structures. Proposition 71 was a good example. The initiative was the brainchild of multimillionaire Robert Klein II, whose son has diabetes and who became convinced that stem cell research offered the best promise for a cure for that disease and many others (Mecoy 2004). Klein eventually spent $3 million dollars on the campaign and enlisted financial backing from Microsoft founder Bill Gates, eBay founder Pierre Omidyar, and venture capitalist William Bowles (Garvey 2004). Opponents of the measure raised money as well; Focus on the Family Action spent $65,000 to mail letters to its 180,000 followers in the state, and Christian conservative activist Howard Ahmanson Jr. gave $50,000 to the campaign. Ultimately, however, initiative supporters outspent their opponents by a whopping $27.5 million to $270,000 (http://cal-access-ss.ca.gov).

This financial discrepancy is nothing new for the Christian Right in California. Opponents of one of the voucher initiatives, Proposition 174, outspent supporters by $24 million to $3 million (www.calvoter.org). The Christian Right has consistently faced well-organized and financed opposition. Opponents of the voucher initiatives, for example, included all of the teacher unions in the state, the state Democratic party, President Clinton, the League of Women Voters, the Mexican American Legal Defense Fund, the National Association for the Advancement of Colored People, Governor Gray Davis, and many others (Allswang 2000, 185). Both of the AIDS initiatives from the 1980s were opposed by civil liberties groups,

gay and lesbian rights organizations, the entire California medical community, U.S. Surgeon General C. Everett Koop, Republican Governor
George Deukmejian, and most of the prominent religious leaders in the
state. This political imbalance of power underscores the larger point that
key opponents of the Christian Right—such as feminists, gay rights advocates, teachers' unions, and environmentalists—are politically powerful in
California. Passage of Proposition 71 reinforced the power imbalance in
the state on cultural and moral issues; California became the first state to
promote such research, and the state's voters repudiated the Bush administration's policy that limited such research on moral grounds.

Several other initiatives were on the ballot in 2004, though none that
were particularly relevant to the Christian Right. What was remarkable
about the propositions was that Schwarzenegger's opposition to a pair of
tribal gambling initiatives was instrumental in their defeat, and the governor's active support proved crucial in passage of a proposition that revised
how the state funds local government. On initiatives, at least, Schwarzenegger proved to have very long coattails. He received far more media
attention around the state than the presidential or senatorial candidates,
and he used this attention aggressively to publicize his views on key initiatives. By contrast, Schwarzenegger did nothing to alter the electoral
outcome for the Republican Party candidates within the state; even those
he endorsed in competitive races did not do particularly well in the election (Block 2004).

At the presidential level, Democrat John Kerry bested Republican
George W. Bush by a comfortable 10-point margin—the fourth consecutive Democratic presidential election victory in the state. Democratic
incumbent Senator Barbara Boxer defeated her Republican opponent, Bill
Jones, by an even larger margin of 20 percentage points. The partisan
makeup of the state's congressional delegation and both houses of the
state legislature remained virtually unchanged after the 2004 elections.
The state's congressional delegation comprises thirty-three Democrats
and twenty Republicans, the State Senate has twenty-five Democrats and
fourteen Republicans, and the State Assembly includes forty-eight Democrats and thirty-two Republicans. One explanation for this lack of change
is that the architects of legislative districts have successfully eliminated
competitive districts in the state. According to one estimate (Block 2004,
6) "only 14 out of the 153 district contests for Congress, state Senate, or
state Assembly generated any real competition." Even in those rare competitive races, Schwarzenegger's support for Republican candidates had
very little impact. The governor's postelection response to this challenge
was to compel the newly elected state legislature to change the reappor-
tionment process by placing it in the hands of "independent" jurists; if that

fails, the governor has vowed to take the issue directly to the voters in a proposition on the 2006 ballot.

As in previous years, in 2004 belonging to the Christian Right dramatically increased one's chances of voting for a Republican candidate. Also as in earlier elections, this pro-GOP influence remains robust after statistically correcting for the effects of education, income, gender, ethnicity, and age (see table 11.2). The logistic regression coefficients in the first column of table 11.2 indicate, for instance, that a forty-year-old, white, non–Christian Right Protestant woman who holds a bachelor's degree and has a household income of $40,000 per year would have a 40 percent chance of voting for George W. Bush. If this hypothetical voter were the same on all characteristics except that she belonged to the Christian Right, however, she would almost certainly cast her ballot for Bush (92 percent likelihood). Thus, membership in the religious right strongly influenced one's vote for president (as well as for U.S. Senate and gubernatorial candidates and the stem-cell initiative), and its impact was almost twice that of its closest competitors—being Jewish ($b = -1.501$; $p < .05$) or African American ($b = -1.683$; $p < .05$).

Prospects for the Future of the Christian Right in California

The Christian Right in California currently finds itself in a tenuous position. Although the movement has won a place at the party table over the past several decades, this gain coincided with the severe electoral decline of the state Republican party. When Christian Right voters have helped to nominate social issue conservatives for statewide elective office, those candidates invariably have lost. More troubling than those defeats, perhaps, was Arnold Schwarzenegger's electoral success in 2003. His election proved that a social issue moderate fares better than a social issues conservative in a statewide race; Schwarzenegger also demonstrated that white, Christian conservatives voters will not abandon the GOP over even the most liberal candidate. Absent the threat of defecting to a Democratic candidate or staying home from the election, Christian conservative voters have little leverage within the GOP.

A "clean break" between the GOP and the Christian Right is unlikely in the immediate future, however. Conservative Christians remain an important part of the state GOP; white conservative Christians provide considerable resources for the party and its candidates, and they represented one-quarter of all GOP votes in the 1994 and 2004 elections. The movement is a substantial part of the party's coalition within the state, and it is likely to continue to pressure the party to take more conservative

Table 11.2   Determinants of Presidential, U.S. Senate, Stem Cell,
and Recall Votes, California

Determinants	GOP Presidential Vote	GOP Senate Vote	"No" Stem Cell Vote	Schwarzenegger Vote
Independent Variables				
Christian Right	2.855**	2.644**	1.542**	.932**
Catholic	−.328**	−.281*	.006	.006
Jewish	−1.501**	−1.266**	−1.493**	−1.030**
Other religion	−1.235**	−1.173**	−.460**	−.238**
Secularist	−.894**	−.581**	−.376**	−.721**
Education	−.588**	−.413**	−.198**	−.193**
Income	.225**	.274**	.091**	.154**
Female	−.295**	−.487**	−.171	−.380**
African American	−1.683**	−1.833**	−.282	−1.602**
Latino	−.897**	−1.084*	−.193	−.922**
Asian	−.212	−.819**	−.148	−.086
Other race	−.253	−.347	.138	−.149
Under age 30	−.308**	−.017	−.167	.085
Over age 64	−.383**	.017	−.018	−.233
Constant	1.563**	.427	.057	.556**
Model Statistics				
Sample size (*N*)	1527	1456	1462	4030
% correctly predicted	72.7	74.0	66.2	65.6
χ^2	461.9***	448.2***	160.8***	536.6
Degrees of freedom	14	14	14	14
Pseudo R^2 (Nagelkerke)	.347	.355	.139	.168

Note: Data from 2004 National Election Pool and 2003 Los Angeles Times Recall Election exit polls. Christian Right voters described themselves as "white," "conservative," and "Protestant" or "other Christian." Estimates obtained by dichotomous logistic regression. Education ranges from 1 to 5 (2004) or 6 (2003), and Income varies from 1 to 8 (2004) or 6 (2003). Cases with missing data deleted listwise. Data weighted to achieve demographically representative sample.
*$p < .10$, two–tailed test   **$p < .05$, two–tailed test   ***$p < .05$, one–tailed test.

positions on social and moral issues. The governor's decision to veto the same-sex marriage bill in 2005 demonstrates that there may be wisdom in the Christian Right sticking with the Republican Party; a Democratic governor would have been unlikely to veto that bill. Moreover, California's political climate and institutions will continue to provide opportunities for any movement that can muster support at the local level. Because the state's institutional structures are porous and open to mobilization of committed activists, there will always be a place in California politics for a social movement, like the Christian Right, that can effectively organize group members for political activism.

In the short run, the Christian Right, the state Republican party, and Arnold Schwarzenegger are consigned to an unusual relationship. Like a *ménage à trois*, it is a living arrangement of sorts—but it is not normative, and it is not the healthiest of relationships for anyone involved. The Christian Right might find itself in the unusual position of having to wish ill on Schwarzenegger because his electoral success reinforces the party's movement in a socially liberal direction. In years to come, the Christian Right might conclude that it would be better for the movement to be vilified by the Democrats than to be all but ignored by a fellow Republican.

In the long run, the Christian Right could try to expand its base by including ethnic minorities. The most notable demographic feature of California in recent decades has been the rapid growth in the numbers of Latinos and Asians and the decline of Anglos as a percentage of the state's population. California is now a "majority-minority state." After the 2000 census, whites made up 47 percent of the state population, Latinos 32 percent, Asians 11 percent, and African Americans 7 percent. The minority electorate, particularly Latinos, has expanded rapidly in the past several decades. Although Latinos historically have lagged well behind non-Hispanic whites in voter participation, that situation is slowly changing. The state's demographics, in short, make it virtually impossible for a political movement of white evangelical Christians alone to have a dramatic political impact in California. The capacity of the Christian Right to succeed in the Golden State will be a function of the ability of movement leaders to increase support among Latino, Asian, and African American Christians.

Fortunately for the Christian Right, Latinos, Asians, and African Americans are more socially conservative as a whole than non-Hispanic whites, and they are more likely than non-Hispanic whites to identify with the Christian Right. In the 2000 election, for example, exit polls indicate that 31 percent of Latinos, 23 percent of African Americans, and 17 percent of Asians considered themselves part of the "conservative Christian political movement." Only 13 percent of white voters, by comparison, identified themselves in this way. In that election, Hispanics represented 25.5 percent of voters who identified with the religious right; 10.2 percent were African Americans, and 5.1 percent were Asians. In some respects, Latinos in particular are natural allies of the Christian Right. They are more religious than non-Latinos, less liberal ideologically, and have more conservative views on social issues such as homosexuality and abortion (Field Poll 2000). When California voters approved Proposition 22, which banned recognition of same-sex marriages, Latino voters gave the measure stronger support than non-Latinos (Meyerson 2001). In other words, there is a Christian conservative constituency in California; it is found increasingly outside the white, evangelical Protestant world that historically has propelled the Christian Right political movement.

On the surface, a political movement by the Christian Right that crosses ethnic lines seems highly unlikely. For the past several decades the Christian Right has worked hard to increase its presence within the state Republican party, but that affiliation limits the movement's capacity to mobilize Latinos and African Americans, who vote overwhelmingly Democratic, and Asians, who are slightly more Democratic than Republican. Although Latinos and African Americans lean to the right on social issues, they are to the left of the electorate on economics and the rights of ethnic minorities.

Creation of a new kind of Christian Right that might mobilize Latino, Asian, and African American evangelicals probably would require a new leadership cadre that is not as bound to the GOP or as narrowly focused on the social issues of abortion and gay rights. A first-generation Salvadoran American interviewed at a Pentecostal-oriented, Spanish-speaking church in Los Angeles explained that he had voted for Governor Gray Davis to avoid rewarding the Republicans for their dirty methods of electioneering. The twenty-year U.S. resident also preferred many of Davis' policies, such as his stand on bilingual education. Although this Latino Pentecostal was not dead-set against voting for a Republican candidate in the future (and actually was fond of Ronald Reagan), he did not see himself supporting the GOP unless Republicans adopted "more just" positions on immigration and welfare reform. Given the extent to which the state's Republicans and the Christian Right have shown themselves to be hostile to immigrants and welfare recipients, however, such a "kinder, gentler" GOP is not likely to appear anytime soon.

For at least the medium term, then, California's Latinos and African Americans are likely to remain solidly in the Democratic fold, despite their socially conservative views. What remains to be seen is whether a new kind of Christian Right can emerge that will cross ethnic lines to take advantage of those institutional openings. Without this attempt to bridge the ethnic divide among evangelical Protestants, any future political movement among evangelical Christians will be limited in impact.

References

Allswang, John M. 2000. *The Initiative and Referendum in California, 1898–1998.* Stanford, Calif.: Stanford University Press.

Barabak, Mark A. 2001. "State Republicans Search for Beacon amid Gloom." *Los Angeles Times*, 2 February, A1.

Block, A. G. 2003. "California in Crisis." *California Journal* 34 (August): 18–27.

———. 2004. "Much Ado about Nothing." *California Journal* 35 (December): 6–8.

Bruzzone, Arthur. 2003. "Blood Feud: California Republicans' Unholy War." Available at www.rightturns.com/columnists/bruzzone/ab20030115.htm.

California Journal. 2002. "Election 2002: Governor." *California Journal* 33 (April): 14–17.

California Opinion Index. 1997. "Gay and Lesbian Rights Issues." Release no. 1832 (May).

———. 2005. "Vote in 2004 Presidential Election." Release no. 2150 (January).

California Republican Party. 2001. California Republican Party 2004 Platform. Available at www.cagop.org/about/platform.

Cannon, Lou. 1998. "The Two Faces of the California GOP." *California Journal* 24 (November): 18–21.

———. 2002. "Reagan Rerun?" *California Journal* 33 (April): 18–21.

———. 2003. "There We Go Again?" *California Journal* 34 (September): 28–29.

———. 2004. "Riding Herd on California's GOP." *California Journal* 35 (March): 34–38.

Conger, Kimberly H., and John C. Green. 2002. "Spreading Out and Digging in: Christian Conservatives and State Republican Parties." *Campaigns and Elections* 23 (February): 58–60, 64–65.

Dunlap, David W. 1994. "Minister Stresses Anti-Gay Message." *New York Times*, 19 December, A8.

Elazar, Daniel J. 1972. *American Federalism: A View from the States*, 2nd ed. New York: Thomas Y. Crowell Co.

Field Poll. 1997. "Majority of Voters Continue to Approve of Abortion During 1st Trimester." Release no. 1835 (March 1997).

———. 2000. "The Expanding Latino Electorate: California's New Latino Voters Differ from Their Predecessors in Many Ways." Release no. 1525 (May).

———. 2004. "Voters Remain Pro-Choice." Release no. 2118 (June).

Field, Mona. 2005. *California Government and Politics Today*, 10th ed. New York: Pearson Longman.

Garvey, Megan. 2004. "Stem Cell Initiative Attracts Backers." *Los Angeles Times*, August 31, B1.

Garza, Jennifer. 2003. "Church and State: How Much Do Voters Care about the Religious Beliefs of Candidates?" *Sacramento Bee*, 4 October, E1.

Gerston, Larry N., and Terry Christenson. 1995. *California Politics and Government*. Belmont, Calif.: Wadsworth Publishing Co.

Gilbert, Christopher P. 1993. *The Impact of Churches on Political Behavior*. Westport, Conn.: Greenwood Press.

Green, John C. 2000. "The Christian Right and the 1998 Elections: An Overview." In *Prayers in the Precincts: The Christian Right in the 1998 Elections*, ed. John C. Green, Mark J. Rozell, and Clyde Wilcox. Washington, D.C.: Georgetown University Press, 1–19.

Haddock, Vicki. 2003. "Arnold Shows a Bit of the Right (wing) Stuff." *San Francisco Chronicle*, 31 August, D1.

Hyink, Bernard L., and David H. Provost. 1998. *Politics and Government in California*. Menlo Park, Calif: Longman.

Lesher, David. 2003. "The Rise of Voters." *California Journal* 34 (September): 20–25.

Los Angeles Times Poll. 2000. "Study #449/Exit Poll. General Election: Nation and California, November 7, 2000." Available at www.latimes.com/extras/timespoll.

Marinucci, Carla. 2003. "Religious Right Opposes Schwarzenegger." *San Francisco Chronicle*, 1 October, A12.

Marquez, Jeremiah. 2003. "Women's Groups, Religious Leaders Galvanize Opposition to Schwarzenegger." Associated Press state and local wire, 3 October.

Matthews, Joe, and Megan Garvey. 2004. "Schwarzenegger Backs Stem Cell Study." *Los Angeles Times,* 19 October, A1

Mayhew, David. 1986. *Placing Parties in American Politics*. Princeton, N.J.: Princeton University Press.

McGirr, Lisa. 2001. *Suburban Warriors: The Origins of the New American Right*. Princeton, N.J.: Princeton University Press.

Mecoy, Laura. 2004. "Multimillionaires Fuel Initiatives." *Sacramento Bee*, 29 October, A3.

Meyerson, Harold. 2001. "California's Progressive Mosaic." *The American Prospect* 12 (18 June): 17–23.

National Annenberg Election Survey. 2004. "Welcome to the NAES 2004." Available at www.annenbergpublicpolicycenter.org/naes/.

Nollinger, Mark. 1993. "The New Crusaders—The Christian Right Storms California's Political Bastions." *California Journal* 24 (January): 6–11.

Persinos, John C. 1994. "Has the Christian Right Taken Over the Republican Party?" *Campaigns and Elections* 15 (September): 20–24.

Peterson, Larry. 1991. "The Dannemeyer-Seymour Race: Do Republicans Face an Unpalatable Choice?" *California Journal* 22 (January): 30–34.

Rich, Frank. 2003. "Top Gun vs. Total Recall." *New York Times*, 14 September, A19.

Russo, Michael A. 1995. "California: A Political Landscape for Choice and Conflict." In *Abortion Politics in American States*, ed. Mary C. Segers and Timothy A. Byrnes. Armonk, N.Y.: M. E. Sharpe, 168–81.

Salladay, Robert. 2004. "Schwarzenegger Could Accept Gay Marriages If Voters, Courts Approve It." *San Francisco Chronicle*, 2 March, A5.

Schuparra, Kurt. 1998. *Triumph of the Right: The Rise of the California Conservative Movement, 1945–1966*. Armonk, N.Y.: M. E. Sharpe.

Sheldon, Lou. 2004. "California Governor Signs Drag Queen/Hate Crime Law." Available at www.traditionalvalues.org/modules.php?sid=1920.

Skelton, George. 2000. "State Republicans Find Waking Up Is Hard to Do." *Los Angeles Times*, 13 November, A3.

———. 2005. "Gov's Taken Himself Out of the Game on Same-Sex Marriage." *Los Angeles Times*, 8 September, B2

Soper, J. Christopher. 1995. "California: Christian Conservative Influence in a Liberal State." In *God at the Grass Roots: The Christian Right in the 1994 Midterm Elections*, ed. Mark J. Rozell and Clyde Wilcox. Lanham, Md.: Rowman and Littlefield, 211–26.

Soper, J. Christopher, and Joel S. Fetzer. 2003. "The Christian Right in California: Dimming Fortunes in the Golden State." In *The Christian Right in American Politics: Marching to the Millennium*, ed. John C. Green, Mark J. Rozell, and Clyde Wilcox. Washington, D.C.: Georgetown University Press, 209–30.

Weintraub, Daniel. 2004. "Conservatives Stuck with Social Liberal Schwarzenegger." *San Gabriel Valley Tribune*, 30 September, A10.

Wildermuth, John. 2001. "Moderates Rebuffed in Bid to Lead State GOP." *San Francisco Chronicle*, 26 February, A1.

CHAPTER TWELVE

South Carolina

Integration and Success?

JAMES L. GUTH

FOR ALMOST FOUR DECADES SOUTH CAROLINA HAS PROVIDED A MAR-velous case study of the Christian Right's fortunes within the Republican party. The movement appeared earlier, manifested more variation, and sustained greater influence in the Palmetto State than almost anywhere else in the country. Indeed, the South Carolina GOP often is characterized as "dominated" or at least "strongly influenced" by the Christian Right (Conger and Green 2002). As a result, the Christian Right has established a firmer position within the Republican party in South Carolina and, per-haps, had greater electoral impact than in other states (Smith 1997).

The contemporary reality is more complex, however. As demographic changes visibly erode the numerical dominance of conservative Protestants, Christian Right forces sometimes still clash with the GOP's business wing and seldom exhibit monolithic unity, especially in electoral campaigns. The price of the movement's integration into the party is a more pragmatic orientation among some activists that alienates them from more purist colleagues. Moreover, the Christian Right often has been constrained by external events or countermobilization by political opponents.

After briefly reviewing South Carolina's religious makeup, we review highlights of the Christian Right's history in the state, concluding with its successes and failures in the 2000 and 2002 elections. We then focus on the influence of Christian conservatives in the 2004 presidential contest and, especially, the crucial U.S. Senate contest to replace retiring Democratic Senator Fritz Hollings. These episodes reveal that although the electoral machinery of movement groups has broken down, Christian conservatives have become a vital part of the GOP's electoral majority.

Religion in South Carolina

South Carolina has long been fertile ground for the Christian Right. Although economic growth and in-migration have diversified the urban population, residents of the state still are predominantly evangelical Protestants, especially Southern Baptists—the state's (and nation's) largest Protestant body, claiming almost 49 percent of all South Carolina church members in 2000. There also are numerous (and mostly uncounted) independent fundamentalist congregations, usually Baptist, along with many new nondenominational megachurches in the burgeoning suburbs. Other evangelical groups, such as the Presbyterian Church in America (PCA), also have benefited from suburbanization and sometimes play a noticeable political role.

South Carolina also claims many mainline Protestants, especially members of the United Methodist Church (16 percent of church members) and the Presbyterian Church in the U.S.A. (5 percent), as well as evangelical Lutherans and Episcopalians (about 3 percent each). The African American community is served by several Baptist denominations (perhaps 16 percent of all church members) and others such as the African Methodist Episcopal Church, Zion (compare Bradley et al. 1992, 31, with Jones et al. 2002, 36–37), and African American clergy retain their historic political role. Recent years also have seen the steady growth of the Catholic community (7 percent of adherents), both Anglo and Hispanic, although these groups have not yet become distinct political forces. Some data suggest a rise in the number of secular voters as well.[1]

Organization of the Religious Right

For most of the twentieth century, the centrality of race in South Carolina politics precluded any large role for religion. This dynamic changed in the 1960s and 1970s, however, as Republicans challenged the historic Democratic monopoly on public office. At first the revitalized GOP reflected the religious hues of its new urban, often "immigrant," leadership: upper-status mainliners such as Episcopalians, Presbyterians, Methodists, and some "First Church" Southern Baptists. More conservative religious forces soon crashed the party (Guth 1995), however, taking advantage of the openness of the nascent Republican party to any organized group.

The Bob Jones Contingent

The Christian Right first appeared in the 1960s as Barry Goldwater's presidential candidacy excited religious conservatives, especially at Greenville's

Bob Jones University (BJU)—a mecca for the strictest wing of historic fundamentalism. After a decade of growing involvement, in 1976 BJU forces infiltrated precinct meetings and took control of the Greenville county GOP—the state's largest Republican beachhead. Some activists supported Ronald Reagan's 1976 challenge against incumbent President Gerald Ford; most sought to push the GOP platform to the right, and many hoped to thwart federal interference with the burgeoning Christian school network (Smith 1997). The BJU encroachment met fierce resistance from GOP regulars, who were accustomed to running their own show, but Ford's electoral defeat in 1976 forced the two factions together.

The eventual assimilation of the "BJU crowd" into the GOP reflected several factors. First, BJU activists were too few to control local party committees statewide, although they were numerous enough to establish a presence. Even where they were dominant in local organizations, their candidates for office usually lost. Second, Republican leaders such as Congressman (later Governor) Carroll Campbell and Governor James Edwards astutely cultivated BJU activists, patiently mediating intraparty disputes and rewarding cooperative behavior. Finally, BJU's militant religious separatism discouraged loyalists from joining other religious conservatives in a broader Christian Right organization—in effect encouraging individual activism in the GOP.

As a result, BJU leadership soon was dominated by savvy politicians rather than "religious amateurs," permitting easier accommodation with party regulars, who gladly traded platform concessions for loyal support. Although the fundamentalists were more preoccupied with moral issues than most party regulars were, the routine governmental implications of this fact often were hard to detect, and some BJU politicos soon gained the respect of even their staunchest opponents. One GOP legislative leader, the late Terry Haskins, observed that the fundamentalists and party regulars soon "agreed on everything except where to go to church" (Ehrenhalt 1991, 98). BJU produced a large cadre of activists, who usually backed the most conservative entrant in GOP primaries—unless that candidate had unacceptable religious traits, such as Pentecostal beliefs. Then they behaved as loyal pragmatists, supporting the GOP primary winner in the general election (Smith 1997). By the mid-1980s, then, BJU Republicans were a distinct but fairly integrated GOP faction—a development encouraged by some "moderation" in the university's social and political stances, initiated by President Bob Jones III (Guth 2000a).

Ironically, the presence of BJU fundamentalists preempted Jerry Falwell's Moral Majority, which was heavily dependent on the very independent Baptists who were monopolized by the BJU network in South Carolina. As a result, the Moral Majority had virtually no grassroots organization in the state during the early 1980s, aside from a few pastors in Falwell's Baptist Bible Fellowship. Moreover, the occasional candidate with Falwell connections failed at the polls, especially in BJU precincts, as religious competition between the Jones and Falwell networks precluded any merger of forces.

The Christian Coalition

Just as the GOP was assimilating the BJU folks, a more challenging insurgency emerged when the charismatic forces of religious broadcaster Marion G. "Pat" Robertson infiltrated 1987 precinct meetings, almost capturing the state convention. They were narrowly repelled by GOP regulars (with BJU help), largely through astute legal maneuvering. Robertson's organizational prowess was not matched by his performance in the 1988 presidential primary in South Carolina, however. He finished a poor third, with only one-fifth of the vote; he failed to expand his base much beyond its original charismatic and Pentecostal core, which was quite small in South Carolina. Most conservative Christians, including Southern Baptist clergy and their parishioners, voted for the primary winner, George H. W. Bush. To keep peace, Governor Campbell, acting at Bush's behest, gave Robertson supporters some party offices, including delegate slots to the 1988 national convention.

The "merger" did not go smoothly, however. In 1991 Robertson loyalists reorganized as the state Christian Coalition, led by Roberta Combs. Whereas rivals often criticized national Christian Coalition executive Ralph Reed for being far too accommodating to Republican leaders, Combs was more belligerent. Buoyed by apparent successes in the 1992 election, in organizing the state's three metropolitan areas, and in recruiting some Southern Baptists and other conservative Protestants—especially anti-abortion activists—the Christian Coalition struck hard. Members flooded the 1993 GOP precinct meetings, narrowly controlled the state convention, and helped elect Henry McMaster as state chair over Greenvillian Knox White—a Campbell protégé and moderate conservative who nevertheless had strong ties with BJU (Graham, Moore, and Petrusak 1994). Yet although McMaster added Christian Coalition activists to his staff, he proved independent, staving off persistent Christian Coalition efforts to gain control of the GOP executive committee while mollifying disgruntled party regulars.

Although national and state Christian Coalition leaders strongly supported GOP presidential primary winner Bob Dole in 1996, tension between Christian Coalition forces and party regulars reappeared at the state convention, where nineteen of the thirty-seven national convention delegates were to be selected. Governor David Beasley—elected with strong Christian Coalition support in 1994—and Roberta Combs negotiated furiously over a "gubernatorial/Coalition" slate that would include some elected officials but favored Christian conservatives. The agreement fell apart at the convention, however. The consensus slate was distributed to all delegates, but to Beasley's surprise each county Christian Coalition leader provided followers with a slate limited to Christian Coalition activists and "friends" (including some BJU activists). There were slots for Beasley and Senator Strom Thurmond but not for former governor Campbell or Southern Baptist activist Cyndi Mosteller—a Beasley appointee to the state Health Board, chair of the platform committee, and antiabortion leader (Guth and Smith 1997).

The subsequent vote revealed the Christian Coalition's clout. Several unknown members outpolled both Campbell (twelfth in the balloting) and GOP Congressman Floyd Spence. Another GOP congressman had to settle for a position as alternate, and the incumbent national committeewoman and committeeman were excluded altogether. The resulting delegation was staunchly conservative, lukewarm toward Dole, and very "Christian Right."

Over the succeeding four years, the Christian Coalition fought sporadic skirmishes with the state leadership but gradually lost ground—reflecting, in part, the decline in the national organization after Ralph Reed's departure. Roberta Combs' appointment to take Reed's place did little to revive the national Christian Coalition and accelerated the decline of the state unit. Although the Christian Coalition mustered some activity in 2000, especially in assisting George W. Bush's primary victory over John McCain, by 2002 it had virtually disintegrated; its partisans continued to seek advantage in the state executive committee, usually without success. When GOP chairman McMaster resigned in 2002 to run (successfully) for state attorney general, the Christian Coalition offered no candidate to replace him in a contest won overwhelmingly by Katon Dawson, a party regular, who handily beat two other candidates—including prolife leader Cyndi Mosteller (Vinson and Guth 2003). Nevertheless, two national committee posts remained in the hands of Christian Coalition allies (and remained so in 2005).

The Southern Baptists

The third major Christian Right element, the vote-rich Southern Baptist contingent, has always been more difficult to assess. The powerful state Baptist convention clearly has moved to the right politically, and like their brethren elsewhere, South Carolina Baptist clergy have become increasingly active. Surveys reveal that a large majority of ministers consider themselves Republicans and feel close to most national Christian Right groups—although not to the Christian Coalition. Clergy and laity have been prominent in the antiabortion movement, antigambling campaigns, and on other social issues, but Baptists still lack any central organizing forum. Efforts by prominent Baptist activists to politicize the convention's Christian Life Committee structure have been partially successful, and several Baptist conservatives have become prominent politicians, especially in the state legislature. The state Baptist Convention itself recently has adopted a somewhat higher lobbying profile in the state capital, often in conjunction with other Christian Right groups, and it has substantially increased publicity about conservative causes in the state *Baptist Courier.* Other Baptist laity, however, are leading business and professional people with closer ties to the old party establishment. The same could be said for PCA activists, who are much less numerous but constitute a major element in GOP organizations, especially in the upstate region.

Other Christian Right Organizations

The BJU, Christian Coalition, and state Baptist forces have been complemented by many smaller and sometimes overlapping organizations. The Palmetto Family Council, which is loosely affiliated with James Dobson's Focus on the Family, has maintained a modest presence on moral issues in the legislature, often working with the state's Southern Baptists and other groups on issues such as gay marriage. The American Family Association, Eagle Forum, and National Right to Life Committee have had small local units that also have contributed at times to Christian Right activism.

Thus, as the new millennium dawned, the South Carolina GOP remained a hybrid organization—though a "hardy" hybrid: part BJU, part Christian Coalition, and part conservative Southern Baptist, with minor strains of other conservative Christians—all grafted on the basic stock of business Republicans. The Christian Right's long history in South Carolina has revealed some clear patterns. Although Christian activists do not dominate party functions, they are a major force within the GOP, especially in primaries, and they are an essential part of any winning coalition—both for GOP nominations and for Republican victory in general elections. Christian conservatives have given "moral" and "family values" issues a higher visibility; no Republican candidate (and probably few Democrats) can avoid these issues entirely. Although the Christian Coalition is moribund, conservative Christians of many stripes are firmly embedded in the state's politics, holding GOP leadership posts and public offices.

Integration of the Christian Right within the GOP was epitomized by the 2002 Republican gubernatorial primary. Although no Christian Right group explicitly endorsed any of the seven candidates—and the Christian

Coalition appeared to be absent entirely—all of the candidates vigorously sought conservative Christian support. They all emphasized the role faith plays in their lives, their regular church attendance, and roles as Sunday school teachers or elders—or, in one case, minister in training. Even the (successful) Episcopalian candidate, former U.S. Representative Mark Sanford, ran TV ads highlighting his "Christian values" and discussed his faith in press interviews. Moreover, all of the candidates scrambled for endorsements from prominent Christian conservatives. Both Sanford and his friend Lindsey Graham, a Southern Baptist who won an uncontested GOP nomination to run for the Senate seat vacated by Strom Thurmond, had solid, if quiet, support from Christian conservatives in November. By 2004, then, the GOP appeared almost a model of internal harmony, with many conservative Christian activists well integrated into party machinery, though certainly not in control—or necessarily always pleased by party policy.

The Election of 2004

The 2004 election was the first in recent memory in which no Christian Right organization played a major role in grassroots mobilization. Thus, the campaign provided an interesting test for the staying power of Christian conservatives in the GOP. Because President Bush had the active support of virtually every Republican faction and, in any event, faced no primary opponent and virtually no prospect of losing the state's electoral votes in November, there was little drama in the presidential race. Indeed, except for the national media's coverage, the paraphernalia of the presidential contest was mostly absent from South Carolina.

The Senate race was a different matter. The retirement of veteran Fritz Hollings offered a rare opportunity for state politicians to move to the upper chamber of Congress. Given growing Republican dominance (Kuzenski 2003), Democrats regard the contest as a crucial test of their ability to remain competitive. Naturally the GOP primary attracted the most combatants; the Democrats sought their most attractive candidate, quickly settling on state Superintendent of Education Inez Tenenbaum—a proven voter getter in 1998 who actually bolstered her majority during the 2002 Republican landslide.

The GOP race attracted six candidates, with varying appeals to the Christian conservative and business wings and different "regional" strengths, which remain important in South Carolina. Fastest out of the gate was Greenville's Jim DeMint, first elected to the U.S. House of Representatives in 1998 and self-limited to six years in office. DeMint had compiled a record as a strong economic and social conservative in Washington.

Although he focused on taxes, health care, and social security reform, he also was active in the Pro-Life Caucus and sponsored legislation to encourage adoptions. DeMint also was a convinced free trader, casting the deciding House vote that gave President Bush fast-track trade authority in 2001. This action by a legislator from a city that once billed itself the "textile capital of the world" elicited a challenge in the 2002 Republican primaries from Phil Bradley, a state public service commissioner who had massive financial support from textile interests, especially billionaire Roger Milliken. DeMint, for his part, had solid backing from many small businesses, Greenville's large and growing international business community, and national business groups, including the U.S. Chamber of Commerce and the politically aggressive Club for Growth. His closeness to the White House and frequent meetings with Karl Rove suggested Bush's implicit endorsement. Perhaps as a result, DeMint started the race aided by most of the state GOP's expert fundraisers and many party officials.

DeMint's ties with Christian conservatives also were solid. An active member of a PCA congregation, he had served as a deacon, elder, and Sunday school teacher. The numerous PCA political activists in the Fourth District had been an asset in his initial House race, just as they had assisted his mentor and predecessor, Bob Inglis. Moreover, although BJU forces had supported an opponent in DeMint's first run for the GOP nomination, he developed fairly cordial relationships with that group, although some BJU Republicans joined Phil Bradley's 2002 primary challenge. In Washington DeMint roomed with other religious conservatives, participated in prayer groups, and maintained contact with Christian Right organizations, such as Focus on the Family.

The PCA and BJU constituencies were important in the Fourth Congressional District but were less help in a statewide race. DeMint struggled to build support in other regions. Indeed, each area produced at least one candidate hoping to turn local prominence into a first- or second-place primary finish, thereby emerging into the runoff and its increased visibility for the survivors. Former state Attorney General Charlie Condon, a resident of the Charleston area, hoped his years in state office in Columbia had given him name recognition across the state, especially in the Midlands. His official responsibilities also had provided opportunities—which he used aggressively—to promote conservative policies on law and order, social issues, and constitutional questions. Despite being Catholic in an overwhelmingly Protestant state, he had drawn considerable Christian Right support in his failed bid for the 2002 gubernatorial nomination, which he hoped to expand upon in the Senate primary.

While DeMint combined emphases on economic and social conservatism and Condon stressed the latter, other candidates concentrated on the GOP's business wing. Thomas Ravenel of Charleston enjoyed strong name recognition: His father, Arthur Ravenel, was a former U.S. Representative, state legislator, and unsuccessful candidate for the 1994 GOP gubernatorial nomination. Although Thomas Ravenel listed connections with an old French Huguenot congregation in his campaign literature, like his father he built his appeal around business issues, leavened with a major dose of patriotism. He downplayed social issues, on which he took conventional conservative stances. Like his father, however, he hoped to rally Republicans who were uncomfortable with the GOP's religious tone, but without offending religious conservatives. His campaign was well funded, in part because of his ability to invest vast amounts of personal wealth. Two other candidates also entered the contest: Mayor Mark McBride of the resort city of Myrtle Beach—the only candidate who sometimes showed hints of moderation, especially on social issues—and Orly Benny Davis, a Bluffton businesswoman who took conventional GOP positions on most issues. Neither McBride nor Davis generated much activist enthusiasm or financial support, and they quickly became marginal players.

Although many Christian conservatives made early commitments, usually either to DeMint or Condon, others were either dissatisfied with the choices available or convinced that neither could match the demonstrated vote-getting prowess of the putative Democratic nominee, Inez Tenenbaum—a conviction reinforced by some early polls. As a result, many Christian Right leaders encouraged the candidacy of an old favorite: former governor David Beasley. Beasley had ridden to power in 1994 with support from a coalition of Christian conservatives and party regulars—in a good Republican year. During four years in office, however, he had combined some courageous stands—such as proposing to remove the Confederate flag from the Statehouse and outlaw video poker—with a host of political missteps in advocating these and other policies. His success in irritating or even antagonizing vital GOP constituencies allowed Democrat Jim Hodges, riding on a flood of campaign money from gambling interests, to defeat Beasley in 1998. (Hodges himself was a one-term governor; he was defeated by Republican Mark Sanford in 2002.)

Beasley's failures had not dampened Christian activists' enthusiasm for him (Hoover 2003). After his 1998 defeat he revived a successful business career and devoted much energy to religious causes, including mission stints in the United States and abroad. His official policies subsequently were vindicated, at least in part, when his successor and the legislature settled issues that had vexed his tenure: The Confederate flag was removed from the statehouse, the blight of video poker was eradicated, and a lottery for educational funding was implemented. Indeed, Beasley himself received a "Profile in Courage" award for efforts on the flag issue from the

John F. Kennedy Library—although it was not clear how this would play among GOP voters (Hoover 2004c). Several polls suggested that Beasley was the only Republican who was capable of beating Mrs. Tenenbaum, which provided some regular Republicans with reasons to support him.

Beasley's late entrance, in mid-January 2004, reconfigured the race. As the best-known candidate and with a fervent political base of conservative Christian activists and wealthy textile executives, Beasley immediately became the frontrunner, forcing other candidates to fight for a second-place finish in the hope that Beasley would come up short of a majority, forcing a runoff. Nevertheless, his late entrance did cost him potential backers and financial support. As BJU dean and GOP activist Bob Taylor noted, by the time Beasley got in, most Christian activists had commitments they were unwilling to break—although a few, including State Senator Mike Fair and prolife leader Lisa Van Riper, did shift to Beasley (Hoover 2004a). Some Christian Right activists opposed Beasley, however, out of dislike for his gubernatorial actions on the flag, his failure to take more aggressive action on abortion, or his "flip-flopping" on the lottery.

The contest gradually settled into a three-candidate race, with Beasley seeking an absolute majority on June 8 and DeMint and Ravenel vying for the runoff spot if Beasley failed to win an absolute majority. As the candidates traversed the state debating, each emphasized his strong suit: Beasley focused on family values and protection for the textile industry, consistently tying DeMint to his free-trade votes in Congress. DeMint kept plugging tax and social security reforms. Ravenel emphasized other business issues, attempted to avoid being identified on the trade question, although his views were closer to DeMint's than to Beasley's. Condon emphasized terrorism and law and order, as well as cutting federal spending. The candidates seldom discussed social issues, but when they did all the candidates took conservative positions (Hoover 2004b). For example, the four leading candidates all endorsed a federal constitutional amendment prohibiting same-sex marriage. (Although Mayor McBride agreed on the substance, he didn't want to clutter up the U.S. Constitution.)

Beasley did "win" the first primary, but he got only 36 percent of the vote, with DeMint (26 percent) and Ravenel (24 percent) close behind and Condon falling to single digits (9 percent). The runoff between Beasley and DeMint promised to be close. Although DeMint had more ground to make up, several factors worked to his advantage: His economic stances were much closer to Ravenel's than were Beasley's more populist trade policies; he had solid support from many Christian conservatives, undermining Beasley's base, especially in the vote-rich upstate region; finally, DeMint garnered the endorsements of Ravenel, Condon, and McBride, which suggested that Beasley might not pick up enough votes from the third-, fourth-, or fifth-place camps. DeMint also won the endorsement of most state newspapers.

The runoff campaign was short and intensive and became almost a referendum on foreign trade—the only issue on which there were substantial differences between the candidates. Although each candidate attacked the other's political judgment, the race was a virtual seminar on the relative merit of different trade policies. As the day of the runoff approached GOP voters moved decisively toward DeMint, who won going away, 59 percent to 41 percent. DeMint won handily among the ideological conservatives who dominate the state GOP, carried urban and suburban areas, and won among voters with at least some college education. Although available poll data contain no religious measures, the fact that substantially more than half of all GOP identifiers who called themselves "conservatives" come from the evangelical camp hints that DeMint must have done very well among them, even against a Christian Right favorite.

The choice for Christian Right activists in the general election was clear. All the unsuccessful primary candidates—including Beasley—warmly endorsed DeMint's bid, leaving few factional scars for the Democrats to exploit. Moreover, the Democratic candidate confronted several difficulties in appealing to a religiously conservative electorate. Tenenbaum tried to present a moderate image on social issues, distancing herself from presidential candidate John Kerry, opposing gay marriage, backing capital punishment, and even supporting a ban on partial-birth abortion (Bandy 2004)—stands that caused her problems among liberals, especially gay rights groups. Yet even these concessions were not enough to move her very far beyond her party's core religious constituency of black Protestants, other religious minorities, and secular voters. First, as Superintendent of Education she held a post whose incumbent Christian conservatives—dissatisfied with public schools and tied to the Christian school movement—inevitably distrusted. She also had few effective religious appeals of her own: Brought up a Methodist, she was married to a prominent Jewish business leader who had long been an important figure in the state Democratic Party. Although she occasionally highlighted her "mainline" Protestant background, this tack proved ineffective.

Even Tenenbaum's social issue moderation was belied by substantial financial support from Emily's List and other prochoice groups, as well as by her own service as a lobbyist/litigator for feminist groups earlier in her career. Although she was able to build a relatively extensive campaign organization of paid canvassers and volunteers, these activists themselves were overwhelmingly liberal, resisted being "gagged" by the campaign hierarchy, and often sought to tie Tenenbaum more closely to Kerry's candidacy—a sinking ship in South Carolina waters (Anderson 2005).

Although both DeMint and Tenenbaum had run impeccable campaigns in earlier races, the general election contest saw missteps on both sides. Although the contenders maintained unusual civility in public statements and broadcast debates, some fairly sharp differences emerged. DeMint tried to keep the campaign focus on economic policy, defending his free trade policies and promoting tax cuts and Social Security reform. He counted on his uniformly conservative record on social issues to keep Christian conservatives in his camp—with the help of visits by Christian Right favorites such as former U.S. House Majority Leader Dick Armey. Tenenbaum countered with protectionist appeals, tying South Carolina's employment woes to recent trade pacts—in the process picking up major financial backing from usually Republican textile executives, led by Roger Chastain, former president of the American Textile Manufacturers' Institute. When protectionism failed to provide any more traction for her than it had for David Beasley, she focused on DeMint's tax-cutting panacea—a 23 percent national sales tax to replace federal income taxes—suggesting that this "new tax" would be on top of existing levies. This somewhat misleading characterization produced a clear boost in the polls and left DeMint to explain a complicated proposal with no appeal to most voters.

Social issues played little overt role in the race—at least until late in the campaign, when DeMint was asked whether he supported the state GOP platform plank that would prohibit gays from teaching in the public schools. DeMint replied that he did and added that he thought unmarried pregnant teachers also should be banned. These statements immediately aroused media controversy, and DeMint backed off, arguing that these issues were local matters and should not be the topic of a U.S. Senate debate. He also recounted his own experience of being raised by a single mother to assert his sympathy with such parents. Although the media reaction was adverse to both DeMint's original statement and his "retraction," his stance probably did not hurt him among Christian conservatives (Hurt 2005).

During the campaign there was little visible organizational activity by Christian Right groups. DeMint himself spoke in a few churches, addressing religious and social issues. The national Christian Coalition published a voter guide on its website that compared DeMint most favorably against the Democratic candidate, urging visitors to make copies and distribute the guide themselves—a far cry from the days of massive church distribution. James Dobson of Focus on the Family released a public letter praising DeMint and blasting Tenenbaum because of her support from prochoice groups (Hoover 2004d). More important, perhaps, DeMint had financial support from prolife and Christian Right groups, including the Campaign for Working Families, the National Right to Life Political Action Committee (PAC), the Eagle Forum PAC, the Susan B. Anthony List, and

Focus on the Family Action. Although the sums involved—both direct contributions and independent expenditures—were large, they were submerged in a sea of individual, business PAC, and other organized contributions that gave DeMint a considerable financial advantage over Tenenbaum, who relied on Emily's List, textile executives, and labor PACs for campaign cash to supplement individual contributions. In any event, on November 2, DeMint won the Senate seat easily, defeating Tenenbaum by 54 percent to 44 percent.

Religious Voting in the 2004 Election

The 2004 South Carolina races were fought in a new environment: There was limited grassroots involvement by Christian Right groups, and social issues usually were in the background. Although national debates over abortion and gay marriage penetrated the state through the press, in the absence of either a real presidential contest or a state ballot question, neither issue was a visible part of the state presidential campaign, modest as it was. Even the Senate race focused on international trade, taxes, and economic questions; the GOP primary contenders were all agreed on social issues, and Tenenbaum eschewed social liberalism in a conservative state, looking to economic policy as the vehicle for overcoming the "normal" Republican majority.

In the absence of both intensive religious organizing and social issue debates, did the outcomes of the presidential and senatorial races fall out along religious lines? Did evangelicals turn out for the GOP? Which religious groups chose the Democratic candidates? Although the National Election Pool exit poll's religious measures are not ideal, they do permit some insight into the religious coalitions underlying contemporary Palmetto State politics—which here, as elsewhere, have been shaped by long-term efforts by the Christian Right to realign the party system.

As table 12.1 shows, there were distinct religious differences in the two-party vote for president and U.S. Senate. Evangelicals voted overwhelmingly Republican, accounting for almost half of the GOP coalition; mainline Protestants also voted strongly for the GOP, providing another quarter of the total vote. The Republicans also drew majorities from smaller groups of Mormons, white Catholics, and "other Christians." Kerry and Tenenbaum won majorities among Jewish voters, voters of other non-Christian faiths, black Catholics, secular voters, and, most important, black Protestants. Indeed, both Democratic candidates drew significantly more than 70 percent of their total support from religious groups other

Table 12.1 Religious Voting in 2004 South Carolina Elections

Religious Tradition	% of Voters	Bush	DeMint	Proportion of GOP Coalition
		%		
Evangelical	32.4	87.7	82.5	48.3
Mainline	19.8	73.0	65.2	24.6
Latter-Day Saints	1.2	73.7	73.7	1.5
White Catholic	8.5	70.4	60.3	10.0
Other Christian	3.7	61.8	62.1	3.6
Jewish	1.2	42.1	31.6	0.8
Other Faiths	4.6	31.0	32.9	2.3
None	4.8	22.4	17.8	1.8
Black Protestant	22.4	18.2	14.6	6.9
Black Catholic	1.4	9.1	30.0	0.2
Total	100.0	59.4	55.0	100.0
N		(1,596)	(1,550)	

Source: 2004 National Election Pool exit polls.

than the large evangelical and mainline Protestant traditions—almost half of it from black Protestants alone (45 percent for Kerry).

Even among these predominantly Democratic groups there was some weakness, however, especially among more devout voters. For example, black Protestants who claimed to be "born again" gave Bush 20 percent of their votes and DeMint 16 percent, compared to 13 percent and 8 percent among black Protestants who did not claim that label. Similarly, 83 percent of the significant minority of born-again white Catholics favored Bush, compared to 67 percent of other Catholics (the comparable figures for DeMint were 70 and 59 percent). Among "Other Christians" Bush received 62 percent from "born agains" and only 18 percent from others.

Table 12.1 also shows that evangelicals are the core of the GOP in loyalty as well as numbers. The falloff from the presidential vote to the Senate vote was only 5 percentage points among evangelicals, compared to 8 percentage points among the smaller mainline contingent and 10 percentage points among white Catholics, who are newer to the GOP family. There was less variation among Democratic religious groups by office, although Bush did better among Jews than DeMint did, and some black Catholics, who are sensitive to parochial school issues, voted for Kerry but defected from Tenenbaum.

Although the religious coalitions delineated in table 12.1 provide a *prima facie* case for the impact of religious values on the electoral process, other factors may modify, reinforce, or even counteract those influences. Table 12.2 reports results from a multivariate analysis that entailed adding demographic and political variables to religious affiliation to explain partisanship and voting patterns. If religious factors have reshaped party affiliation and electoral behavior, religious affiliation should persist as an influence even when socioeconomic factors such as family income and demographic factors such as gender and age are included. Unfortunately, the 2004 exit polls had no question about whether voters thought of themselves as part of the "Christian Right." As a reasonable proxy, therefore, we used two dummy variables: one for those who said "moral values" were most important to their presidential vote and another for respondents who said the most critical trait of their presidential candidate was that "he has strong religious faith." The first column in table 12.2 reports the results for predicting Republican identification; the second, Bush presidential vote; the third, a vote for DeMint in the senatorial race; and the fourth, for straight-ticket GOP voting.

The results are consistent. Evangelicals are distinctly more Republican than any other group, and mainliners always fall on the GOP side but with much more variation. The coefficients for party identification and Bush vote are stronger than those for DeMint (not even statistically significant) and for straight-ticket voting. White Catholics actually are more Republican than mainliners in party identification when all other variables are controlled, though slightly less so in the election, where the coefficients are not all statistically significant but are still positive. Interestingly, black Catholics do not match the strong Democratic tendencies of their Protestant counterparts, who are joined by secular voters as the staunchest Democratic "religious" constituency.

What about the historic "class basis" of the New Deal party system? At the bivariate level, the poorest voters tend to be more Democratic, but this result is almost entirely because of the presence of African Americans. Once black Protestants and Catholics are included the regression, the class basis of the South Carolina party system is nonexistent—that is, it does not matter among whites. As table 12.2 shows, family income has virtually no relationship to any partisan measure. Recent economic experience, on the other hand, does make a difference: Voters who reported declines in personal economic fortunes are significantly more likely to identify as Democrats and vote for Democratic candidates. Women also are marginally more Democratic: Although Bush virtually erased the gender gap, Tenenbaum benefited from it. Age has virtually no predictive power; clearly, the days of the aging "yellow-dog" Democratic holdovers from the "Solid South" are over. (In fact, older voters were slightly more likely to vote a straight GOP ticket.) Finally, regionalism lives: Upstate

Table 12.2   Determinants of Party Identification, Presidential and Senate Voting, and Straight Party Republican Voting in 2004

Independent Variable	GOP ID	Bush Vote	DeMint Vote	Straight GOP
Religious Tradition				
Evangelical	1.032***	1.647***	1.005***	1.174***
Mainline	0.660**	0.921***	0.329	0.572*
White Catholic	0.848***	0.859**	0.198	0.362
Black Catholic	-0.359	-1.915*	-0.339	-1.466
Black Protestant	-1.277***	-1.471***	-1.660***	-1.611***
None	-1.479***	-1.267***	-1.476***	-1.461***
Demographics				
Finances worse	-0.841***	-1.302***	-1.001***	-1.227***
Family income	0.044	-0.024	0.034	0.021
Female	-0.267*	-0.264	-0.404**	-0.403**
Age	-0.019	0.039	0.042	0.084*
Upstate	0.303*	0.454**	0.419***	0.347*
Election Concerns				
Moral issues	0.659***	1.540***	1.227***	1.247***
Faith of candidate	0.511*	2.114***	1.524***	1.454***
Constant	0.997**	2.349***	1.915***	1.767***
Model Statistics				
Sample size (N)	1,495	1,464	1,443	1,495
% predicted	74.0	83.5	79.8	80.7
Pseudo R^2	.390	.591	.503	.542

Note: Data are from 2004 National Election Pool exit polls. Estimates are coefficients from dichotomous logistic regression. Pseudo R^2 is Nagelkerke estimate.
$*p < .05$; $**p < .01$; $***p < .001$.

residents were significantly more Republican, even when all other variables are incorporated.

What about the impact of "moral values" and the candidate's "religious faith"? Not surprisingly, evangelicals were most likely to report these priorities (38 percent for moral values, 24 percent for candidate faith), followed by white Catholics (21 percent and 8 percent, respectively) and mainline Protestants (21 percent and 6 percent). Yet even when religious traditions are included in the equation, voters making these choices were significantly more likely to identify as Republican and to vote for Bush and DeMint. (In fact, the 7 percent of the state electorate who named both moral values and candidate's faith voted *unanimously* for Bush.) Even among "Democratic" religious constituencies, such as black Protestants, voters who named moral issues and/or presidential faith were significantly more Republican. Moreover, when other issue priorities and candidate traits are added to the analysis, these measures of religious importance remain strongly significant (data not shown).

Conclusion

The 2004 election in South Carolina exhibits the maturation of relationships between Christian conservatism and the GOP. Although organized Christian Right mobilization activity was negligible, at least in comparison with previous election years, the movement has deposited a distinct but fairly well-integrated residue in the state GOP organizational structure, buttressed by the voting power of evangelicals and other religious conservatives. Although the party is not in Christian Right hands, it clearly is in conservative Christian hearts. Moreover, the party hierarchy pays attention: As state GOP chairman Katon Dawson boasted after the election, "We do not take our evangelical, Christian right vote for granted" (Davenport 2004).

In the pivotal U.S. Senate race, all the GOP candidates took socially conservative positions, and all made deferential nods toward Christian conservatives. Yet the primary confirmed again that candidates who depend primarily on Christian conservatives (e.g., Condon and Beasley) were unlikely to win statewide GOP nomination—though so were candidates who rely only on the party's business wing (Ravenel and McBride). Christian conservatives' contribution to the GOP's presidential landslide and striking victory in the Senate contest against the state's most attractive Democratic candidate confirmed the political value in the merger of Christian Right and traditional Republican forces. At the advent of the 109th Congress, the GOP controlled six of eight seats in the South Carolina congressional delegation; all six members were evangelical, not mainline, Protestants—three Southern Baptist, two PCA, and one Associate Reformed Presbyterian. All put at least some priority on social issues, and all maintained voting records that were more than acceptable to Christian Right scorekeepers.

Despite such success within the GOP, Christian conservatives still confront challenges to their future influence. Although the state's economic modernization continues to foster Christian Right sentiments among many first-generation suburbanites, that process also has produced increasing religious diversification. Growing numbers of Catholics, Jews, Muslims, and other religious minorities, as well as secular citizens, have bolstered the ranks of potential opponents, who naturally gravitate toward the Democrats. Nevertheless, for the foreseeable future competitive Democratic candidates will have to reduce Republican majorities among evangelicals and mainliners—a fact emphasized in state Democratic leaders' overwhelmingly hostile reaction to National Democratic Chairman Howard Dean's critique of the GOP as "pretty much a white Christian party" (Hoover 2005). Democrats also will have to prevent further encroachments by the GOP among the more devout voters in their own religious constituencies.

Moreover, even friendly faces in the legislature and Congress do not guarantee policy success for the Christian Right. South Carolina's adoption of a lottery and its repeal of blue law restrictions are just two harbingers of declining evangelical dominance. Although the most recent state legislature overwhelmingly approved a state constitutional amendment prohibiting same-sex marriage, it also rejected Governor Sanford's proposal for tax credits for private and religious school students ("Put Parents in Charge")—a bill many Christian conservatives vocally favored. Even the Republicans in the state's congressional delegation occasionally defy Christian Right prescriptions. For example, Lindsey Graham's support of a compromise to end the Senate Democratic filibuster of President Bush's judicial nominees in early 2005 elicited screams of disapproval from Christian conservatives, both nationally and in the state. Thus, even within the GOP, Christian Right leaders will have to tend their alliances to achieve policy objectives. In large part, how well they adapt to the new religious environment of the state and use their points of leverage within the GOP will determine the future of the movement.

Notes

Although this analysis derives in part from my "participant observation" in GOP politics, many observers have supplied essential information and perspectives. Dan Hoover of the *Greenville News* and Lee Bandy of the Columbia *State* are cited frequently here and in earlier analyses (Guth 1995, 2000b; Guth and Smith 1997). Congressman Bob Inglis and Senator Jim DeMint, former Lieutenant Governor Nick Theodore, and former Governor and Secretary of Education Dick Riley also have been helpful over the years. I also thank several former students: Greenville County Democratic chair Johnnie Fulton, Beasley cabinet member Lewis Gossett, and former state Democratic chair Frank Holloman, who ran the Tenenbaum Senate campaign. My colleague Brent Nelsen has provided the useful insights of a Republican activist and academic. Another colleague, Danielle Vinson, who coauthored a previous iteration of this chapter, has shared ideas gleaned from her own projects in state politics and, as a native South Carolinian, often corrects the mistaken notions of a transplanted Badger.

1. Membership estimates are based on the decennial Glenmary survey of religious membership for 2000; these estimates leave much to be desired,

however, because they undercount independent congregations and often lack the cooperation of African American and conservative Protestant groups. Even trends between decades are murky, given variations in each survey.

References

Anderson, Chris. 2005. "Congressional Campaigns: A Case Study of Field Organiz-
    ing." Unpublished senior honors essay, Furman University, Greenville, South
    Carolina.
Bandy, Lee. 2004. "Tenenbaum Vows Independent Course." *The* [Columbia] *State*,
    2 May.
Bradley, Martin, Norman M. Green Jr., Dale E. Jones, Mac Lynn, and Lou McNeil.
    1992. *Churches and Church Membership in the United States, 1990.* Atlanta: Glen-
    mary Research Center.
Conger, Kimberly H., and John C. Green. 2002. "Spreading Out and Digging In:
    Christian Conservatives and State Republican Parties." *Campaigns and Elections*
    23, no. 1 (February): 58–64.
Davenport, Jim. 2004. "More Black Voters Supported Bush Election." Associated
    Press, 7 November.
Ehrenhalt, Alan. 1991. *The United States of Ambition.* New York: Random House.
Graham, Cole Blease Jr., William V. Moore, and Frank T. Petrusak. 1994. "Praise
    the Lord and Join the Republicans." Paper presented at annual meeting of
    Western Political Science Association, Albuquerque, New Mexico.
Guth, James L. 1995. "South Carolina: The Christian Right Wins One." In *God at
    the Grass Roots: The Christian Right in the 1994 Elections*, ed. Mark J. Rozell and
    Clyde Wilcox. Lanham, Md.: Rowman and Littlefield.
———. 2000a. "Letter from Greenville: Living with Bob Jones." *Christian Century*
    117 (March 22–29): 28–29.
———. 2000b. "South Carolina: Even in Zion the Heathen Rage." In *Prayers in the
    Precincts: The Christian Right in the 1998 Elections*, ed. John C. Green, Mark J.
    Rozell and Clyde Wilcox. Washington, D.C.: Georgetown University Press.
Guth, James L., and Oran P. Smith. 1997. "South Carolina Christian Right: Just
    Part of the Family Now?" In *God at the Grass Roots, 1996: The Christian Right
    in American Elections*, ed. Mark J. Rozell and Clyde Wilcox. Lanham, Md.:
    Rowman and Littlefield.
Hoover, Dan. 2003. "Beasley Feels Draft for Senate." *Greenville News*, 14 November.
———. 2004a. "Beasley Elects to Enter Senate Race." *Greenville News*, 15 January.
———. 2004b. "Senate Hopefuls United on Gay Marriage Ban." *Greenville News*,
    29 February.
———. 2004c. "'Vindicated' Beasley Dogged by Protesters." *Greenville News*, 4
    April.
———. 2004d. "Campaigns Clash over National Ties." *Greenville News*, 25 October.
———. 2005. "Dean Visit Mixed Bag for Dems." *Greenville News*, 26 June.

Hurt, Charles. 2005. "DeMint Found Virtue in Telling Truth on Trade." *Washington Times,* 6 January.

Jones, Dale E., Sherry Doty, James E. Horsch, Richard Houseal, Mac Lynn, John P. Marcum, Kenneth M. Sanchagrin, and Richard H. Taylor. 2002. *Religious Congregations and Membership in the United States, 2000.* Nashville: Glenmary Research Center.

Kuzenski, John C. 2003. "South Carolina: The Heart of GOP Realignment in the South." In *The New Politics of the Old South,* 2nd ed., ed. Charles S. Bullock III and Mark J. Rozell. Lanham, Md.: Rowman and Littlefield.

Smith, Oran P. 1997. *The Rise of Baptist Republicanism.* New York: New York University Press.

Vinson, C. Danielle, and James L. Guth. 2003. "Advance and Retreat in the Palmetto State: Assessing the Christian Right in South Carolina," In *The Christian Right in American Politics: Marching to the Millennium,* ed. John C. Green, Mark J. Rozell and Clyde Wilcox. Washington, D.C.: Georgetown University Press.

Contributors

DAVID BEER is a Ph.D. candidate in the Department of Government at Georgetown University.

KIMBERLY H. CONGER is assistant professor in the Department of Political Science at Iowa State University.

DEBASREE DAS GUPTA is a Ph.D. candidate in the School of Public Policy at George Mason University.

MATTHEW DESANTIS is a Ph.D. candidate in the Department of Government at the University of Florida.

JOEL S. FETZER is Frank R. Seaver associate professor of political science at Pepperdine University.

CHRISTOPHER P. GILBERT is professor of political science at Gustavus Adolphus College.

JOHN C. GREEN is director of the Ray Bliss Institute for Applied Politics at the University of Akron.

JAMES L. GUTH is professor of political science at Furman University.

CARIN LARSON is a Ph.D. candidate in the Department of Government at Georgetown University.

LINDA M. MEROLLA is a Ph.D. candidate in the Department of Government at Georgetown University.

SUSAN ORR is a Ph.D. candidate in the Department of Political Science at the University of Florida.

JAMES M. PENNING is professor of political science at Calvin College.

DONALD RACHETER is president of the Public Interest Institute.

MARK J. ROZELL is professor of public policy at George Mason University.

SHAD B. SATTERTHWAITE is visiting assistant professor of political science at the University of Oklahoma.

RICHARD K. SCHER is professor of political science at the University of Florida.

CORWIN SMIDT is professor of political science at Calvin College.

J. CHRISTOPHER SOPER is professor of political science at Pepperdine University.

KENNETH D. WALD is distinguished professor of political science at the University of Florida.

CLYDE WILCOX is professor of government at Georgetown University.

Index